DISARM—OR DIE

Other Volumes by the Author

The Wit and Wisdom of Gandhi (1951)
An Albert Schweitzer Festschrift (1955)
The Gandhi Reader (1956)
Religion and Peace (1966)
World Religions and World Peace (1968)
Religion for Peace (1973)
The Disarmament Workbook (1978)
World Religion/World Peace (1979)
Religion in the Struggle for World Community (1980)

DISARM—OR DIE

The Second U.N. Special Session on Disarmament

By Homer A. Jack

with a Foreword by Ambassador
Alfonso Garcia Robles

World Conference on Religion and Peace
New York
1983

World Conference on Religion and Peace
777 United Nations Plaza
New York, N.Y. 10017, U.S.A.

ISBN: 0-935934-07-3
ISBN: 0-935934-08-1 (softcover)
Library of Congress Catalog Card Number 83-60689
Manufactured in the United States of America

The logotype on the front and back covers is the U.N. prize-winning poster for SSD II. It was conceived by designer Gerhard Voight of the German Democratic Republic.

Acknowledgment is made to Alex Jack for publishing this manuscript and to Renate Belck for typing it.

Photographs courtesy of the United Nations except those taken by Jennifer Warburg.

To
My Grandchildren,
Michael and Molly Williams.
May their lives be as long
—and rich—as mine!

Contents

Foreword

In the last day of June 1978, the General Assembly of the United Nations closed its First Special Session devoted to disarmament with the adoption, by a consensus which included all five nuclear weapon States, of a "Final Document." Thus for the first time in its history, the United Nations succeeded in forcefully proclaiming a number of objectives, principles, priorities, and conclusions whose validity henceforth it will be impossible to question.

The Final Document through peremptory and inequivocal provisions asserted—that the stockpiling of weapons, particularly nuclear weapons, far from helping to strengthen international security, actually undermines it;—that existing nuclear arsenals and the continuing arms race threaten the very survival of mankind;—that while the final objective should continue to be general and complete disarmament under effective international control, the immediate goal is the elimination of the danger of a nuclear war;—that there is a close relationship between disarmament and development and that any resources that may be released as a result of the implementation of disarmament measures must urgently be used to reduce the economic imbalance between developed and developing countries;—that, in accordance with the Charter, the United Nations has a central role and primary responsibility in the field of disarmament and Member States must therefore keep it duly informed of all measures—whether unilateral, bilateral, regional, or multilateral—taken outside its auspices;—and that all the peoples of the world have a vital interest in the success of disarmament negotiations.

What could be called the United Nations philosophy on disarmament, particularly on nuclear disarmament, thus defined in the Final Document was of such a revolutionary nature that Philip Noel-Baker called it "the greatest state paper of all time."

Unfortunately, all the main provisions of the Final Document have remained a dead letter. The sound advice expressly given by the Gen-

11

eral Assembly that "the pressing need now is to translate into practical terms" the provisions of the Document and "to proceed along the road of binding and effective international agreements in the field of disarmament" has been totally ignored.

This sad conclusion became strikingly evident at the Second Special Session devoted to disarmament which was held four years after the first, from June 7 to July 10, 1982. That Assembly failed hopelessly in what had from the outset quite rightly been regarded as the fundamental objective of the session: the adoption of a Comprehensive Program of Disarmament which would reflect faithfully the requirements set forth in paragraph 109 of the Final Document.

In the light of this situation, perhaps the most encouraging results of the Second Special Session were two-fold. It was still possible, as explicitly stated in the "Concluding Document," to secure "the unanimous and categorical reaffirmation by all Member States of the validity of the Final Document of the Tenth Special Session as well as their solemn commitment to it and their pledge to respect the priorities in disarmament negotiations as agreed to in its Program of Action." Also the Special Session launched the World Disarmament Campaign, for which Mexico had the privilege to take the initiative in 1980 at the thirty-fifth session of the General Assembly. The World Disarmament Campaign will no doubt help to ensure that the mobilization of world public opinion on behalf of disarmament becomes in the future sufficiently strong as to avoid the repetition of the unfortunate experience of the Second Special Session in the spring and early summer of 1982.

To facilitate an effective contribution from the non-governmental organizations and peace and disarmament research institutes to the achievement of the aim of mobilizing world public opinion, the present volume prepared by Homer A. Jack—with his customary thoroughness, expertise, and objectivity—constitutes an invaluable tool which I would recommend without hesitation.

Alfonso Garcia Robles
Permanent Representative of Mexico
to the Committee on Disarmament
1982 Nobel Peace Laureate

Geneva
March 31, 1983

Introduction

Never in the history of disarmament deliberations have so many worked so hard to produce so little. More than 5,000 representatives of 157 Member States, the Secretariat, and non-governmental organizations (NGOs) participated in the Second U.N. Special Session on disarmament (SSD II) held at U.N. Headquarters from June 7th through July 10, 1982. SSD II began with high hopes, not only because of the appearance of world political leaders, but because of the June 12th march/demonstration which was the largest political rally in North American history. Yet when SSD II adjourned, its obituary notice hardly appeared in the media. SSD II was an abject failure.

The smaller, if longer, 1932 disarmament conference at Geneva was a failure because the League of Nations was unable to deal with Germany and Hitler. It was the harbinger of World War II. The 1982 disarmament conference at New York was a failure because the U.N. was unable to deal with the U.S.A. and the U.S.S.R. If SSD II is not to be a harbinger of World War III, this failure must be carefully analyzed and efforts other than an occasional U.N. Special Session must be used to stave off nuclear holocaust and to end the nuclear arms race.

Perhaps this volume will be most useful to those who might otherwise be disillusioned by the disappointments of SSD II. Do such citizens give up, drop out, and wait for nuclear catastrophe? Or can the very failure of SSD II yet become a basis for further success in disarmament activity? The seeming irrelevance of public opinion on SSD II is making NGOs worldwide wonder what they did wrong and what is missing. Are their methods—educating, political action, lobbying, demonstrating, and committing civil disobedience—inadequate to the task? Are more revolutionary means necessary to make most governments listen?

This rethinking of NGO strategy may be one of the most important by-product of a failed SSD II. While the lack of success may have turned off some NGOs, it may have turned others on who cannot understand the gap between the popular outcry for nuclear disarma-

13

ment and the diplomatic stonewalling to maintain the nuclear status quo. This gap in the end could be destructive to the comfortable diplomacy of the nuclear weapon States and the narrowing sovereignty of most States. Perhaps President Dwight D. Eisenhower was prophetic when in August 1959 he wrote: "I like to believe that people in the long run are going to do more to promote peace than are governments. Indeed, I think that people want peace so much that one of these days governments had better get out of their way and let them have it." Has the failure of SSD II made "one of these days" today?

This volume supplements the author's earlier history of SSD I: "Disarmament Workbook: The U.N. Special Session and Beyond." The author has had rich experiences which have been useful in writing this present volume. He was not only an observer at SSD I, but observed both the 18 months of preparations for SSD II and the five weeks of SSD II itself. He wrote articles and editorials for *Disarmament Times*. He marched and demonstrated. He committed civil disobedience and was arrested. He spoke both to the Prep Comm and to the Ad Hoc Committee of SSD II and frequently lobbied the delegates on specific issues. He even sued U.S. Secretary of State Alexander Haig in an attempt to obtain visas denied to NGOs. Perhaps these experiences, and others, give richness to this history, even if the author was not an official delegate.

Why write, let alone publish or read, a tale of failure? Simply because this one failure must not be allowed to become a pattern in the world disarmament community. There must yet come actual nuclear disarmament. It is the only way to prevent nuclear war. The world can only take seriously the lesson of the Final Document of SSD I: "We must halt the arms race and proceed to disarmament or face annihilation." Disarm—or die!

—H. A. J.

New York, N.Y.
April 25, 1983

Abbreviations Used

CD	Committee on Disarmament
CPD	Comprehensive Program of Disarmament
DC	Disarmament Commission of the U.N.
Freeze	Nuclear weapons freeze
GCD	General and complete disarmament
NGO	Non-governmental organization (or observer)
Prep Comm	Preparatory Committee for the Second Special Session
SSD I	First U.N. Special Session devoted to disarmament. It was technically called the Tenth Special Session of the U.N. General Assembly.
SSD II	Second U.N. Special Session devoted to disarmament. It was technically called the Twelfth Special Session of the U.N. General Assembly.
U.N.	United Nations

1.

Preparations

The Second U.N. Special Session devoted to disarmament (SSD II) was a result of a decision of the First Special Session (SSD I) held in 1978 to convene a second conference. However, it was not until December 1980 that a Preparatory Committee (Prep Comm) was appointed. It held one organizational session in 1980, two substantive sessions in 1981, and a third in 1982. The preparations for SSD II were not, of course, confined to the Prep Comm, but were made on many U.N., governmental, and NGO levels throughout the world.

1. The Prep Comm

The Final Document of SSD I, in paragraph 119, called for the convening of SSD II: "A Second Special Session of the General Assembly devoted to disarmament should be held on a date to be decided by the General Assembly at its thirty-third session." Some Non-Aligned States which helped pilot SSD I through the political reefs of the 31st and 32nd regular sessions of the General Assembly in 1977 and 1978 made sure that paragraph 119 would be implemented in the 33rd session late in 1978.

Both the years 1981 and 1982 were then informally discussed as the date for SSD II. A consensus soon emerged for 1982. Then Yugoslavia introduced a draft resolution into the First Committee on November 24, 1978 which, inter alia, dealt with SSD II, including its date. Since this resolution combined several disarmament questions, the resolution was not adopted unanimously. It did receive, however, a total of 129 affirmative votes, with no negative ones and 13 abstentions. The appropriate section on SSD II is as follows: "Bearing in mind the decision adopted at its Tenth Special Session . . . Desiring to contribute to the furthering and broadening of positive processes initiated . . . at its Tenth Special Session, 1. Decides to convene a Second Special Session of the General Assembly devoted to Disarmament in 1982 at U.N. Headquarters in New York; 2. Decides also to set up, at its thirty-fifth session, a Preparatory Committee for the Special Session . . ."[1]

Almost two years later, in 1980, one agenda item of the 35th session of the General Assembly was "Review of the implementation of the recommendations and decisions adopted by the General Assembly at its Tenth Special Session." Under this item, Yugoslavia introduced a draft resolution. This was co-sponsored by some Non-Aligned States, at least one Third World State then not Non-Aligned (Pakistan), and one Socialist State (the German Democratic Republic.) For some reason, no Western State was a co-sponsor.

There were some immediate pressures to expand the Prep Comm beyond a membership of 54 States (which comprised the Committee for SSD I.) Accordingly, the draft resolution did not initially include the number of Member States in the Prep Comm. Negotiations were begun by Pakistani Ambassador Niaz A. Naik, Chairman of the First Committee, to determine an adequate ceiling to the number of members. Finally, he announced that agreement had been reached with the five regional groups at the U.N. for the Prep Comm to be composed of 78 Member States. With this decision, the draft was adopted by consensus.[2] For text, see Appendix F below.

Ambassador Naik announced the allocation of places on the Prep Comm by regional groupings: Africa 19 (up five places from 1976–78), Asia 16 (up five), Eastern Europe 10 (up four), Latin America 15 (up five), and Western European and Other States 18 (up five). Still, there continued to be considerable jockeying by individual States for membership within their group. By the time the vote was taken on the draft resolution in the plenary, the President of the General Assembly was able to announce the list of 78 States appointed to the Prep Comm.

The list of members of the Prep Comm is given in Table 1. Every member of the Prep Comm for SSD I was included. Among the 24 additional States were China, Czechoslovakia, Finland, Indonesia, and the Netherlands. Of the 78 States, a total of 36 belonged to the Non-Aligned caucus, not including three Observer States to that caucus (e.g., Mexico.) Of the 78 members, 12 were members of NATO and seven belonged to the Warsaw Pact. Also of the 78, 39 were members of the Committee on Disarmament (CD) at Geneva. Indeed, the only member of CD which was not a member of the Prep Comm was Burma.

2. Organizational Session[3]

The Prep Comm held a brief organizational session—three meetings—shortly after the 35th session adopted the resolution establishing its existence. This was held on December 4-5, 1980. Ambassador Olu

TABLE 1
MEMBERSHIP OF STATES ON THE PREPARATORY
COMMITTEE FOR SSD II.

African States (19)	Asian States (16)	Eastern European States (10)
*Algeria Nc	*Bangladesh N#	Bulgaria cW
*Benin N	China c	Byelorussia
*Burundi N#	*Cyprus N	Czechoslovakia cW
Congo N#	Fiji	*German D.R. #cW
*Egypt N#c	*India N#c	*Hungary cW
*Ethiopia N#c	Indonesia N#c	*Poland cW
Kenya N#c	*Iran c	*Romania #cW
*Liberia N	*Iraq N	Ukraine
*Libya N	*Japan c	*U.S.S.R. cW
*Mauritius N	Lebanon N	*Yugoslavia N#c
*Morocco N#c	*Malaysia N#	
*Nigeria N#c	Mongolia #c	
Senegal N#	*Nepal N	
Sierra Leone N	*Pakistan N#c	
*Sudan N	*Philippines	
*Tunisia N	*Sri Lanka N#c	
Tanzania N		
*Zaire N#c		
*Zambia N#		

*—Also member of Preparatory Committee for SSD I
#—Co-sponsor of resolution establishing Preparatory Committee for SSD II
N—Member of Non-Aligned caucus
NO—Observer State in Non-Aligned caucus
c—Member of the Committee on Disarmament at Geneva
NA—State belongs to NATO
W—State belongs to Warsaw Pact

(continued)

MEMBERSHIP OF STATES ON THE PREPARATORY
COMMITTEE FOR SSD II. *(Cont'd)*

Latin American States (15)	Western European and Other States (18)
*Argentina Nc	*Australia c
*Bahamas #	*Austria
*Brazil NO#c	*Belgium cNA
*Colombia	*Canada NA
Costa Rica #	Denmark NA
*Cuba N#c	Finland
Ecuador #	*France cNA
*Guyana N#	*German F.R. cNA
Honduras	Greece NA
Jamaica N#	*Italy cNA
*Mexico NO#c	Netherlands cNA
*Panama N	New Zealand
*Peru N#c	*Norway NA
Suriname	*Spain
*Venezuela NO#c	*Sweden c
	*Turkey NA
	*U.K. cNA
	*U.S.A. cNA

Adeniji of Nigeria—representative at the time of Nigeria to the U.N. at Geneva and also to the CD—was elected Chairman. He had recently been Chairman of the largely-successful U.N. conference on inhumane and indiscriminate weapons. (Ambassador Carlos Ortiz de Rozas, then representing Argentina at the U.N., was Chairman of the Prep Comm for SSD I.) While it was decided to form a Bureau consisting, in addition to the Chairman, of 13 Vice-Presidents and a Rapporteur, not sufficient time was available to conclude negotiations on these nominations. However, Mr. Pal Csillag of the U.N. Centre for Disarmament was appointed secretary of the Committee. Mr. Jan Martenson was Assistant Secretary-General for disarmament affairs throughout SSD II.

It was agreed that the two sessions of the Prep Comm for 1981 would be held in May and October, so as not to coincide with meetings of the CD. Also an initial statement was made by the Chairman on the participation of NGOs. (See Chapter 10 below for a full discussion of the evolution of the role of NGOs in the Prep Comm and at SSD II itself.) Ambassador Alfonso Garcia Robles of Mexico raised the question of what documents were required for use by the Prep Comm and by SSD II itself. The ample documentation for SSD I was recalled and some delegates felt that many of these could easily be updated. Also new topics were suggested. During these first three meetings of the Prep Comm not much more could be accomplished.

3. First Substantive Session[4]

The first substantive session of the Prep Comm was held at U.N. Headquarters from May 4–15, 1981. It met in an acknowledged gloomy international atmosphere for any hope of progress in disarmament. The accomplishments of the session were chiefly two-fold: identifying some elements of the provisional agenda for SSD II and determining, provisionally, the time and duration of the conference.

After adopting its agenda, the Prep Comm elected additional members of its Bureau. Of a total of 15 members, including the Chairman and the Rapporteur, three would come from each of the five political/geographical groupings of the U.N. Thus in addition to the Chairman, earlier elected from Nigeria, and the Rapporteur, Mr. Omer Ersun, elected from Turkey, 13 Vice-Chairmen were elected as States, not individuals. They came from Australia, Bahamas, Bangladesh, Benin, Bulgaria, German Democratic Republic, India, Italy, Japan, Mexico, Morocco, Peru, and Yugoslavia. During this two-week, ten-day session, there were 14 formal meetings and two informal meetings, and two meetings were suspended for regional caucuses. Also three disarmament caucuses emerged—as they did at recent disarmament deliberative forums: the Non-Aligned group, the Eastern European group, and the Western European and Other States group.

More time was spent discussing the provisional agenda for SSD II than any other topic. The replies of 42 Member States to a communication from the U.N. Secretary-General were before the Committee.[5] Several conference room papers were issued about the provisional agenda, but no decision was made by the time the session adjourned.

The time and duration of SSD II was also debated. It was decided not to make a firm decision, but to block out an eight-week period beginning May 10th 1982 at U.N. Headquarters in New York. It was also concluded that the duration should be "up to five weeks."

No further studies on disarmament for use by SSD II were authorized, although NGOs had submitted proposals for three: the dynamics of unilateral measures for progress in disarmament, the history and development of a convention for general and complete disarmament, and the feasibility of a verifiable bilateral or multilateral nuclear weapons freeze.

The NGO role at the Prep Comm was also discussed, at the urging of NGOs present. At the final meeting of the session, the Chairman reported that the Bureau had agreed to allow NGOs to make oral statements at the next session of the Prep Comm, with the NGOs themselves being asked to decide which of their number would speak. Additional NGO proposals for a U.N. cover sheet and symbol number for their statements and for admittance to working groups were not granted. The proposal of some NGOs for the Prep Comm to urge that religious leaders be especially invited to SSD II was informally considered, but no action was taken.

4. Second Substantive Session[6]

The Prep Comm held its second session on October 5–16, 1981, at U.N. Headquarters. Its principal tasks were to complete the provisional agenda for SSD II and to set the final dates. It also drafted its report to the 36th regular session of the General Assembly which was meeting concurrently.[7]

The provisional agenda was finally completed. The first seven agenda items were routine for special sessions of the General Assembly: 1) Opening of Session, 2) Minute of Meditation, 3) Credentials, 4) Election of President, 5) Organization, 6) Report of the Prep Comm, and 7) Adoption of Agenda. However, the other substantive items were debated at some length.

Agenda item 8. General Debate. There was intensive discussion about whether the item should consist of solely the two words, general debate, or whether there should be a larger annotation. After much debate and negotiation, the following annotation was adopted: "including review and appraisal of the present international situation in the light of the pressing need for specific generally agreed measures to eliminate the danger of war, in particular nuclear war, halt and reverse the arms race and to achieve substantial progress in the field of disarmament, especially in its nuclear aspects, taking due account of the close interrelationship between disarmament, international peace and security, as well as between disarmament and economic and social development, particularly of the developing countries."

9. Review of the Implementation of the Decisions and Recommendations Adopted by the General Assembly at its First Special Session Devoted to Disarmament. Four sub-items or annotations were

Top Left: Ambassador Inga Thorsson of Sweden
Top Right: Ambassador Alfonso Garcia Robles of Mexico
Below: Meeting of Preparatory Committee (left to right): Under Secretary-General for Political and Security Council Affairs Mikhael Sytenko; Chairman, Ambassador Olu Adeniji of Nigeria; Secretary Pal Csillag

Top: Diplomats in negotiation: Ambassador R. M. Timerbaev of the U.S.S.R.; Ambassador Viktor Issraelyan of the U.S.S.R.; Ambassador Alexander Akelovsky of the U.S.A.; Senator John W. Warner of the U.S.A.; Ambassador Ed Fuelner of the U.S.A. (Jennifer Warburg Photo)

Bottom: Special meeting of the First Committee of the 37th General Assembly: General Assembly President Imre Hollai of Hungary; Chairman, Ambassador James V. Gbeho of Ghana; U.N. Secretary-General Javier Perez de Cuellar

given: disarmament negotiations, report on the Committee on Disarmament, report on the Disarmament Commission, and studies.

10. Consideration and Adoption of the Comprehensive Program of Disarmament. This was considered the centerpiece of SSD II, and occasioned most debate. The proposal was enshrined in the Final Document of SSD I, and a draft was elaborated in part both by the Disarmament Commission and the Committee on Disarmament.

11. Implementation of the Declaration of the 1980s as the Second Disarmament Decade as well as Consideration of Initiatives and Proposals of Member States. Originally these were proposed as two items.

12. Enhancing the Effectiveness of Machinery in the Field of Disarmament and Strengthening the Role of the U.N. in this Field, including the Possible Convening of a World Disarmament Conference. There was brisk debate on including mention of the World Disarmament Conference, since this has been a none-starter for several years and only kept on the U.N. agenda at the insistence of the Eastern European group.

13. Measures to Mobilize World Public Opinion in Favor of Disarmament. This included three sub-items: disarmament education, seminars, and training; world disarmament campaign; and other public information activities.

14. Adoption, in an Appropriate Format, of the Document(s) of the Second Special Session of the General Assembly Devoted to Disarmament. There was much discussion about how to separate the contemplated Comprehensive Program from the other work of the Special Session. The above rendering was a compromise.

The final dates of SSD II were also fixed. Certain conflicts were considered, including a meeting of the foreign ministers of Non-Aligned States in Havana late in May. (Significantly, NATO members present did not mention a Summit meeting of NATO scheduled for the second week of June.) Also there was a desire to keep the CD at Geneva in session as long as possible, in the hope that its negotiations would make SSD II more successful. Given these constraints, the dates of the session were set for a little later than earlier planned: from June seventh to July ninth.

Certain other administrative details were decided upon. It was agreed that an earlier practice would be followed of electing as President of SSD II the President of the regular session of the General Assembly. Thus Ambassador Ismat Kittani of Iraq would be named President. Also the subsidiary groups of SSD II were discussed. It was agreed to form an Ad Hoc Committee—sometimes also called the

Committee of the Whole. It was felt that a working group on the Comprehensive Program would be necessary and as many other open-ended groups or subsidiary organs as might be useful. It was also agreed that the Chairman of the Ad Hoc Committee would be the same as the Chairman of the Prep Comm. Thus Ambassador Adeniji would also be Chairman.

The rules of procedure are always a worrisome problem for special U.N. bodies. It was also agreed that the rules of procedure for the General Assembly would apply to SSD II, "without amendments, on the understanding that, regarding the adoption of decisions by the Assembly at the Special Session, every effort should be made to ensure that, in so far as possible, decisions on matters of substance will be adopted by consensus." There was remarkable agreement by most States to work through consensus (unanimity), except for a few Non-Aligned States (and some NGOs), even though the Special Session, like the First Committee of the regular session, is a deliberative body and not one negotiating actual disarmament agreements. In other words, the Special Session could vote at any time to take a vote, but pressures to work by consensus were overwhelming.

The level of representation was also agreed upon—Member States to be represented at the "highest possible political level." It was re-called that, during the general debate at SSD I, participants included four Heads of State, 16 Prime Ministers, four Vice-Presidents and Deputy Prime Ministers, and 49 Ministers of Foreign Affairs.

At this Prep Comm session, by previous agreement, one meeting—October 9, 1981—was set aside for oral statements by representatives of NGOs and peace and disarmament research insititutions. Eleven made statements and these were published in the verbatim report.[8] Many other NGOs and institutions submitted written statements. These were made available for the delegates and they were indexed for circulation.[9]

The preliminary report of the Prep Comm[10] was discussed by the 36th General Assembly. The latter adopted by consensus a resolution endorsing the report and its recommendations, including the provisional agenda.[11] For the text, see Appendix F below.

5. Final Session[12]

The final session of the Prep Comm was held on April 26th through May 14th, 1982. It came at the conclusion of a session of the CD at Geneva, just before a shortened meeting of the Disarmament Commission also at New York, and only a few weeks before the opening of SSD II itself. This tended to be an euphoric, relaxed session, although the unfinished accumulated tasks before the Prep Comm were formidable.

Few organizational details had to be solved. It appeared that a number of Heads of State and Government would attend SSD II. The dates for the general debate were fixed, as were two days immediately thereafter for statements from NGOs and research institutions in the Ad Hoc Committee. It was agreed that, after the general debate, all other agenda items would be taken up by the Ad Hoc Committee and its working groups, except for the last item on the final document(s).

The CD was unable to finish drafting a Comprehensive Program,[13] although it was still acknowledged to be the centerpiece of SSD II. The Prep Comm initially did not know how to handle the matter, since it felt that the CD document on the Program had to be transmitted to the SSD II without changes. Finally, an informal working group was established to discuss the matter. This was formed on the condition that it would not in any way interfere with the results of the work of the CD on this topic. This working group created several contact groups to discuss such issues as measures to be contained, time frames, and the nature of the Program. Also there was a discussion on how binding the Program should be on Member States. The working group, in its report to the full Prep Comm,[14] reaffirmed that the elaboration of a Program was "one of the central tasks" of SSD II. It also urged that the working group on the Program be established at SSD II as rapidly as possible after its convening.

The Prep Comm also decided to establish an informal working group on reviewing the implementation of the recommendations and decisions of SSD II, especially since no other body had begun to discuss this obviously contentious issue. Many working papers were submitted to this working group, and its drafting group. A composite working paper was drafted, but could not be agreed upon. There was consensus only that this long paper would be placed in the annex of the report of the Prep Comm to SSD II[15]

The Prep Comm also dealt with the World Disarmament Campaign. At the very end of the session, after a good deal of negotiations, the Chairman announced in behalf of the Bureau that the President of SSD II would be asked to launch the Campaign at the opening meeting. He was also asked to carry out consultations on the best modalities to collect funds for the Campaign. (For further details, see Chapter 7 below.)

The Prep Comm also had to receive and certify the list of NGOs and research institutions making oral statements to SSD II. The Ad Hoc NGO Liaison Group submitted a list and the Prep Comm endorsed it, adding six research institutions. (For further details, see Chapter 11 below).

Finally, the Prep Comm drafted and adopted by consensus its report to SSD II.[16]

6. Costs

The convening of a U.N. Special Session is an expensive affair, but insignificant in cost compared to that of the most elemental military hardware.

When the U.N. General Assembly discusses a resolution involving costs, the Secretary-General must submit a statement of its administrative and financial implications. This Secretary-General Kurt Waldheim did on 19th November 1981.[17] The total estimate was $5,686,900. These costs were based on three assumptions about the five-week 1982 session at U.N. Headquarters: 1) Interpretation would be required in six languages for four simultaneous meetings a day, including one plenary meeting, the Ad Hoc Committee, the working group on the Comprehensive Program, and a second working group to be established; 2) Documentation in the six languages would be 500 pages for the pre-session period, 1,000 pages during the session, and 200 pages after the session; and 3) Verbatim records would be provided for two plenary meetings and two meetings of the Ad Hoc Committee each day.

The greatest cost dealt with so-called conference servicing, totaling $4,932,400. The pre-session documentation was estimated to be 200,000 words, costing $554,200. The servicing of the meetings of the session—interpretation into six languages—was estimated to be $1,066,400. The documentation during the session, or 400,000 words, was estimated to cost $1,078,000. The documentation after the session, or 80,000 words, would cost $215,300. The verbatim records for 100 meetings might cost $2,018,500.

There were, of course, other costs. By tradition, the U.N. provides one round-trip ticket to Headquarters for every Member State to send one delegate to a Special Session (or Emergency Session). This costs $450,000. Certain miscellany expenses were estimated for the Office of the Secretary-General ($35,000) and for the Office of General Services ($92,000 for additional sound technicians, overtime for security services, information clerks, and messengers). The extra costs of the

Office of Public Information were estimated at $176,700, including press and publications, radio and visual services, communications engineering, etc. Thus the grant total was estimated to be $5,686,900.

In addition to the above estimates, others were made during December 1981,[18] but these did not differ appreciably from those originally made by the Secretary-General. After SSD II was held, attempts were made to estimate the actual costs incurred. The Director of the Budget of the Office of Financial Services submitted an approximation of the costs of SSD II. In addition to the above estimate of $5,686,900, it was further estimated that approximately four months of the time of the Centre for Disarmament was devoted exclusively to SSD II. This was the equivalent of $1,440,000. In addition, the Centre had earlier been provided with temporary assistance of about $200,000. Thus the total cost to the U.N. for convening SSD II was $7,326,900.

The above costs to the U.N. do not, of course, include much more than an equal amount spent by the 157 Member States, members of the press, and hundreds of NGOs. The NGO Committee on Disarmament (at U.N. Headquarters)—to cite only one known and small example—raised and spent more than $125,000.

To repeat, the extra costs of the Special Session to the normal U.N. budget amounted to several million dollars, but less than the wing of a single bomber.

7. Conclusions

The Prep Comm during its three substantive sessions did "prepare" well for SSD II. Given the experience of SSD I, the 78 Member States had a much more concrete concept about SSD II than its predecessor Prep Comm had for SSD I. The Non-Aligned group did not claim that SSD II was its initiative as much as the group did for SSD I. At times, most Non-Aligned States seemed to side-step any responsibility; at other times, it assumed some initiatives. The work of the Prep Comm was business-like and adequate, but hardly imaginative.

During most of 1981 the international climate was so bleak that, intermittently, questions were raised about the possibility of postponing SSD II beyond mid-1982. However, during the spring of 1982, with the growing popular disarmament demonstrations, there appeared much more optimism about the success of SSD II. However, the Prep Comm in retrospect can be faulted, at its final session, for not realizing the seriousness of the impasse on the elaboration of a Comprehensive Program. No real effort was made to reconsider the agenda of SSD II. Originally put together in October 1981, this agenda was not changed—even during the opening days of SSD II.

There were certain warnings about the possible failure of SSD II in the final weeks of its preparations. The Stanley Foundation, at a conference of key SSD II diplomats in May 1982, questioned the feasibility of continuing to make the Comprehensive Program "the highest priority" of SSD II.[20] Several observers urged, in light of public demands for a lessening of the threat of nuclear war, that a "short list" of achievable nuclear measures be discussed and adopted, for early negotiations at CD.

In the end, the Prep Comm made no efforts to anticipate any failure of SSD II and, indeed, showed no inkling of any possible disaster.

8. The Non-Aligned Caucus

Even though the Non-Aligned caucus played less of a leading role in the preparations for SSD II, and in SSD II itself, than in SSD I, that group is an important actor in the U.N. and other international circles. However, the caucus is not well understood and even its exact membership is known to a relatively few observers.

The Non-Aligned Group or caucus—it does not like to be called a bloc—was established at a Summit meeting of Heads of State or Government at Belgrade, Yugoslavia, in 1961. At the time the group consisted of 25 States. Since that time, an increasing number of States have joined the movement as their leaders have attended a succession of summit conferences, the last being at New Delhi in March 1983. A list of the 93 Member States of the Non-Aligned grouping as of SSD II is given in Table 2.

The Non-Aligned Group, beginning in 1961, is sometimes confused with those States which attended the Asian-African Conference held at Bandung, Indonesia, in 1955. These consisted of both Aligned and Non-Aligned States and a second conference was never successfully held. Thus Bandung never emerged as a sustained, continuing movement.

The Non-Aligned caucus also should not be confused with the Group of 77, although all Non-Aligned States belong to the 77. The latter was formed in 1964 at the First U.N. Conference on Trade and Development (UNCTAD) and ever since has been an important caucus on economic issues in the U.N. and other international circles. The accompanying table also lists the 124 Member States of the Group of 77.

The "Third World" is not a formal caucus at the U.N., but constitutes most States in Africa, Asia (and the Pacific), and Latin America, except—for differing reasons—China, Israel, Japan, and South Africa.

TABLE 2
STATES MEMBERS OF CAUCUSES AT SSD II.*

I. THE NON-ALIGNED STATES (93 PLUS TEN OBSERVER STATES)

African (50)

c p Algeria ('62)** 7 21
Angola ('76) 7
p Benin ('60) 7
Botswana ('66) 7
p Burundi ('62) 7
Cape Verde ('75) 7
Cen. African Republic ('60) 7
Chad ('60) 7
Comoros ('75) 7
p Congo ('60) 7
Djibouti ('77) 7
c p Egypt ('45) 7 21
Equatorial Guinea ('68) 7
c p Ethiopia ('45) 7 21
Gabon ('60) 7
Gambia ('65) 7
Ghana ('57) 7
Guinea ('58) 7
Guinea-Bissau ('74) 7
Ivory Coast ('60) 7
c p Kenya ('63) 7 21
Lesotho ('66) 7
p Liberia ('45) 7
p Libyan Arab Jamahiriya ('55) 7
Madagascar ('60) 7
Malawi ('64) 7
Mali ('60) 7
Mauritania ('61) 7
p Mauritius ('68) 7
c p Morocco ('56) 7 21

Mozambique ('75) 7
Niger ('60) 7
c p Nigeria ('60) 7 21
Rwanda ('62) 7
Sao Tome & Principe ('75) 7
p Senegal ('60) 7
Seychelles ('76) 7
p Sierra Leone ('61) 7
Somalia ('60) 7
p Sudan ('56) 7
Swaziland ('68) 7
Togo ('60) 7
p Tunisia ('56) 7
Uganda ('62) 7
Un. Rep. of Cameroon ('60) 7
p Un. Rep. of Tanzania ('61) 7
Upper Volta ('60) 7
c p Zaire ('60) 7 21
p Zambia ('64) 7
Zimbabwe ('80) 7

Asian and Pacific (27)
Afghanistan ('46) 7
Bahrain ('71) 7
p Bangladesh ('74) 7
Bhutan ('71) 7
p Cyprus ('60) 7
Democratic Yemen ('67) 7
c p India ('45) 7 21
c p Indonesia ('50) 7 21
c p Iran ('45) 7 21

---

*—Only States are listed, not independence movements
**—Date of membership in the U.N.
#—Voted into membership of Non-Aligned caucus in March 1983
c—Member of the Committee on Disarmament in Geneva
o—Observer State at the U.N.
p—Member of the Preparatory Committee for SSD II
7—Member of the Group of 77 (now approximately 124 States)
f1—South Africa is not a member of the African group at the U.N. and it seldom partici-
pates in the U.N., although it remains a Member State
f2—Israel is not a member of the Asian group at the U.N.
21—Member of Group of 21 at CD, composed of Non-Aligned and independent States

TABLE 2
STATE MEMBERS OF CAUCUSES AT SSD II.* *(cont'd)*

p Iraq ('45) 7
  Jordan ('55) 7
  Kuwait ('63) 7
  Lao People's Dem. Rep. ('55) 7
p Lebanon ('45) 7
p Malaysia ('57) 7
  Maldives ('65) 7
p Nepal ('55) 7
  Oman ('71) 7
c p Pakistan ('47) 7 21
  Qatar ('71) 7
  Saudi Arabia ('65) 7
  Singapore ('65) 7
c p Sri Lanka ('55) 7 21
  Syria ('45) 7
  United Arab Emirates ('71) 7
  Viet Nam ('77) 7
  <u>Yemen ('47) 7</u>
  Korea, Peoples Rep. (o) 7

Latin American (14)
c p Argentina ('45) 7 21
  Belize ('81) 7
  Bolivia ('45) 7
c p Cuba ('45) 7 21
 p Ecuador ('45) 7

  Grenada ('74) 7
p Guyana ('66) 7
p Jamaica ('62) 7
  Nicaragua ('45) 7
p Panama ('45) 7
p Peru ('45) 7 21
  St. Lucia ('79) 7
p Suriname ('75) 7
  Trinidad & Tobago ('62) 7

European (2)
  Malta ('64) 7
c p Yugoslavia (45) 7 21

Observer States (10)
  Barbados ('66) 7#
c p Brazil ('45) 7 21
 p Colombia ('45) 7#
 p Costa Rica ('45) 7
  Dominica ('78) 7
  El Salvador ('45) 7
c p Mexico ('45) 7 21
  Philippines ('45) 7
  Uruguay ('45) 7
c p Venezuela ('45) 7 21

II. THE WESTERN EUROPEAN AND OTHER STATES (16 AND 3)

c p Belgium ('45)
c p Canada ('45)
 p Denmark ('45)
c p France ('45)
c p Germany, Fed. Rep. ('73)
 p Greece ('45)
  Iceland ('46)
c p Italy ('55)
  Luxembourg ('45)
c p Netherlands ('45)
 p Norway ('45)

  Portugal ('55)
 p Spain ('55)
 p Turkey ('45)
c p U.K. ('45)
c p <u>U.S.A. ('45)</u>
c p Australia ('45)
c p Japan ('56)
 p New Zealand ('45)

III. THE EASTERN EUROPEAN STATES (8)

c p Bulgaria ('55)　　　　　　　　c p Hungary ('55)
　p Byelorussia ('45)　　　　　　　c p Poland ('55)
c p Czechoslovakia ('45)　　　　　　p Ukraine ('45)
c p German Dem. Rep. ('73)　　　　c p U.S.S.R. ('45)

IV. OTHER STATES (27)

African (1)
South Africa ('45) (f1)

Eastern European (2)
Albania ('55)
c p Romania ('55) 7

Asian & Pacific (12)
c Burma ('48) 7 21
c p China ('45)
　　Democratic Kampuchea ('55) 7
　p Fiji ('70) 7
　　Israel ('49) (f2)
c p Mongolia ('61)
　　Papua New Guinea ('75) 7
　　St. Vincent ('80) 7
　　Samoa ('76) 7
　　Solomon Islands ('78) 7
　　Thailand ('46) 7
　　Vanuatu ('81) 7#

Korea, Rep. of (o) 7

Latin American (8)
Antigua & Barbuda ('81) 7
p Bahamas ('73) 7#
　Chile ('45) 7
　Dominican Republic ('45) 7
　Guatemala ('45) 7
　Haiti ('45) 7
p Honduras ('45) 7
　Paraguay ('45) 7

Western European and Other (4)
p Austria ('55)
p Finland ('55)
　Ireland ('55)
c p Sweden ('46) 21
　Holy See (o)
　Monaco (o)
　Switzerland (o)

REFERENCES

1. General Assembly resolution 33/71 H.

2. Resolution 35/47.

3. Detailed information in Section 1 above and in this section is given in the author's WCRP Report on "The Initial Preparations for the Second Special Session on Disarmament." New York: WCRP. January 1981. 14 pp.

4. Detailed information in this section is given in the author's WCRP Report on "'Opening May 11 or 18 and Lasting Up to Five Weeks:' The Work of the First Substantive Session of the Preparatory Committee of the Second Special Session on Disarmament." New York: WCRP. June 1981. 21 pp.

5. A/AC.206/2 and Add. 1–9.

6. Detailed information in this section is given in the author's WCRP Report on "The Provisional Agenda of the Second Special Session on Disarmament: The Preparatory Committee Continues Its Deliberations." New York: WCRP. October 1981. 30 pp.

7. A/36/49 and Corr. 1.

8. A/C.206/SR.25, pp. 1–17.

9. A/C.206/INF.1 and Add. 1–4.

10. A/36/49. Also in A/S-12/1.

11. 36/81 A.

12. Detailed information in this section is given in the author's WCRP Report on "The Final Meetings of the Preparatory Committee for the Second Special Session on Disarmament." New York: WCRP. June 1982. 17 pp.

13. The report and text on the CPD from the CD is CD/283. 53 pp.

14. Annex II, A/S-12/1, p. 55.

15. Annex I, A/S-12/1, pp. 18–54.

16. A/S-12/1, 58 pp.

17. A/C.1/36/L.49. 3 pp.

18. A/C.5/36/87. 4 pp.

19. A/C.5/36/105.

20. "The U.N. Second Special Session on Disarmament and Beyond." Muscatine, Iowa: The Stanley Foundation. 1982. 23 pp.

2.

Opening and General Debate

SSD II was opened on June 7th at an afternoon meeting in the great hall of the General Assembly.[1] The first seven agenda items were discussed and, for the most part, completed. Then for the next 24 meetings the general debate was held. The opening meeting and the general debate took more than one-third of the time of the entire SSD II.

1. Opening Meeting

The Special Session was opened by its Temporary President, Ambassador Ismat Kittani, Chairman of the delegation of Iraq and President of the 36th session of the U.N. General Assembly. This was an afternoon meeting scheduled for 3:00 p.m., but which began at 3:35 p.m. He then invited representatives to stand and "observe one minute of silent prayer or meditation." (This is routine for openings of the regular and special sessions of the General Assembly.)

The third item on the agenda was the credentials of representatives to the session. The Temporary President indicated that, in accordance with rule 28 of the rules of procedure and taking into account the recommendations of the Prep Comm, endorsed by the 36th regular session, the Credentials Committee would consist of the same nine members as those appointed for the 36th session: China, Ghana, the Netherlands, Niger, Panama, Papua New Guinea, Paraguay, the U.S.S.R., and the U.S.A. There were no objections.

33

The fourth agenda item was the election of the President of the Special Session. Ambassador Olu Adeniji of Nigeria, Chairman of the Prep Comm, obtained the floor and nominated Ambassador Kittani, indicating that this was the unanimous view of the members of the Prep Comm. (This has also been the precedent.) He asked that Ambassador Kittani be elected by acclamation. This was also agreed upon.

The President

Then President Kittani delivered an address.[2] A few excerpts follow:

". . . As we speak of disarmament, war is all around us . . . The presidency of this body involves not only privileges and honors but also duties and responsibilities. This afternoon I feel one such responsibility very strongly—that of reflecting the deep preoccupation of all the millions of people in the world who are following these deliberations with hope, with concern, and with fear: hope that we shall take meaningful steps towards the solution of the most dangerous dilemma of our time; concern over the consequences for humanity if the arms race is not checked; and fear that we may fail. Everything—the world, civilization—is at stake. This is not empty rhetoric, it is a fact.

". . . Many of the representatives present were here in this hall when the [First Special Session] adopted a Final Document which was hailed by many as a breakthrough in the frustrating search for a workable formula for halting the arms race. What has happened in the intervening four years? . . . We all know the answer, but I want to state it loudly and clearly for the world to hear. Nothing. Not a single weapon has been destroyed over the past four years as a result of a disarmament agreement. Nothing of significance has been done to reduce the imminent threat of self-extinction that makes the present so dangerous and the future so uncertain. It is a sorry record of failure.

"Indeed, in a perverse way we should be forced to regard it as an achievement if our world were in as good a condition today as it was four years ago. Sadly, that is not the case . . .

"Despite this gloomy picture, I am not fundamentally pessimistic about the future . . . First, the economic factors related to the arms race are working in favor of rationality and moderation . . . My second reason . . . is the growing and increasingly organized and assertive public movement against the arms race. This groundswell of public opinion is world-wide and cuts across the entire political spectrum. It is, to me, particularly significant that in many countries religious leaders are in the forefront of this movement. We are witnessing the truly democratic process of public opinion moving governments to adopt more—not less—rational approaches . . . My third reason . . . is my deep belief in the rationality of the human mind and of human beings, a rationality which, if we do not wait too long, can lead us to apply ourselves to the business of disarming this world . . .

"I am likewise pleased to note the broad and impressive representation and activities of non-governmental organizations at this session, both in this hall and outside. That alone is an indication of public interest and concern. I should like to welcome them and tell them that their participation is most important, and on behalf of the Assembly I want to thank them for their continuing efforts in the cause of peace.

"We still have a chance. We still have time, but not much. The odds are lengthening against humanity. It is time to put an end to the arms race and begin the peace race."

The Secretary-General

Mr. Javier Perez de Cuellar, Secretary-General of the U.N. then addressed the meeting.[3] Some excerpts follow:

". . . I invite the Assembly to husband the necessary political will to cut through the undergrowth and to treat the subject at hand with the boldness which is required in a situation of emergency . . . Before the invention of the nuclear weapon, man was concerned with the death of the individual, alone or in groups. In the nuclear age, however, he is faced with the very real and mounting threat of the death of the whole species. Apocalypse is today not merely a biblical depiction; it has become a very real possibility . . .

"Since 1945, no nuclear bomb has been used in military action but the world has experienced well over 100 wars fought with conventional weapons. These have caused vast suffering and destruction and the loss of an untold number of human lives. I do not, therefore, support the opinion that disarmament is a problem exclusively for the industrialized countries . . .

"This Assembly faces the question: Is there to be no end to this folly? . . . Yet we, gathered here in the U.N., most somehow cut this Gordian knot, if we cannot unravel it . . . We must not ignore the hopeful signs in recent developments. Outstanding among these are the public pronouncements on disarmament matters, including specific proposals for negotiations . . .

"The General Assembly is meeting in this Special Session at a time when there is a great wave of public concern over the measureless perils of the arms race. What is felt to be in danger is not only peace, stability, social progress, and civilization, but human survival itself.

"Millions of people in all walks of life—scientists, physicians, and other experts not least among them—have voiced a growing fear and anxiety about the present disastrous course . . . There are indications now that popular concern is no longer settled in that fatalistic pose . . . This new expression of popular concern and resolve is an encouraging phenomenon. In a divided and distracted world we witness an upsurge of feelings over an issue that transcends all political differences and is related to common survival. This should enable Governments to look at their arms policies in a fresh perspective. At the same time, it places an unparalleled responsibility on this gathering. If we fail to rise to it, if we continue to temporize, there will be massive disillusionment about the credibility of the professed allegiance of Governments to the aims of peace and progress around the world . . .

"The powerful expressions of public opinion on this issue which we have witnessed recently have been accompanied by an outpouring of new ideas for enduring the present impasse. Many of these innovative ideas can be useful, as they are put forward by public figures with long experience of arms negotiations . . . The heavy responsibilities that representatives bear are, therefore, not solely to Governments but also to humanity itself. Enormous public concern and attention is now focused on the U.N. and on you, the representatives who have gathered here to consider these issues. Perhaps this concern, arising from the mass of humankind and expressing itself through you, will serve at last, like the sword of Alexander in the old Greek history, as the instrument with which the Gordian knot of the arms race can be severed.

"The significance of your deliberations here reaches far beyond the five-week period of this session itself. World statesmanship faces a new challenge, so it must think anew and act anew. All the peoples ask for a creative response which would give a fresh and hopeful direction to human affairs."

At this point the President took up the next two agenda items: organization of the session and report of the Prep Comm. He again called upon the Chairman of the Prep Comm, Ambassador Adeniji. The latter submitted the report.[4] It was endorsed, with the recommendations it contained. The President then named the 21 Vice-Presidents of the session, being representatives from Australia, Benin, Botswana, China, Cuba, Cyprus, France, Indonesia, Mexico, Morocco, Pakistan, Panama, Papua New Guinea, Rwanda, Seychelles, Sweden, Togo, the Ukrainian Soviet Socialist Republic, the Union of Soviet Socialist Republics, the United Kingdom of Great Britain and Northern Ireland, and the United States of America. These were also the Vice-Presidents of the 36th regular session.

Cuba then nominated Ambassador Adeniji to be Chairman of the Ad Hoc Committee of the session. This nomination, recommended by the Prep Comm, was supported by representatives from the German Democratic Republic (for the Eastern European bloc), Malta (for the Western European and Other States), and Turkey (for the Asian States). Ambassador Adeniji was then elected as Chairman of the Ad Hoc Committee. With his election, the General Committee of SSD II was completed: the President, the 21 Vice-Presidents, the Chairmen of the seven main committees (hold-overs from the 36th regular session), and the Chairman of the Ad Hoc Committee.

The provisional agenda, proposed by the Prep Comm, was adopted without change or debate, and without referral to the General Committee, as the seventh item of the provisional agenda.

The final business of the first meeting dealt with the World Disarmament Campaign. The President read the relevent recommendation of the Prep Comm, including the Campaign being launched at the opening meeting. The meeting endorsed the recommendation of the Prep Comm on the Campaign. President Kittani then said: "I have the honor and pleasure solemnly to declare that, as the first substantive step taken by this Second Special Session of the General Assembly, devoted to disarmament, the World Disarmament Campaign has been officially opened." Then he announced that the general debate would begin the next morning. The meeting adjourned at 5:10 p.m.

2. The General Debate

The sessions of many U.N. bodies begin with a general debate. This is an opportunity for the States members of the body to discuss the topic of the session in general or specific terms. Often an important official gives the address, not necessarily the person who is the chief representative of the State for the duration of the session.

General debates have sometimes been criticized for being time-consuming and containing too general material. Yet the values of the general debate are often great. It forces the State to think through policy matters in advance and put, in a sense, its best foot forward on the issue involved. It often brings a Head of State or Government or another key policy maker to the session, if only for a few days. The general debate gives time—perhaps too much time—for the session to become organized for the important work to be attempted, and this sometimes begins before the general debate has closed. Finally, the general debate is watched carefully by members of most delegations to see if some new positions are being advocated by key States. The general debate is an important political weather-vane.

The general debate began on June 8th and lasted through June 26th—covering 24 meetings. In this period, a number of Heads of State or Government and other high officials spoke. The list is given in Table 3.

Significantly lacking from the list are leaders from Eastern Europe and also the Non-Aligned caucus. Perhaps the declining health of President Brezhnev caused the socialist States not to send their highest representatives to SSD II, despite their keen interest. It is harder to explain the absence of the highest officials of most of the Non-Aligned States, since many more attended SSD I. Those few States which sent their top officials to both SSD I and SSD II included Canada, Federal Republic of Germany, Sweden, and the U.K.

Under U.N. rules, each Member State has the "right of reply" if in its judgment it feels unfairly criticized by another State in the debate. Five States used this prerogative. Morocco objected to some of the comments of Mozambique about the conflict in the Western Sahara. China and Democratic Kampuchea criticized the address of Viet Nam. Also Argentina and the U.K. debated the war in the Falkland Islands/Malvinas which was still occurring.

A total of 132 countries participated in the general debate. The lapsed time was more than 63 hours, or an average of 29 minutes for each address. Those 25 States which did not participate in the general debate are the following: Bahrain, Belize, Cape Verde, Central African Republic, Chad, Comoros, Djibouti, Dominica, El Salvador, Equatorial Guinea, Gambia, Guatemala, Guinea-Bissau, Haiti, Ivory Coast, Lesotho, Malawi, Paraguay, St. Lucia, Sao Tome and Principe, Saudi Arabia, Solomon Islands, South Africa, Swaziland, and Vanuatu. Some of these States may not have participated at all in SSD II.

In addition to Member States, certain observer States, other recognized entities, and U.N. agencies were given special permission by the plenary to give statements in the general debate. These included the Holy See as an observer State; the Palestine Liberation Organization and the League of Arab States; UNESCO, U.N. Institute for Training and Research (UNITAR), International Atomic Energy Agency (IAEA), U.N. Environment Program (UNEP), and the U.N. Development Program (UNDP). Significantly, UNICEF voted not to send a representative to speak and the debate on this issue in the Executive Committee of that children's agency was not one of its finest hours.[5]

TABLE 3
HEADS OF STATE OR GOVERNMENT AND OTHER HIGH OFFICIALS ADDRESSING SSD II
(IN ORDER OF APPEARANCE)

Mr. Thorbjorn Falldin—Prime Minister of the Kingdom of Sweden

Mr. Zenko Suzuki—Prime Minister of Japan

Mr. Peter Stambolic—President of the Presidency of the Socialist Federal Republic of Yugoslavia

Mr. Kalevi Sorsa—Prime Minister of the Republic of Finland

Mr. Charles J. Haughey—Prime Minister of Ireland

Mr. Spyros Kyprianou—President of the Republic of Cyprus

Mr. Aristides Royo Sanchez—President of the Republic of Panama

Mr. Helmut Schmidt—Chancellor of the Federal Republic of Germany

Mr. Anker Jorgensen—Prime Minister of the Kingdom of Denmark

Mr. Otema Allimadi—Prime Minister of the Republic of Uganda

Mr. Giovanni Spadolini—President of the Council of Ministers of the Italian Republic

Mr. Andreas A. M. van Agt—Prime Minister and Minister for Foreign Affairs of the Kingdom of the Netherlands

Mr. Carlos Rafael Rodriguez—Vice-President of the State Council and of the Government of the Republic of Cuba

Mr. Ronald Reagan—President of the United States of America

Lieutenant-General Hussain Muhammad Ershad—Chairman of the Council of Ministers and Head of Government of the People's Republic of Bangladesh.

Mr. Menachem Begin—Prime Minister of the State of Israel

Mr. Pierre Elliot Trudeau—Prime Minister of Canada

Mrs. Margaret Thatcher—Prime Minister of the United Kingdom of Great Britain and Northern Ireland

Mr. Ahmed Sékou Touré—President of the Revolutionary People's Republic of Guinea

---

All of the addresses in the general debate deserve mention, and often quoting, but space limits excerpts from only a representative group of countries, given below.

Mr. Huang Hua, Foreign Minister of the People's Republic of China[6]

". . . No objective and unbiased observer can deny the fact that there has been sustained international tension during these years [since SSD II]. This has been mainly due to the acts of expansion and aggression by the hegemonists and to the intensified arms race and fierce rivalry between the two super-Powers. One super-Power has been pressing forward to expand its sphere of influence. Not wishing to be outdone, the other super-Power has exerted its utmost to build up its strength and try to regain its former position of world supremacy. The two super-Powers have been contending for world hegemony. Their rivalry extends to all parts of the globe, thus threatening the independence and sovereignty of small and medium-sized countries as well as world peace and security . . ."

"In recent years the people of Europe, Japan, and the U.S., and elsewhere have launched a mass movement against the nuclear-arms race of the two super-Powers and for preventing nuclear war. We fully understand and sympathize with their concern for peace and for the prevention of war. . . .

"Historical experience tells us that a party which gains the upper hand in an arms race would seek to freeze the status quo and maintain its superiority while the party in an unfavorable position would try to change the status quo, catch up with the other, and redress the imbalance. Now, one super-Power stresses that an arms freeze should come first, while the other insists on priority for arms reduction. . . .

"People often say that this super-Power is launching a 'peace offensive' when it strikes a posture in favor of disarmament. We have a saying in China: it is the mark of a swindler always to present a respectable facade to cover up his misdeeds. The fact that this super-Power is so fond of such 'peace offensives' does not mean it is genuine about disarmament, or that it is prepared to turn over a new leaf and abandon its policy of aggression and expansion. . . .

"The Chinese Government has long since repeatedly pledged to the world that at no time and under no circumstances will China be the first to use nuclear weapons and that it undertakes unconditionally not to use such weapons against non-nuclear States. This amply shows the good faith of the Chinese Government on the question of disarmament. I would like to announce here that, if the two super-Powers take the lead in halting the testing, improving, or manufacturing of nuclear weapons and in reducing their nuclear weapons by 50 per cent, the Chinese Government is ready to join all other nuclear States in undertaking to stop the development and production of nuclear weapons and to reduce further and ultimately destroy them altogether. . . ."

Mr. P. V. Narasimha Rao, Minister for External Affairs of India[7]

"An enormous sense of insecurity and uncertainty oppresses the people of the world in both the industrialized and the developing

Top: Delegates stand for moment of silence as Second Special Session opens on June 7, 1982

Bottom: U.N. Secretary-General Javier Perez de Cuellar and President of the Second Special Session, Ambassador Ismat Kittani of Iraq

Top Left: Chairman Lieut-Gen. Hussain Muhammad Ershad of Bangladesh

Top Right: Prime Minister Pierre Elliott Trudeau of Canada

Bottom Left: Foreign Minister Huang Hua of China

Bottom Right: Chancellor Helmut Schmidt of the Federal Republic of Germany

Top Left: President Ahmed Sékou Touré of Guinea
Top Right: Prime Minister Zenko Suzuki of Japan
Bottom Left: Prime Minister Menachem Begin of Israel
Bottom Right: Prime Minister Thorbjorn Falldin of Sweden

THE
UNIVERSITY OF WINNIPEG
PORTAGE & BALMORAL
WINNIPEG, MAN.   R3B 2E9
CANADA

Top Left: Foreign Minister Andrei A. Gromyko of the U.S.S.R.
Top Right: Prime Minister Margaret Thatcher of the United King-
dom
Bottom Left: President Ronald Reagan of the U.S.A.
Bottom Right: President Peter Stambolic of Yugoslavia

countries. The question today is, shall we allow the nuclear weapon to be the destroyer of the world? This is not an academic question. The number of false alarms that have resulted in nuclear forces being placed on stepped-up alert clearly indicate the risks involved and warn mankind that, whatever the degrees of sophistication attained in safeguard systems, the man-machine combination will not remain fail safe for all time to come. . . .

"Outstanding military commanders, scientists, and policy makers, including many who had earlier propounded these concepts, have now challenged the very notion that a nuclear war can be fought and won. Theories dealing with nuclear war, such as those concerning limited nuclear war and war in outer space, are fantasies, but they are capable of leading to reality of all-out nuclear war. . . .

"Nuclear war doctrines are in essence doctrines of terrorism practiced by nation States. They are based on subjecting the populations of entire countries to the terror of obliteration. If nation States practice terrorism in their international dealings, can this fail to have a deep and unwholesome impact on individuals and societies?

". . . The first and most urgent step in the efforts to root out the menace of nuclear weapons is to agree immediately upon the total prohibition of their use. While there is the Geneva Protocol of 1925 prohibiting the use of both chemical and biological weapons, and there are ongoing negotiations to prohibit, inter alia, the use of radiological weapons, it is strange that the banning of the use of nuclear weapons has not been seriously considered so far . . .

"Early this year, in its communication to the Secretary-General, India proposed the concept of a freeze on nuclear weapons. This proposal provided for a complete stoppage of any further production of such weapons combined with a complete cut-off in the production of fissionable material for weapon purposes. These combined measures would mean that no more nuclear weapons would then be produced anywhere in the world and nuclear facilities everywhere whether in nuclear weapon States or non-nuclear-weapon States would become peaceful and stay peaceful for all time. . . .

"It is India's conviction, therefore, that the focus of disarmament must be clearly directed on nuclear weapons and other weapons of mass destruction. This is not to say that an ever-spiraling arms race in conventional weapons and the increasing sophistication of these weapons systems is not a matter for concern. . . .

"Mrs. Indira Gandhi . . . has asked me to convey the following personal message from her to this gathering: . . . 'Never has a feeling so deeply affected people, across divisions of class, political ideology, and even of international frontiers. It may not yet encompass the whole of the human race, but its numbers are increasing . . . As a first step towards the eventual cutting of existing stockpiles, there must be a freeze on nuclear weapons, providing for the total stoppage of any further production of nuclear weapons, combined with a cut-off in the production of fissionable material for weapons purposes . . . On behalf of the growing world community which is calling for peace, I appeal to leaders of all nuclear-weapon Powers and their allies to help pull the world back from the precipice. Let us all cooperate to save humanity. In a war, the dominant thought is to win. Can we do less for peace?'"

Mr. Zenko Suzuki, Prime Minister of Japan[8]

". . . During these four years [since SSD I] the arms race has exacerbated the threat to peace, heightening the anxieties of peoples, and imposing heavier burdens on each nation at the expense of its economic and social development. This is truly regretable. I am fully aware that it is easier to talk about disarmament than to achieve it . . .

"The two Houses of the Japanese Diet, prior to my departure for this Special Session, unanimously adopted identical resolutions on the promotion of disarmament, in particular nuclear disarmament, as an expression of the aspirations of the Japanese people to a lasting peace. I stand here today in this Assembly Hall representing the collective will of the Japanese people as expressed in those resolutions. I am convinced from the bottom of my heart that the common aspiration to peace of all the peoples of the world is concentrated in this chamber. Our mission here is to combine our efforts in response to this common aspiration of mankind and to move decisively together on the road to peace . . .

"There are today three aspects to our efforts towards enduring peace through disarmament: first, reversal of the trend of the ever-increasing arms race by promoting mutual confidence among States, in particular disarmament of nuclear weapons, those weapons which pose the greatest threat to the survival of mankind, should be pursued with the utmost urgency; secondly, utilization of the human and physical resources released by disarmament to alleviate the poverty and social instability which breed conflict; thirdly, the strengthening and reinforcement of the peace-keeping functions of the U.N. in order to promote disarmament . . .

"In anticipation of this Special Session, voices for the elimination of nuclear weapons have risen in Japan like a flood-tide. Many people from all walks of life in Japan, who greatly outnumber those who came here from Japan on the occasion of the First Special Session, are now visiting here, and many of them are present in this Assembly Hall in order to convey their earnest wish to the U.N.

"During the Second World War, my country had its land reduced to ashes and lost millions of irreplaceable human lives. The cities of Hiroshima and Nagasaki experienced the unprecedented horror of nuclear weapons. As a consequence, we Japanese pledged never to go to war again, and we pray that a nuclear holocaust will never again be inflicted on mankind. These feelings are deeply etched in the mind of every Japanese and they will never be erased. In keeping with our pledge, Japan established after the war a Constitution that proclaims peace as the national commitment. This Constitution states: 'We, the Japanese people, desire peace for all time and are deeply conscious of the high ideals governing human relationships, and we are determined to preserve our security and existence, trusting in the justice and faith of the peace-loving peoples of the world.' My country is determined under this Constitution not to become a military Power, and to continue to maintain the three non-nuclear principles of not possessing nuclear weapons, not producing them, and not permitting their introduction into Japan. . . ."

Mr. Andrei Gromyko, Minister of External Affairs of the U.S.S.R.[9]

". . . President Leonid Illyich Brezhnev has sent a message to the Second Special Session. . . 'This session is faced with great and responsible tasks. Its agenda includes a number of items of paramount importance. But if we are to single out what is the most important, the most urgent, what now animates people in all corners of the globe, what preoccupies the minds of statesmen and public figures in many countries of the world, it is the concern for halting the endless build-up of ever more destructive types of weapons, ensuring a breakthrough in improving international relations and averting a nuclear disaster. . . . Guided by the desire to do all in its power to deliver the peoples from the threat of nuclear devastation and ultimately to exclude its very possibility from the life of mankind, the Soviet Union solemnly declares: the Union of Soviet Socialist Republics assumes an obligation not to be the first to use nuclear weapons. This obligation shall become effective immediately, at the moment it is made public from the rostrum of the U.N. General Assembly. . . .

"'The peoples of the world have the right to expect that the decision of the Soviet Union will be followed by reciprocal steps on the part of the other nuclear States. If the other nuclear Powers assume an equally precise and clear obligation not to be the first to use nuclear weapons, that would be tantamount in practice to a ban on the use of nuclear weapons altogether, which is espoused by the overwhelming majority of the countries of the world. . . . In the search for measures which would actually halt the arms race, many political and public figures of various countries have recently turned to the idea of a freeze, in other words, of stopping a further build-up of nuclear potentials. The considerations advanced in this connection are not all in the same vein; still, on the whole, we believe they go in the right direction. We see in them the reflection of peoples' profound concern for their destinies. To use a figure of speech, people are voting for preserving the supreme value in the world, which is human life. The idea of a mutual freeze of nuclear arsenals as a first step towards their reduction and, eventually, complete elimination is close to the Soviet point of view. However, our country was the initiator of concrete proposals aimed at stopping the nuclear arms race in its quantitative and qualitative aspects. . . . '

"'Every year an overwhelming majority of States in the U.N. has been expressing concern lest mankind trip up and fall into the abyss, concern for preserving the most precious thing on earth, namely, peace or, in other words, life . . . How can that peace be achieved? One should not expect miracles. One has to work for peace. . . .

"'One can hear statements to the effect that arms limitation is not enough, that deep and impressive cuts are needed. The words themselves are not that bad. A closer look reveals, however, that it is the Soviet Union—and it alone—that is to make those deep and impressive cuts. . . . It is asserted, for example, that the Soviet Union has gained an edge in armaments, although that is a fraud, since both facts and figures totally disprove that argument. The obvious intention is to mislead people. . . . What all this adds up to is a desire to wreck the existing parity in the field of nuclear arms, which is determined by the totality of the arms that the two sides possess, rather than by the quantities of some of the individual types. Why is this truth concealed from people? Why is it kept under lock and key? They do not want people to know it. In this way it is easier to see decisions in favor of the arms race and easier to defend bloated military budgets. . . . '

"It is the unprecedented arms race launched in the U.S. that constitutes the destabilizing factor. . . . Each day brings new evidence that the U.S. foreign policy is becoming pervaded more and more with a spirit of militarism. This militaristic frenzy breeds all sorts of frenzied military doctrines. A first nuclear strike is being talked about as if it were something casual or routine, whereas what is involved here is a criminal concept of unleashing nuclear war. The idea that a nuclear war is winnable provided the theatre of that war is moved to some place further away from home—for example, to Europe—is being presented as something of a masterpiece of military strategy. . . .

"The situation in the world causes legitimate concern among peoples. It has found its expression in parliamentary debates, discussions at international forums, and in the upsurge of a mass anti-war movement for which the Soviet people has profound esteem. . . . The Special Session . . . should not become an ordinary event in international relations. This will not happen, given the will of the States represented in this hall. This session will leave a visible imprint on world politics if it gives a significant impetus to solving the most pressing problems of curbing the arms race and of disarmament. The U.N. has adopted quite a few well-intentioned resolutions, yet, no matter how good a resolution may be, it will remain on paper unless followed by deeds. This entirely depends on States and on whether or not they recognize the fact that any chance offered by history in the name of the triumph of life must be seized. That is what the Soviet Union is calling for."

Mr. Ronald Reagan, President of the United States[10]

" . . . America has no territorial ambitions. We occupy no countries and we have built no walls to lock our people in. Our commitment to self-determination, freedom, and peace is the very soul of America. That commitment is as strong today as it ever was. . . .

"The pain of war is still vivid in our national memory. It sends me to this Special Session of the U.N. eager to comply with the plea of Pope Paul VI when he spoke in this chamber nearly 17 years ago. 'If you want to be brothers,' His Holiness said, 'let the arms fall from your hands.' We Americans yearn to let them go. . . .

"The decade of so-called détente witnessed the most massive Soviet buildup of military power in history. They increased their defense spending by 40 per cent while American defense spending actually declined in the same real terms. Soviet aggression and support for violence around the world have eroded the confidence needed for arms negotiations. While we exercised unilateral restraint, they forged ahead and today possess nuclear and conventional forces far in excess of an adequate deterrent capability. Soviet oppression is not limited to the countries they invade. At the very time the Soviet Union is trying to manipulate the peace movement in the West, it is strifling a budding peace movement at home. In Moscow, banners are scuttled, buttons are snatched, and demonstrators are arrested when even a few people dare to speak out about their fears. . . .

"Let me stress that for agreements to work, both sides must be able to verify compliance. The building of mutual confidence in compliance can only be achieved through openness. I encourage the Special Session on disarmament to endorse the importance of these principles in arms control agreements . . .

"The Soviet Union and its allies are violating the Geneva Protocol of 1925, related rules of international law, and the 1972 biological weapons convention. There is conclusive evidence that the Soviet Government has provided toxins for use in Laos and Kampuchea, and are themselves using chemical weapons against freedom fighters in Afghanistan. . . .

"Today the U.S. proposes an international conference on military expenditures to build on the work of this body in developing a common system for accounting and reporting. We urge the Soviet Union in particular to join this effort in good faith, to revise the universally discredited official figures it publishes, and to join with us in giving the world a true account of the resources we allocate to our armed forces. . . .

"During my recent audience with His Holiness Pope John Paul II, I gave him the pledge of the American people to do everything possible for peace and arms reductions. The American people believe forging real and lasting peace to be their sacred trust. . . .

"Is it not time for us really to represent the deepest most heartfelt yearnings of all our people? Let no nation abuse this common longing to be free of fear. We must not manipulate our people by playing upon their nightmares; we must serve mankind through genuine disarmament. With God's help we can secure life and freedom for generations to come."

Mr. Peter Stambolic,
President of the Presidency of the Socialist
Federal Republic of Yugoslavia[11]

" . . . We must approach this session with a sense of responsibility for the future of mankind—responsibility to present generations and to generations to come. . . . We believe that this representative gathering is in itself proof that we share such a feeling of responsibility and that, in spite of differences and disagreements and often even crises in mutual relations, we do not forget what we have in common, nor do we neglect our constant commitment to surmount all that divides us. Today more than ever before the destiny of the world is indivisible and every nation has the right to participate in resolving international problems . . .

"The arms race is being intensified as the consequence and reflection of deeply-rooted contradictions and lack of confidence between the blocs and, above all, between the two big Powers that are fully responsible for this development. . . . The nuclear-weapon States have continued to increase their arsenals, regardless of the recommendations and commitment to reduce armaments. The Treaty on the Non-Proliferation of Nuclear Weapons is flagrantly violated. . . .

"One of the gravest consequences of the arms race . . . is the serious deterioration of the position of Non-Aligned and other developing countries with respect to their security. The forces threatening freedom, as well as the instruments of military intervention, have been growing much faster than the national defense capabilities of threatened countries. . . .

"Proceeding from the original principles and goals of the policies of non-alignment, the Non-Aligned countries have always placed in the focus of their activity the strengthening of peace and international security and cooperation. They have pointed to the untenability of the bloc concept of international security and relations based on domination and hegemony. Non-alignment is essentially a negation of such a policy. The present crisis in international relations unequivocally discloses all the dangers inherent in the bloc division of the world and in the system of security based on the balance of force and terror. Being unreconciled to such a system of security, the Non-Aligned countries have offered a new concept of international relations, the essence of which is active and peaceful co-existence, equitable cooperation, and equal security for States and peoples. . . .

"It is precisely the population of Europe that has strongly manifested its awareness of the fact that disarmament is not a matter of concern to Governments only but it is the vital interests of all people. The streets of cities in Europe have been crowded with hundreds of thousands of people of different political orientation demanding strongly and resolutely that the race in the production of means of destruction be stopped and greater security for all be ensured. . . .

"We consider that a decision on convening the Third Special Session devoted to disarmament should be adopted at this session. It seems to us that the four-year interval has proved to be practical and politically acceptable to all participating States.

"In conclusion I should like to quote certain ideas from the message of President Tito addressed to the First Special Session which, I believe, are equally topical and valid at this moment: 'I am convinced that the present and future generations will not judge countries or statesmen by the destructive power of weapons in their possession, but rather by their genuine efforts and contribution towards stopping destruction and self-annihilation and towards placing human energy, wisdom, and wealth at the service of the security and prosperity of all countries, of all peoples, at the service of the most humane ideals of man.' "

3. Computerized Index

For several years the U.N. Centre for Disarmament (since January 1, 1983, the U.N. Department for Disarmament Affairs) has been compiling a computerized index of substantive issues in disarmament debates. During SSD II an index was made of verbatim records both of the general debate and of the Ad Hoc Committee.[12]

These are an unofficial compilation, for even the subject headings or titles have varying political implications. Thus the unofficial compilation on the general debate contains the caveat: "no official character and serves only as a tool of convenience." The index items are based on those used for several years by the Centre/Department especially to compile the annual "Disarmament Yearbook." However, several new headings are being introduced to cover new developments. In compiling the index, the primary consideration is on comprehensiveness. Some passages are indexed under two or more subject-related headings; on the other hand, references which are not meaningful are omitted. Since some topics are closely related, certain topics need cross-checking.

Each subject heading is indexed alphabetically by Member State or agency, and, then by the number of the provisional verbatim record, followed by the page. The 31 major subject headings, but not the many sub-headings, are given in Table 4.

The index for the general debate of SSD II is admittedly not up to date in terminology. It is also flawed by containing some sub-headings which, by logic if not by tradition, should be full headings, such as items under general and complete disarmament as comprehensive pro-

TABLE 4
MAJOR SUBJECT HEADINGS FOR THE INDEX TO THE GENERAL DEBATE

1. Annual Report of the Secretary-General
2. U.N. Role in Disarmament
3. Conference of the Committee on Disarmament
4. First Special Session on Disarmament
5. Committee on Disarmament
6. Disarmament Commission
7. World Disarmament Conference
8. Nuclear Arms Limitation and Disarmament
9. Nuclear-weapon-free Zones
10. Non-proliferation of Nuclear Weapons
11. Peaceful Uses of Nuclear Energy
12. Cessation of Nuclear-Weapon Tests
13. Security Guarantees for Non-nuclear-weapon States
14. Biological Weapons Convention
15. Prohibition of Chemical Weapons
16. Geneva Protocol of 1925
17. Certain Conventional Weapons
18. Peace Zones
19. Prohibition of Environmental Warfare
20. New Weapons of Mass Destruction
21. Outer Space
22. General and Complete Disarmament
23. Arms Race in the Sea-bed
24. Reduction of Military Budgets
25. Economic and Social Consequences of the Arms Race
26. Disarmament and Development
27. Arms Race, Disarmament, and International Security
28. Program of Studies
29. Information
30. Regional Approach to Disarmament
31. Technological Aspects of the Arms Race

gram of disarmament, international transfers of conventional arms, elimination of foreign military bases, confidence-building measures, etc. These may well be given full categories in subsequent indices.

The index of the general debate in SSD II listed, for example, 49 States mentioning the non-first-use of nuclear weapons. This listing begins with Afghanistan and ends with Zambia. The index, used together with the provisional verbatim reports, constitutes a rich lode of

information. However, although technology is now available to retrieve the substantive statements by computer, this is not yet available
because of financial limitations. Today, even under the present system,
it takes more than the pushing of a button to retrieve the actual substance of the debate on any one issue.

4. The Ad Hoc Committee

After the general debate concluded, all additional agenda items—9
through 13—were dealt with by the Ad Hoc Committee except for the
last item—14—on the adoption of documents of SSD II. Thus when
the plenary concluded the general debate at its 25th meeting on June
23rd, it met only twice until June 9th—the day scheduled for closure.
One additional meeting of the plenary, on June 29th, was to hear an
address by the President of the Republic of Guinea. The other, on June
9th, was to recess for the final meetings on June 10th.

The first and organizational meeting of the Ad Hoc Committee was
held on June 8th. The Committee consisted of all Member States of the
U.N. present for SSD II. (This was somewhat less than 157 Member
States, since an unidentified few were absent for the entire session.)
Ambassador Olu Adeniji of Nigeria had been elected Chairmen of the
Ad Hoc Committee and Mr. Omer Ersun of Turkey Rapporteur. The
other members of the Bureau were the 13 Vice-Chairman. All fifteen
were identical to the Bureau of the Prep Comm. The Bureau met twice
before the second meeting of the Ad Hoc Committee on June 14th.

The work of the Ad Hoc Committee included the following:

○ To constitute the venue for certain oral statements made to SSD
II, but not to its plenary. These consisted of statements by NGOs and
peace and disarmament research institutions, and by the Inter-
Parliamentary Union, the Independent Commission on Disarmament
and Security Issues (the Palme Commission), the Second U.N. Conference on the Exploration and Peaceful Uses on Space (UNISPACE),
and the Director-General for U.N. International Economic and Social
Affairs.

○ To organize working groups and receive their weekly and final
reports.

○ To discuss items which were not directly assigned to the working
groups, especially agenda items 11 and 12 on initiatives and proposals
by Member States and on machinery.

○ To discuss and adopt a concluding document on SSD II to be
recommended to the plenary.

o To help move SSD II to a successful outcome. This role was performed chiefly by the Chairman, Ambassador Adeniji.

The Ad Hoc Committee held 15 meetings as follows:[13]

o June 8th—Opening and organizational meeting.

o June 14th—Introduction of report of CD and organization of work.

o June 17th—Organization of work.

o June 23rd—Oral statements.

o June 24th–25th—Oral statements by NGOs and research institutions.

o June 28th—Reports of working groups, oral statements, and beginning of discussion of initiatives by Member States.

o June 29th and 30th—Proposals and machinery.

o July 2nd—Reports of working groups and initiatives.

o July 6th—Organization of work and presentation of reports of working groups.

o July 7th—Reports by working groups.

o July 9th—Adoption of concluding document for presentation to plenary.

REFERENCES

1. The provisional verbatim record is A/S-12/PV.1. 48 pp.
2. *Ibid.*, pp. 6–13.
3. *Ibid.*, pp. 14–28.
4. A/S-12/1. 58 pp.
5. "Disarmament and Children: UN-ICEF Attempts to Remain Unpolitical," by Homer A. Jack. WCRP Report. 1981. 14 pp.
6. A/S-12/PV.8, pp. 31–45.
7. A/S-12/PV.9, pp. 76–95.
8. A/S-12/PV.5, pp. 16–40.

9. A/S-12/PV.12, pp. 21–62.
10. A/S-12/PV.16, pp. 2–13.
11. A/S-12/PV.6, pp. 2–17.
12. Index to Statements on Disarmament at the Plenary Meetings of the Twelfth Special Session. U.N. Centre for Disarmament. June/July 1982. 52 pp. Index to Statements on Disarmament at the Meetings of the Ad Hoc Committee of the Twelfth Special Session. U.N. Centre for Disarmament. July 1982. n.p.
13. A/S-12/AC.1/PV.1–15.

3.

Assessment of the First Special Session

It was early suggested that, among the agenda items of SSD II, there be one on an assessment of why the Final Document of SSD I failed to be implemented. At the time, few delegates perceived that this seemingly simple evaluation would constitute one of the principal failures of SSD II.

1. The Prep Comm

The Prep Comm put together the provisional agenda of SSD II during its 1981 session. The proposal to include an item on implementation of SSD II was made early. The item, as finally designated, was annotated as follows: "9. Review of the implementation of the decisions and recommendations adopted by the General Assembly at its First Special Session devoted to disarmament as contained in the Program of Action and bearing in mind the priorities set out in the Program; Consideration of the report of the Committee on Disarmament, in particular any draft instruments transmitted by the Committee; Consideration of the report of the Disarmament Commission; Consideration of the implementation of resolutions of the General Assembly on specific tasks, in particular studies, aimed at the realization of the Final Document and their follow-up."[1]

It was not until the final session of the Prep Comm, only a few weeks before SSD II was scheduled to begin, that its members realized that the item on reviewing the implementation of the Final Document was a formidable one and could not entirely wait for negotiations in SSD II itself. Accordingly, on April 30th it was decided to establish an open-ended working group on this topic. (Open-ended meant that any Member State of the Prep Comm could participate.) Indian Ambassador A.P. Venkateswaran was named Chairman.

On the basis of the creation of this working group, a number of delegations and groups of delegations submitted proposals for incorporation in any preliminary document.

In order to bring some rationalization out of the deluge of proposals, an open-ended drafting group was created and met between May 6th and 11th. This put together a composite paper incorporating all the elements contained in the different working papers submitted as well as oral submissions, amendments, additions, and reformulations.

The Prep Comm at its 38th meeting on May 12th heard a report from the Chairman of the working group and took note of the composite paper.[2] It was understood that the paper was compiled to assist SSD II. It was further understood that the paper "did not prejudge the position of any delegation" on any point. The Prep Comm decided to annex the paper in the report of the Prep Comm to SSD II itself.[3]

2. The Composite Paper

The composite paper, appearing as Annex I of the final report of the Prep Comm, is a lengthy document, consisting in English of 36 pages, single-spaced. It is divided into the sections of the Final Document: introduction, principles, program of action, machinery, and conclusions and recommendations. The paper is an inventory giving the lack of progress, except for the completion of a convention against some use of inhumane weapons and for the implementation of some of the suggested disarmament machinery.

The inevitable political nature of the review is evident by the number of square brackets—indicating that one Member State, or a group, placed reservations on the word, sentence, or paragraph. In most cases, the negotiations did not reach the stage of differing over separate words, but varied over whole concepts. Often in a section or sub-section of the paper, the paragraphs within brackets constituted alternatives.

A reading of the composite paper makes clear the huge, and perhaps fruitless, task before SSD II itself. Each caucus, if not individual State, viewed each section, or sub-section, from its own ideological and national security viewpoint. While a description of the failure to implement the Final Document was in itself controversial—to some—certainly the effort to assign blame on one group of States, or another, compounded the political complexity.

Below are a few sentences—all in brackets—from the composite paper, while essentially correct, could hardly emerge as a consensus document:

○ "The policies and actual deeds of the States with the largest military arsenals constitute the main obstacle to the progress of disarmament and the main threat to international peace and security."

○ "Almost every objective, priority, and principle endorsed by the Final Document has neither been faithfully (universally) respected nor observed."

○ "Unfortunately, the cause of disarmament has become an important casualty of the present climate of international tension and confrontation."

○ "The major Powers continue to perceive their security in terms of their own narrow interests and concerns and those of their allies."

○ "The notion that the road to disarmament lies through the build-up of armaments and so-called 'deterrence' must be firmly rejected."

○ "Doctrines of nuclear deterrence are dangerous anomalies, and far from being responsible for the maintenance of international peace and security, they lie at the root of the continuing escalation of the quantitative and qualitative development of nuclear armaments and lead to greater insecurity and instability in international relations."

○ "In parallel with the further refinement and the qualitative development of nuclear weapons and nuclear-weapons systems, credence has been given to the acceptability of so-called limited nuclear war and increasing reliance placed on dangerous doctrines of nuclear deterrence."

○ "The Committee on Disarmament has been prevented from undertaking multilateral negotiations on a treaty on a nuclear test-ban as a result of the opposition of some nuclear-weapon States, which have endeavored to overturn the priorities established for negotiations on nuclear disarmament, by relegating the nuclear test-ban as a long-term objective which must be dealt with as part and parcel of the whole range of nuclear issues. This is clearly contrary to both the letter and spirit of the Final Document."

○ "Non-nuclear-weapon States have a right to participate in multilateral negotiations on nuclear disarmament."

○ "Several instances in the recent past involving the failure of the control and safeguard systems for nuclear weapons demonstrate the need for further urgent action in this area."

o "The general optimism concerning the work of the Committee [on Disarmament] with respect to the prohibition of chemical weapons has been considerably marred by recent evidence that the world may be on the brink of a new and potentially alarming chemical weapons race. The political climate within which such negotiations are taking place has also been vitiated by the recent allegations concerning the use of chemical and biological weapons in certain regions of the world."

o "The increasing number of resolutions adopted each year (in the General Assembly) should not overshadow the very fact that the working methods and procedures of the First Committee need to be improved substantially."

o "Although consensus on all important and substantive issues is to be welcomed, the pursuit of consensus should not become a pretext for inaction or a means to dilute, or worse, to overturn the principles, objectives, and priorities in the field of disarmament, which have long been accepted and endorsed by the international community."

o "One can foresee in the future an increase in the involvement of the international community in the field of disarmament. New responsibilities could be given to the international community, for instance, in the verification area or in the implementation of the relationship between disarmament and development. Such tasks call for corresponding innovations in the institutional framework."

3. The Special Session

The Ad Hoc Committee of SSD II immediately established Working Group II to consider a review of the implementation of the Final Document. It held seven meetings from June 18th to July second, under the chairmanship of Australian Ambassador D. Sadleir. Soon the working group established two drafting groups. Drafting Group A, with Ambassador A. T. Jayakoddy of Sri Lanka as coordinator, was entrusted with considering section III of the composite paper. This dealt with the implementation of the Program of Action of the Final Document. Drafting Group B, with Ambassador Nana S. Sutresna of Indonesia as coordinator, dealt with sections I, II, IV, and V of the composite paper as well as the question of studies.

Drafting Group A held eight meetings and Drafting Group B held seven. Then a Chairman's working paper was produced which served as the basis for subsequent deliberations. The Chairman reported to the 12th meeting of the Ad Hoc Committee on July second[4] that "a large amount of work remained to be accomplished." He added: "Despite a constructive spirit, I can not hide from this Committee the fact that progress was very limited." He also suggested that "because of the very great amount of work before us, the Ad Hoc Committee might wish to consider . . . other alternatives so that the working group might complete its work as requested." Consequently, the Ad Hoc Committee decided to establish a contact group to conclude negotiations on this agenda item. This consisted of the Chairman of the working group and a delegate from the U.S.A. (representing the Western group), a delegate from the Soviet Union and Bulgaria (representing the Eastern European group), the two coordinators (from Sri Lanka and Indonesia to represent the Non-Aligned group), and a delegate from China.

On July seventh, Chairman Adeniji informed members of the Ad Hoc Committee that "the drafting group worked very, very hard and for very long hours throughout the holidays." He added that "some progress was made when the drafting group first started its work, but, according to the convenor of the drafting group, the group lost momentum during the last two days." He reported that the Chairman of the working group "felt that there was no possibility that the informal drafting group would fulfill the mandate in time for it to be considered by this Special Session."[5]

All the Ad Hoc Committee could recommend was that the documents transmitted on this item to SSD II, as well as other proposals, both those submitted and those not fully considered, be submitted to the 37th regular session of the General Assembly.

4. Conclusions

The unfinished documents of Working Group II were not transmitted officially to posterity—as were those of Working Group I on the CPD, since the latter appear unabridged and at length as an annex in the Concluding Document. However, at least the Ad Hoc Committee inserted several paragraphs on the implementation of SSD I in its section on conclusions in the Concluding Document. These were written by Ambassador Adeniji, based on some of the wording elaborated in the negotiations on the assessment. The wording was adopted by consensus at the final meeting of the Ad Hoc Committee and remains the only substantive reflection of these negotiations. The five paragraphs relating to the assessment are found in paragraphs 57–61. (See full text in Appendix B.)

It may have been an illusion to attempt any evaluation of the results of SSD I by SSD II. Certainly the highly political evaluation apparently preferred by the Non-Aligned members (compared to less insistence on strong language by both the Western and Eastern European groups) could not easily result in compromise. Perhaps if the CPD were on the verge of adoption by consensus in the other working group, it might have been more possible to reach consensus on a statement about implementation. Given the impasse on the CPD, the impasse on the assessment was more likely if not completely inevitable.

REFERENCES

1. A/S-12/1, p. 7.
2. *Ibid.*, Annex I, pp. 18–54.
3. A/AC.206/SR.38, p. 2.

4. A/S-12/AC.1/PV.12, pp. 31–35.
5. A/S-12/AC.1/PV.14, p. 42.

4.

Comprehensive Program of Disarmament

The Comprehensive Program of Disarmament—CPD—was to be the centerpiece of the SSD II. As history would reveal, the inability to agree on a CPD constituted the biggest failure of SSD II.

1. Origins

A CPD is not to be equated with general and complete disarmament (GCD), but admittedly the proposals for GCD led to the demand for at least a CPD.

The evolution of "comprehensive" disarmament plans in the nuclear era go back to various disarmament forums in the 1950s. A proposal for GCD was included on the agenda of the 1959 U.N. General Assembly by the Soviet Union and personally introduced by Premier Nikita Khrushchev in September of that year. A resolution was unanimously adopted expressing the hope that "measures leading towards the goal of general and complete disarmament under effective international control will be worked out in detail and agreed upon in the shortest possible time."[1] For the next half-decade the whole U.N. system became increasingly immersed in plans and proposals for GCD. In June 1960, for example, the U.S.A. also proposed a program for GCD. When the new Eighteen-Nation Disarmament Committee (ENDC) was established in 1962, both the Soviet Union and the U.S.A. submitted draft GCD proposals. These remained the basis for discussion during the next three years, until—in the words of Mrs.

Alva Myrdal, one of the ENDC participants—"plans for GCD faded away."[2]

U.N. Secretary-General U Thant in his annual report on the work of the organization for 1968–69 proposed that the decade of the 1970s become the Disarmament Decade. He hoped that the General Assembly would establish "a specific program and time-table dealing with all aspects of arms control and disarmament." The 1969 General Assembly welcomed the suggestion and, proposing to celebrate the 25th anniversary of the U.N. in 1970, proclaimed the Disarmament Decade to parallel the Second U.N. Development Decade.[3] At this time, Italy, Ireland, and Japan co-sponsored a draft resolution requesting the Conference of the Committee on Disarmament (CCD, the successor to the ENDC at Geneva) to work out "a comprehensive program dealing with all aspects of the problem of the cessation of the arms race and general and complete disarmament under effective international control, which would provide the Conference with a guideline to chart the course of its further work and its negotiations."[4]

The CCD in 1969 discussed several working papers on a CPD. In August, Mexico, Sweden, and Yugoslavia submitted a draft CPD.[5] This remained unacceptable to some members of the CCD—which operated by consensus— and the most the negotiating body could do was to refer them to the next session of the General Assembly. Here there was further discussion as Ireland, Mexico, Morocco, Pakistan, Sweden, and Yugoslavia submitted still another draft CPD for discussion.[6] There was sufficient opposition that all the General Assembly could do was, in a resolution, urge the CCD to take into account these several CPD proposals. This action in effect relegated the CPD to oblivion since CCD did very little if anything about a CPD in the immediate years following.

When the Disarmament Decade was at mid-point, the General Assembly again pressed the CCD to elaborate a CPD.[7] In 1978 CCD began seriously to consider its assignment, with an ad hoc working group established to "discuss and elaborate" a CPD. Little was accomplished and the work was truncated by the beginning of SSD I in June 1978. CCD's report to SSD I indicated that 22 working papers on a CPD were submitted to it. In the meanwhile, the Prep Comm for SSD I discussed the CPD and inserted the concept in several provisional sections of what became the Final Document of SSD I.

SSD I in its Final Document discussed a CPD in at least three places. In the Introduction there was expressed the need to "prepare through agreed procedures" a CPD. The Document also indicated that the new Committee on Disarmament (CD) should "undertake the elaboration of a comprehensive program of disarmament encompassing all measures thought to be advisable in order to ensure that the goal of general and complete disarmament under effective international control becomes a reality." Further, the Machinery section of the Final Document asked the reconstituted Disarmament Commission (DC) to "consider the elements of a comprehensive program for disarmament to be submitted as recommendations to the General Assembly and, through it, to the negotiating body, the Committee on Disarmament."[8]

The first session of the new DC, in 1979, spent most of its time elaborating the elements of a CPD. This was a consensus document—with all Member States of the U.N. eligible to participate and concurring—and then was transmitted to the CD through the 1979 General Assembly.[9]

2. Committee on Disarmament

The Committee on Disarmament (CD) at Geneva negotiated a CPD over three years—1980, 1981, and 1982. It took the "elements" of a CPD which the Disarmament Commission in 1979 had elaborated and attempted to make a more complete document—for submission to SSD II.

An Ad Hoc Working Group for CPD was established at the 1980 session of CD and Nigerian Ambassador Olu Adeniji was Chairman. It held ten meetings, but hardly got into the substance of the negotiations.[10] At the beginning of the 1981 session of CD, Mexican Ambassador Alfonso Garcia Robles was made Chairman of the working group. It held 24 meetings."[11] While participants were conscious of the mid-1982 deadline coinciding with SSD II, they showed more urgency at the beginning of 1982 when they convened the working group in January, three weeks before the whole CD was reconvened. The working group held 25 meetings, and many additional meetings of subsidiary groups. In addition to the 40 States members of CD participating, a number of additional States asked to become involved in various stages of the work: Austria, Denmark, Finland, Norway, Spain, Tunisia, and Turkey.

The working papers submitted to the working group were abundant—53 in total.[12] These included memoranda by individual States and by groups of States. In addition to the elements which were before the working group, submitted by the DC, three working papers were especially important: 1) "Draft Comprehensive Program of Disarmament," submitted by Australia, Belgium, Federal Republic of Germany, Japan, and the U.K. on July 31, 1981[13]; 2) "Measures," submitted by the Group of 21 on August 19, 1981[14]; and 3) "Working Paper on the Agenda Item Entitled, 'Comprehensive Program of Disarmament,'" by Bulgaria, Hungary, German Democratic Republic, Mongolia, Poland, U.S.S.R., and Czechoslovakia on February 19, 1982.[15] (The Group of 21 consists of the 21 Non-Aligned and independent States members of the CD.)

The Secretariat was asked to prepare a series of documents for the working group. These totalled eleven and often consisted of tabulations of proposals in the various working papers.[16]

In 1980 the working group adopted an outline of the CPD, based on the elements submitted to it: introduction or preamble, objectives, principles, priorities, measures, stages of implementation, and machinery and procedures. In 1981 the working group completed a preliminary examination of the substantive chapters of the CPD. In 1982, however, it began elaborating the text of the various chapters and established contact groups for various portions, as follows: 1) Objectives, with French Ambassador Francois de La Gorce as coordinator; 2) Principles, with Ambassador Gerhard Herder of the German Democratic Republic as coordinator; and 3) Priorities, with Brazilian Ambassador Celso Antonio de Souza e Silva as coordinator, but with Mr. Tariq Altaf of Pakistan as coordinator of an informal drafting group. The fourth group also was charged with elaborating the chapter on machinery and procedures.

The history of the elaborate negotiations within the working group and its subsidiary organs is beyond the province of this book. However, a comparative outline of the three drafts of a CPD is revealing: the elements adopted by the DC, the truncated draft emanating from the CD at the conclusion of its work in April 1982,[17] and the still unfinished, bracketted draft put in an annex of the Concluding Document of SSD II. This comparative outline is found in Table 5.

While space prohibits a comparison of the texts of each draft, one sample might be instructive, that on the important issue of a nuclear test-ban treaty. See Table 6.

3. Polemic Issues

As soon as the diplomats began seriously to elaborate a CPD, in both the DC and the CD, a number of controversial, polemic issues arose. A few are given below.

TABLE 5
A COMPARATIVE OUTLINE OF THREE DRAFTS OF A CPD, 1979–82.*

Disarmament Commission	*Committee on Disarmament*	*SSD II*
I. INTRODUCTION		
7 paragraphs	To be elaborated	6 paragraphs
II. OBJECTIVES		
5 paragraphs on objectives, principles, and priorities	3 paragraphs	3 paragraphs
III. PRINCIPLES		
See above	48 paragraphs	43 paragraphs
IV. PRIORITIES		
See above	3 paragraphs	Omitted.
Measures **V. MEASURES AND STAGES OF IMPLEMENTATION**		
(No stages)	FIRST STAGE	
	Disarmament Measures	
	A. Nuclear Weapons	
(a) Nuclear test ban	1. Nuclear test ban	1. Danger to mankind
(b) Cessation of n-arms race	2. Cessation of n-arms race	2. Negotiations and verification
(c) Non-nuclear States assurances	3. Limitation of strategic arms	3. Nuclear test ban
(d) Continuation of SALT	4. Intermediate range n-forces	4. Continue strategic agreements
(e) Preventing spread of nuclear weapons	5. Avoidance of use of nuclear weapons and prevention of war	5. Bilateral n-freeze
(f) Nuclear-weapon-free-zones	6. Nuclear non-proliferation	6. Medium range n-forces

*These are taken from the "final" drafts of each body, but even some of the title are in square brackets in columns two and three, and also some of the wording. Only the elements from the Disarmament Commission were approved by consensus.

	7. Nuclear-weapon-free zones	7. N-weapons systems in Europe
	8. Non-Stationing of n-weapons	8. Multilateral negot. in disarmament
		9. Avoidance of use of n-weapons
		10. Nuclear non-proliferation

Other weapons of mass destruction	B. *Other weapons of mass destruction*	B. Other weapons of mass destruction
(a) Chemical weapons	C. *Conv. weapons and armed forces*	C. Conv. weapons and armed forces
(b) New mass dest. weapons	D. *Military expenditures*	D. Military expenditures
(c) Radiological weapons	E. *Related measures*	E. Related Measures

Other Measures

1. Confidence-building measures	1. Confidence-building measures	1. Confidence-building measures
2. Relaxation of international tension	2. Relaxation of international tension	2. Relaxation of international tension
3. Preventing use of force	3. Preventing use of force	3. Preventing use of force
4. Mobilizing world public opinion	4. Mobilization of world opinion	4. Mobilization of world opinion
5. U.N. Disarmament Studies		

Disarmament and Development

| 3 sub-sections | 2 paragraphs | 14 paragraphs |

Disarmanent and International Security

| 4 sub-sections | 2 paragraphs | 5 paragraphs |

INTERMEDIATE STAGE
Disarmanent Measures

A. *Nuclear Weapons*
1. Nuclear Test Ban
2. Cessation of n-arms race
3. Limitation of strategic arms
4. Nuclear non-proliferation
5. Nuclear-free zones

TABLE 5
A COMPARATIVE OUTLINE OF THREE DRAFTS OF A CPD,
1979–82.* *(cont'd)*

Disarmament Commission	Committee on Disarmament	SSD II
	B. *Weapons of mass destruction*	
	C. *Conventional weapons and armed forces*	
	D. *Military expenditures*	
	E. *Related measures*	
	F. *Other Measures*	
	Disarmament and Development	
	Disarmament and International Security	
	LAST STAGE	
	Disarmament Measures	
	A. *Nuclear weapons*	
	B. *Weapons of mass destruction*	
	C. *Conv. weapons and armed forces*	
	D. *Military expenditures*	
	E. *Related measures*	
	Other Measures	
	Disarmament and Development	
	Disarmament and International Security	
Machinery and Procedures	VI. Machinery and Procedures	VI. Machinery and Procedures
A. Role of the U.N.	15 paragraphs and others	13 paragraphs
B. Form of Negotiations		
C. World Dis. Conference		
D. Review and verification		
V. General (3 items on which consensus was not reached)		VII. Verification 5 paragraphs

1. How legally binding can and should a CPD be made? Some of the Non-Aligned delegates felt that a CPD should be legally binding. Thus Ambassador Mansur Ahmed of Pakistan felt that the CPD should "create legally binding obligations." He urged the elaboration of a treaty, including signing and ratification, since "mere 'solemnity' in the adoption of a CPD cannot create confidence among States that inter-linked responsibilities will be discharged by other States." Otherwise, the CPD would "likely meet a fate similar to previous solemn declarations and programs adopted by the U.N." and would "deceive ourselves and our people." Ambassador Henning Wegener of the Federal Republic of Germany, on the other hand, felt that a CPD is "unsuitable for a normal process of ratification." He felt that the most SSD II could do was to adopt the CPD "with a special degree of solemnity in order to raise political commitment."

A concrete proposal was made that a solemn Declaration should accompany the adoption of the CPD and that both should be signed by Heads of State or Government of all Member States and finally noted by the Security Council in a resolution adopted under the provisions of the Charter that are designed to create obligations for States. Other proposals were made, but no conclusions were reached, although the several alternatives were explored.[21]

2. Should the CPD be an outline or contain the results of negotiations on each item? Indian Ambassador A. P. Venkateswaran felt that the CPD "embodies an international strategy for disarmament" which, if meaningful, "then it must map out not only the starting point and the destination, but the route to be followed as well." He asked, "if specific States themselves have to decide that they are going to negotiate, and when they are going to negotiate, why have a CPD?" On the other hand, Ambassador Wegener criticized the draft of the Group of 21 for "not limiting itself to indicating the main trust of negotiations, but anticipates detailed results, thereby prejudging the future decisions of Governments and negotiators." He added that the elements of the CPD worked out by the CD "makes it clear that the CPD should only constitute a framework for substantive negotiations, but should not substitute itself for results that require a concrete negotiation process."

3. Should there be specific stages or phases in the CPD, or is this a meaningless effort? Ambassador Richard H. Fein of the Netherlands failed to see "what over-all criterion could be applied to select a certain set of arms control measures to fit into a certain phase—however, important they may be as such—if abstraction is made of the relevance of arms concerned to a given particular security environment." Ambas-

TABLE 6
DRAFT TEXTS ON A NUCLEAR TEST-BAN TREATY IN THE COMPREHENSIVE PROGRAM

Elements: (a) Nuclear-test ban.[18]

From CD in April 1982: Nuclear test ban. The conclusion of an equitable and non-discriminatory treaty on a nuclear test ban would make a significant contribution to the aim of ending the qualitative improvement of nuclear weapons and the development of new types of such weapons and of preventing the proliferation of nuclear weapons.

(i) The Committee on Disarmament should undertake [without further delay] multilateral negotiations on a treaty on a nuclear test ban. Such a treaty should aim at the general and complete cessation of nuclear [weapons] tests by all States in all environments for all time. It should be able to attract universal adherence. The treaty should include a verification system satisfactory to all parties concerned and provide for the participation of parties directly or through the United Nations system in the verification process.

(ii) The parties who have been engaged in trilateral negotiations on a 'treaty prohibiting nuclear-weapon tests and a protocol covering peaceful nuclear explosions which would be an integral part of the treaty' should [immediately resume and intensify their negotiations [and submit full information on the progress of their talks to the Committee on Disarmament, so as to] contribute to and assist multilateral negotiations on the Treaty].][19]

From SSD II in July 1982: "3. Nuclear test ban: *Text proposed by the Coordinator of Drafting Group C:*

[Conclusion of a multilateral treaty on a nuclear ban [with the participation of all the nuclear-weapon States] [[within the framework of] [as a measure relating to] an effective nuclear disarmament process]. [All possible efforts should be made to achieve this objective.]]

Proposed alternative to the Co-ordinator's text

[The immediate conclusion of a nuclear test-ban treaty would make a significant contribution to the aim of ending the qualitative improvement of nuclear weapons and the development of new types of such weapons and of preventing the proliferation of nuclear weapons.

(a) The Committee on Disarmament should undertake without further delay multilateral negotiations on a nuclear test-ban treaty. Such a treaty should aim at the general and complete cessation of the testing of nuclear weapons by all States in all environments and thus be able to attract universal adherence. The treaty should include a verification system also negotiated in the Committee on Disarmament and to which all States will have access.

(b) The parties that have been engaged in trilateral negotiations on a 'treaty prohibiting nuclear-weapon tests and a protocol covering peaceful nuclear explosions which would be an integral part of the treaty' should immediately resume and intensify their negotiations and submit full information on the progress of their talks to the Committee on Disarmament, so as to contribute to and assist multilateral negotiations on the treaty.][20]

sador Ahmed called the Group of 21 draft of four stages "a rational sequence from beginning to end."

4. Should there be time-frames within the CPD or is this an unrealistic exercise? Most controversy often centered on this issue. Ambassador Wegener admitted that "there must be a dynamic time function built into the CPD," but it must be found rather in the "periodicity of review meetings than in the magic and automatism of a calendar which future events could render useless and futile." He felt that review meetings "with their accompanying public attention and dynamic impact will certainly do more to maintain the momentum of the multilateral and bilateral negotiating process, each time, than a mechanical calendar of negotiating assignments which, if overtaken by reality, would embarrass its former authors." Soviet Ambassador Viktor L. Issraelyan called for a "stage-by-stage achievement of actual disarmament within a fixed time-frame." Ambassador Anwar Sani of Indonesia felt that "if a specific period of time is not set for the CPD as a whole as well as for every stage of the program, it will lose all value as a program." Then the CPD, he declared, "will constitute merely a document containing a list of recommendations without any indication as to when their implementation should be completed." Ambassador Venkateswaran asked, "would it be realistic to expect that an open-ended CPD with not even an indicative time-frame for implementation have any impact on the armament plans of States?" Chinese Ambassador Tian Jin affirmed that "for each stage, an indicative time-frame should be provided."

Ambassador Garcia Robles in the statement of the working group to CD and SSD II reported that "it was generally agreed that the Program should be implemented in the shortest possible time."[22] Elsewhere he stated the working hypothesis was four stages of five years each, while later three stages were posited: first, intermediate, and last.[23]

5. What is a "realistic" CPD and what is an unrealistic one? Ambassador Wegener felt that "in the end, the worth of the CPD will be measured not by the degree of noble intentions embodied in it, but by the real momentum it creates and by the negotiations which it facilitates and fosters." The key word, he felt, was "credibility," and "only a CPD which keeps attainable goals and schedules in mind can meet this test." Ambassador Venkateswaran asserted that the call for realism "in effect implies an indefinite perpetuation of the present status quo; worse, it implies an even further worsening of the security climate for the developing and Non-Aligned nations of the world." In the name of this realism, he added, we are asked to accept the notion of a pernicious balance of nuclear terror and to live indefinitely under the threat

of nuclear war. He concluded that "the realists among us have still not answered a question which has been posed to them repeatedly: is it permissible for any State or group of States to pursue its security interests in a manner that jeopardizes the security of all other States and threatens the survival of the human species itself?"[25]

4. The Prep Comm

The final session of the Prep Comm, meeting in April/May 1982, just a few weeks before the beginning of SSD II, could not avoid discussing the incomplete nature of the Draft CPD which the CD was transmitting to SSD II. Initially the Prep Comm felt some hestiation to deal with the CPD, since the draft was submitted to SSD II and not through the Prep Comm. Yet the highly unfinished character of the CPD compelled the Prep Comm to consider the issue. It decided to establish an open-ended informal working group to "help prepare for the consideration of the CPD." It elected Ambassador D. L. Hepburn of the Bahamas as Chairman. Subsequently a contact group was established within this working group. In the final days of the life of the Prep Comm, the Chairman submitted a document entitled, "Commentary of the Informal Working Group on the CPD." The Committee took note of this document and decided that it should be annexed to the final report of the Prep Comm to SSD II.[26]

The Commentary began by pointing out that its examination of the outstanding issues in the CPD "should not in any way interfere with the results of the work of the CD as reflected in the draft CPD that the Committee has agreed to submit" to SSD II. It wanted to make clear that it was not attempting to tamper with the draft CPD. The working group reported that it had a "useful exchange of views," benefitting "greatly" from the contributions of many delegations beyond the 40 which officially participated in the work of the CD.

Then the Commentary made four conclusions. 1) The elaboration of a CPD was one of the central tasks of SSD II. 2) It was necessary that "no effort should be spared" to reach agreement on the text of a CPD at SSD II. 3) Among the outstanding substantive issues, there were three problem areas: questions relating to measures, time-frames, and the nature of the Program. It added that the successful outcome of the negotiations on the CPD would greatly depend on the resolution of these problems. 4) The working group on the CPD to be established at SSD II should begin its work at the earliest possible time in order to discharge its responsibilities. The Commentary concluded by asserting that "despite the persistence of divergent views, efforts should be made to harmonize the different positions during SSD II."

5. The Special Session

At the second meeting of the Ad Hoc Committee on June 14th, an open-ended working group was established on the CPD, with Ambassador Alfonso Garcia Robles of Mexico as Chairman. Working Group I held four meetings between June 14th and July 7th. However, at the first session, it established four open-ended drafting groups to elaborate a CPD. Drafting Group A considered "objectives" and was coordinated by Ambassador Francois de La Gorce of France. Drafting Group B considered "principles" and was coordinated by Mr. Anatoly Nikitich Sheldov of the Byelorussian Soviet Socialist Republic. Drafting Group C considered sections A to E of Chapter V on "measures and stages of implementation" of the draft CPD and was coordinated by Ambassador Ahmed of Pakistan. Drafting Group D considered the remaining sections of Chapter V as well as Chapter VI on machinery and procedures and was coordinated by Ambassador Curt Lidgard of Sweden.

On his election as Chairman of Working Group I, Ambassador Garcia Robles expressed sincere gratitude for being chosen. He accepted the responsibility because he believed that "the working group is a team effort, in which the responsibility will be shared by all members." He said that the time has now come for every delegation to demonstrate its cooperation by making it possible for us to arrive—as did the Preparatory Committee—at a text free of square brackets in most cases . . . and make it possible for us, despite the existence of fundamental issues remaining to be settled, to put forward solutions which will have won general approval."[27]

On June 28th Ambassador Garcia Robles as Chairman of Working Group I gave an oral progress report.[28] He indicated that "the most substantial progress" was made in Drafting Group A on "objectives," with only the last paragraph in brackets. As for Drafting Group B, dealing with "principles," 23 paragraphs were approved without brackets. With ten others there were no substantive problems, but 11 paragraphs still remained in brackets. In Drafting Group C, two complete readings were made of the text, but it was not possible to make much progress. He called this "understandable" and "not due to lack of industry or skill on the part of the members," but because it is "perhaps the thorniest part of the entire Program." Drafting Group D completed the first reading, but a considerable number of paragraphs remained between brackets. He felt that the discussions held by the group "have brought to light a similarity of views in respect to many of the outstanding issues." He felt that it would be necessary for the informal consultations and scheduled meetings to produce concrete results" in the course of the week "with a view to the adoption of formulas acceptable to all," since only two weeks remained.

At the 14th meeting of the Ad Hoc Committee on July 7th, beginning at 8:45 p.m., the final report of Working Group I was submitted. Since the printed report was not yet available, Ambassador Garcia Robles suggested that the Secretary of the Ad Hoc Committee, Mr. Pal Csillag, read it to the Committee.[29] This brief, almost clinical, report summarized the meetings of the whole group and of the four drafting groups. It recounted the "intensive efforts" to achieve agreement at the sections assigned them. Group A held three meetings, Group B ten meetings, Group C 12 meetings, and Group D 19 meetings. In addition, informal consultations were held.

The report indicated that "progress was achieved on a number of issues, particularly those concerning the chapter on 'objectives' and, to a lesser extent, the chapter on 'principles.'" The report added that "significant differences of opinion persisted on various aspects of the program, notably the chapter on 'measures and stages of implementation.'" The report also indicated that "with respect to the question of time-frames and review mechanisms, informal consultations were held under the guidance of the Chairman of the Working Group, but, while some progress was achieved and promising approaches were explored, it did not prove possible to reconcile divergent views." Also the Chairman composed and submitted a brief draft "introduction."

Together with this report, Working Group I submitted to the Ad Hoc Committee "for its consideration" the texts which were devised— many still containing brackets.

In giving a supplementary oral report, Ambassador Garcia Robles emphasized and described the draft "introduction" which he wrote a few days earlier. (See section below). He expressed thanks to a number of people, but made no explicit comment on the failure of Working Group I.

6. Failure

The above report of Chairman Garcia Robles was high drama. Here was the announcement of the failure of SSD II, but without once using that negative term. Those present sensed the drama, but could not entirely believe it until they heard the dreaded word of failure. This came explicitly, if euphemistically, in the successive comments of delegates who themselves, coming out of a daze, realized the enormity of what had happened in their very presence.

After Ambassador Garcia Robles' announcement, this late-night session on July 7th heard the spontaneous responses of a number of delegates. Their comments consisted of: 1) an expression of disappointment, 2) an apportionment of blame, and 3) a desire that the process of formulating the CPD continue in some other forum.

The expressions of disappointment were many: "regret and disappointment" (Belgium in behalf of the European Community); "saddened" . . . "days of despondency and frustration" (Federal Republic of Germany); "with regret" (Denmark); "our great regret" (Czechoslovakia, speaking for the socialist States); "disappointment" (Canada); "deep regret and disappointment" (Japan); "truly frustrating" (Cuba); "the only thing worse than failure is the temptation to cover it up and to project it as a success" (India); and "keen disappointment" (Ireland).

A few countries were not slow to apportion blame, or to avoid blame: Czechoslovakia: "This was not the fault of the socialist countries." Cuba: "We will not at this juncture name the guilty and the innocent; let each listen to his own conscience to learn who, today, have made it impossible to arrive at a CPD." India: "Some delegations, while professing to further the labors of the Group, have, in fact, been bending their entire efforts and directing their energies towards stonewalling negotiations and preventing progress." Ireland: "For our part we do not wish to apportion responsibility (for this failure)."

Most countries felt that the exercise should and must continue. Federal Republic of Germany: "A project of the utmost importance and does not come to an end during the final stages of this session . . . We must continue our efforts to bring it about." Denmark asked that the CPD be referred "to the CD for further consideration and with an invitation to that body to intensify consideration of the problem." Czechoslovakia: "Despite the complex situation that has arisen we are prepared to participate actively and constructively in the future work on the CPD." Canada: "The process of seeking a CPD has a value of its own provided the negotiations are undertaken with openness and realism." Japan: "We should continue the work on a CPD in some body of the U.N. during the 37th regular session." Cuba: "This temporary frustration will in no way alter the position of the Non-Aligned countries in favor of earnest negotiations to achieve a CPD acceptable to the

entire international community." India: [We] "will continue to strive
and do [our] utmost to . . . achieve a meaningful CPD, whatever may
be the obstacles facing us today." Ireland: "The task on which we
should concentrate our efforts now is to ensure that the elaboration of a
CPD will continue."

Chairman Adeniji of the Ad Hoc Committee, toward the end of the
meeting—at 10:15 p.m.—finally put into words what delegates were
informally saying: "Members will no doubt wish to know, now that we
are about 48 hours from the end of the session, how I see our work
developing during the next two days. First it appears from the report of
the Chairman of Working Group I that the possibility of achieving a
CPD is now out of the question. It is also clear from the report of the
representative of Australia, who has been presiding over that small
drafting group on item 9, the review and appraisal, that that is not
going to be possible. In the circumstances, the two documents which
the Preparatory Committee recommends for adoption by the Special
Session cannot be adopted since we cannot agree on them."[30]

7. Final Action

Between the penultimate meeting of the Ad Hoc Committee, and
its 15th and last meeting, the Chairman and Secretariat had to find a
way of dealing with the failure of SSD II, especially regarding the
CPD. At the final meeting,[31] a draft report of the Ad Hoc Committee
was submitted for its approval and for transmittal to the plenary, meeting the next day.

The Chairman decided that the final report—later called the Concluding Document—would consist of an introduction, a report of the
work of the Ad Hoc Committee, and conclusions, and then six annexes.

When the Ad Hoc Committee held its final meeting on July 9th at
6:55 p.m., the various parts of the final report were distributed for
reading and for approval.

The section on Conclusions contained ten paragraphs. Two dealt
with the CPD.

Paragraph 62 asserted: "The General Assembly regrets that at its
Twelfth Special Session it has not been able to adopt a document on
the Comprehensive Program of Disarmament and on a number of
other items on its agenda." Since, during negotiations of the CPD,
some States acted as if they were repudiating sections of the Final
Document of SSD I, a number of delegates felt it important that SSD
II in its final hours at least reaffirm the Final Document. Thus also in

paragraph 62 was this sentence: "The General Assembly was encouraged by the unanimous and categorical reaffirmation by all Member States of the validity of the Final Document of the Tenth Special Session as well as their solemn commitment to it and their pledge to respect the priorities in disarmament negotiations as agreed to in its Program of Action." As far as known, the only solemn commitment was that, upon reading these words, no Member State broke the consensus when these conclusions (paragraphs 60–64) were adopted.

The entire paragraph 63 also dealt with the CPD: "Member States have affirmed their determination to continue to work for the urgent conclusion of negotiations on and the adoption of the Comprehensive Program of Disarmament, which shall encompass all measures thought to be advisable in order to ensure that the goal of general and complete disarmament under effective international control becomes a reality in a world in which international peace and security prevail, and in which a new international economic order is strengthened and consolidated. To this end, the draft Comprehensive Program of Disarmament is hereby referred back to the Committee on Disarmament together with the views expressed and the progress achieved on the subject at the Special Session. The Committee on Disarmament is requested to submit a revised draft Comprehensive Program of Disarmament to the General Assembly at its thirty-eighth session."

The Concluding Document of SSD II, at the request of the Ad Hoc Committee, also contained an Annex—No. I—called "Texts for the draft Comprehensive Program of Disarmament" submitted by Working Group I." This contained 51 single-spaced pages.

REFERENCES

1. Resolution 1378 (XIV).
2. *The Game of Disarmament*. New York: Pantheon. 397 pp. 1976. p. 305.
3. Resolution 2499 (XXIV).
4. Resolution 2602 E (XXIV).
5. CCD/313.
6. A/8191.
7. Resolution 31/68.
8. Paragraphs 9, 109, and 118.
9. The report of the DC was endorsed by General Assembly resolution 34/83 H.
10. CD/139 or A/35/27. 95 pp.
11. CD/217 and Corr. 1 or A/36/27. 128 pp.
12. A/S-12/2. pp. 62–65.
13. CD/205. 14 pp.
14. CD/223. 23 pp.
15. CD/245. 11 pp.
16. A/S-12/2. p. 66.
17. A/S-12/2. pp. 71–114.
18. A/34/42. Also in *1979 U.N. Disarmament Yearbook*, p. 402.
19. A/S-12/2. p. 79.
20. A/S-12/32. p. 16.
21. A/S-12/2. pp. 68–69.
22. *Ibid.*, p. 68.
23. CD/286.
24. *Ibid.*
25. This section reflects debate in the CD during early 1982, especially in the

150th to 154th meetings. See CD/PV.150–54. See also "Progress Toward a Comprehensive Program of Disarmament," by Homer A. Jack. New York: WCRP. 1982. 17 pp. pp. 10–14.

26. A/S-12/1, Annex II, p. 55.

27. A/S-12/AC.1/PV.2, pp. 21–26.
28. A/S-12/AC.1/PV.9, pp. 3–11.
29. A/S-12/AC.1/PV.14, pp. 2–10.
30. A/S-12/AC.1/PV.14, pp. 43–45.
31. A/S-12/AC.1/PV.15.

5.

Preventing Nuclear War

The Final Document of SSD I in paragraph 56 asserted that "the most effective guarantee against the danger of nuclear war and the use of nuclear weapons is nuclear disarmament and the complete elimination of nuclear weapons." Paragraph 57 observed: "Pending the achievement of this goal, for which negotiations should be vigorously pursued, and bearing in mind the devastating results which nuclear war would have on belligerents and non-belligerents alike, the nuclear-weapon States have special responsibilities to undertake measures aimed at preventing the outbreak of nuclear war."

Given this distinction between nuclear disarmament and "special responsibilities to undertake measures aimed at preventing the outbreak of nuclear war," disarmament deliberative forums have tended to consider both broad types of action. World public opinion also tended recently to give higher priority to preventing the outbreak of nuclear war than to ending the nuclear arms race.

1. 36th General Assembly

The U.N. deliberations about preventing nuclear war came to one climax in the 36th General Assembly in 1981 when three draft resolutions on the topic were discussed and adopted.

Most attention was focused on the Declaration on the Prevention of Nuclear Catastrophe. This was the annual disarmament initiative of the Soviet Union, presented in the general debate by Soviet Foreign

Minister Andrei Gromyko. The Declaration solemnly proclaimed that "States and statesmen that resort first to the use of nuclear weapons will be committing the gravest crime against humanity." The fourth operative paragraph (of five) asserted that "it is the supreme duty and direct obligation of the leaders of the nuclear-weapon States to act in such a way as to eliminate the risk of the outbreak of a nuclear conflict." This resolution[1] was adopted, but by a low affirmative vote: 82, with 19 against and 41 abstentions. Of the nuclear-weapon States, only the Soviet Union voted in favor. France, the U.K., and the U.S.A. voted against, while China was intentionally absent.

A second resolution[2] adopted by the 1981 General Assembly on this topic was that on the "non-use of nuclear weapons and prevention of nuclear war." Presented by India, it declared "once again that the use of nuclear weapons would be a violation of the Charter of the U.N. and a crime against humanity." It urged that SSD II consider the drafting of an international convention or some other agreement on the subject. This resolution was adopted 121 to 19, with six abstentions. China and the Soviet Union voted in favor, with France, the U.K., and the U.S.A. opposed.

The third resolution[3] adopted on the prevention of nuclear war by the 36th General Assembly was introduced by several Non-Aligned States, Sweden, and Romania. This urged the nuclear-weapon States to submit to the Secretary-General for submission to SSD II "their views, proposals, and practical suggestions for ensuring the prevention of nuclear war." It invited other Member States to do likewise. This was adopted without a vote—unanimously.

2. Responses of Nuclear-Weapon States

When the final session of the Prep Comm for SSD II began in April 1982, only one nuclear-weapon State had submitted a response to the Secretary-General. At the final meeting of the session, on May 14th, several States asked why all five nuclear-weapon States did not respond.[4] Indian Ambassador A. P. Venkateswaran felt that the lack of responses, except for China, "showed a lack of sensitivity for the concern of the international community by ignoring the request." He added that "the prevention of nuclear war was one of the main tasks confronting the Second Special Session" since "it was imperative that the session should allay the fears of a nuclear holocaust." Delegates from the Soviet Union, Brazil, Argentina, Pakistan, the German Democratic Republic, and Algeria expressed similar convictions. However, none raised the question, certainly not premature, of giving more emphasis in SSD II to the prevention of nuclear war than was reflected in the provisional agenda.

China, in its response to the Secretary-General, asserted that "only by the complete prohibition and thorough destruction of nuclear weapons can the world be free from the threat of nuclear war."[5] The U.K. subsequently sent in its reply and indicated that "collective defense arrangements founded on the principle of deterrence . . . serve the purpose of preventing war, whether nuclear or conventional." Then the U.K. made this flat assertion: "In the view of the British Government, nuclear war is neither likely nor imminent." The reply suggested that "the actions of others, as demonstrated by the invasion of Afghanistan, the pressures exerted on Poland, and the recent invasion of the Falkland Islands, afford ample proof that the disposition to avoid the use of force, save in self-defense, is not universal." The note added that "as a result, confidence between States is undermined and the search for new measures of arms control and disarmament impeded."[6]

France also replied: "Nuclear deterrence is a keystone in France's security policy." It added that "deterrence, which has kept Europe at peace for over a generation, is not aimed at preventing nuclear conflict while envisaging the possibility of hostilities limited to conventional weapons alone, but rather at the preservation of peace, i.e., the absence of all conflict." France rejected "such deceptive formulae as the non-use of nuclear weapons on a first-strike basis, such formulae ignore the facts and can only mislead as to the true nature of the guarantees supposedly being offered."[7]

Toward the end of SSD II, both the Soviet Union and the U.S.A. finally replied to the query of the Secretary-General.[8] The Soviet Union in a short note pointed to the message of President Brezhnev to SSD II, the statement made by Foreign Minister Andrei Gromyko in the general debate, and the memorandum presented entitled, "Averting the growing nuclear threat and curbing the arms race."[9]

The U.S.A. in a longer note[10] began by admitting that "the fear of nuclear war has compelled all peoples of the world to beseech their leaders to find a remedy." Their fears, the note said, "are understandable, but they should not cause us to ignore the broader goal of seeking means to prevent all wars." The reply then discussed Article 2 of the Charter. The note went on to pledge that "the U.S. will spare no effort in search of measures to prevent any accidental outbreak of nuclear war." It then advocated deterrence: "As long as the threat of war remains a reality and the universal respect for the principles of the U.N. is yet to be achieved, the U.S. must continue to rely on the strategy of deterrence." The latter works because "it makes clear to any potential aggressor that the risks and potential costs far outweigh any gains he might possibly hope to achieve." Until the ultimate goal of effective and verifiable agreements for the control of nuclear arms is reached, "the U.S. must continue to rely on the strategy of nuclear deterrence which has succeeded in helping keep peace since the Second World War."

3. A Subsidiary Body?

At the third meeting of the Ad Hoc Committee of SSD II on June 17th,[11] Soviet Ambassador Viktor L. Issraelyan made a proposal that "consultations be held with regard to the creation of a subsidiary body devoted to the question of the prevention of nuclear war, and that the Ad Hoc Committee return to that question at a subsequent meeting in the near future." Indian Ambassador Venkateswaran at that meeting revealed that the Bureau discussed the matter the day before and that he then supported the creation of a subsidiary body for that purpose. He renewed his request to the Ad Hoc Committee. Brazilian Ambassador Celso Antonio de Souza e Silva also supported the Soviet proposal to find a way to "deal very specifically with the question of the prevention of nuclear war." Argentina listened to the proposal "with great interest." Mexican Ambassador Alfonso Garcia Robles felt that it would be appropriate to consider the best way to deal with the question, "the importance of which can hardly be over-estimated." Also Indonesia and Hungary supported the proposal.

At the meeting of the Ad Hoc Committee on June 28th,[12] Dr. Nikolai N. Blokhin, a physician and President of the Academy of Sciences of the U.S.S.R., delivered a long address on preventing nuclear war. He said that "the central question of contemporary international policy is the prevention of a nuclear war, the curbing of the arms race, and the reduction of military tension." He added that the Soviet delegation at SSD II was insisting, "like many others . . . upon the immediate establishment of a subsidiary body to concentrate on drawing up measures on this most important question (removal or restriction of the threat of nuclear war)."

At the meeting of the Ad Hoc Committee on June 29th,[13] Dr. Jaromir Johanes of Czechoslovakia urged that "all proposals aimed at averting nuclear war should be discussed within the framework of a special subgroup to be set up for this purpose within Working Group III." Mr. Igor I. Ternov of the Byelorussian SSR also said that "at today's meeting" a subsidiary body should be established to deal with the "absolutely key issue" of the prevention of nuclear catastrophe. Ambassador Harry Ott of the German Democratic Republic also made such a proposal.

The 12th meeting of the Ad Hoc Committee on July 2nd[14] dealt at length with how to handle the request to discuss proposals relating to the prevention of nuclear war. Chairman Olu Adeniji reported that the Bureau discussed this issue. He recalled that several delegations asked that a subsidiary body be established to consider the subject (not technically an agenda item.) He did not want to take a position earlier since it might have complicated the creation of the three working groups. Now he asked Chairman Herder of Working Group III to undertake consultations on how to handle the subject, since it came under agenda item 11. He still hoped that a working group might discuss this subject.

Soviet Ambassador Issraelyan asked why the matter had not been dealt with earlier, since so many States on June 17th asked for a subsidiary body. He felt it "should be the central question to be discussed at this session." He pointed out that three draft resolutions submitted at that meeting all dealt with this subject matter. He expressed "great dissatisfaction" that nothing was done since June 17th when not a single delegation raised an objection to the proposal to create a subsidiary body. Thus he failed to understand why the Chairman informed the Committee that on the very last day for the work of the working groups, the third group will, "among a multitude of other proposals, somehow deal with the question of the prevention of nuclear war." He felt that SSD II "somehow dealt in a very cursory manner with a question which is of vital importance."

U.S. Ambassador Kenneth L. Adelman felt that the subject was "our overriding business here at this session" and it is "what the Special Session is all about." He felt that "relegating it to a special working group is just downplaying it too much, and that the issue is so important and vital that it should be in all our main groups" and not "isolated in a small working group." Speakers from the Ukrainian SSR and Poland supported the Soviet position. Ambassador Herder of the German Democratic Republic, Chairman of Working Group III, hoped that, as a result of Ambassador Adelman's statement, the U.S.A. would receive instructions to "take an active part in Working Group III in the elaboration of a document containing concrete measures on the prevention of the outbreak of a nuclear war." The Group would meet the following morning and he looked forward "to a very constructive and active contribution on the part of the U.S. delegation." Ambassador Adelman felt compelled to support the position of Chairman Adeniji "since he has been ganged up on by the Soviet Union, the Ukraine, Poland, and the German Democratic Republic."

Representatives from the Ukrainian SSR, Mongolia, Bulgaria, Hungary, and Cuba supported the setting up of a subsidiary body. At this point Ambassador Adelman made one of his classic statements in SSD II: "We have now heard essentially the same remarks from the Soviet Union, the Ukraine, Poland, the German Democratic Republic, Mongolia, Bulgaria, Hungary, and Cuba. I hope that we can have the remaining countries, Czechoslovakia, Byelorussia, Viet Nam submit the statement for the record while we move on to the more important and substantive issues before the Special Session. I think that having countries make the same speech time and time again only delays the work of the Second Special Session, although I, for one, am quite willing to hear the Czechs, Byelorussians, and Vietnamese if they wish to proceed along these same lines."

In the meantime French Ambassador Francois de La Gorce felt that no special treatment should be reserved at the procedural level for the question of the prevention of nuclear war. It could be discussed first under the list of initiatives in agenda item 11. He objected to having a specific procedural decision confer a special status on the proposal made by one State in relation to proposals made by other States. Thus he "very firmly" supported the position of the Chairman. Ambassador F. van Dongen of the Netherlands said he would prefer the subject to be "prevention of war" since nuclear war is fortunately not yet with us "but war, alas, is." He urged that the Committee not lose any more time, but accept the Chairman's proposal.

Ambassador Issraelyan responded by pointing out that his country did not propose discussing an initiative put forward by any one delegation, but the prevention of nuclear war was one subject "that was touched upon by almost every delegation during the course of the general debate." He felt that, had the subject been given the attention it merits, the result would "have contributed to the over-all success of the work of the Special Session." He asserted that attempts to "turn this important question into a matter for frivolous and humorous discussion are out of place." He regretted that the Chairman's proposal was made at such a late date, but he proposed that the discussion be concluded and that the Committee try the method the Chairman suggested or other ways. He wanted the question to be included in the final document of SSD II.

Chairman Adeniji said that when the Soviet Union proposed a subsidiary organ to discuss the subject, he was not consigning it to the waste-paper basket. He tried to hold consultations, but he encountered "the kind of problem we have witnessed in the open debate that we have had this afternoon." He recalled that Ambassador Herder as Chairman of Working Group III had difficulty in getting delegations to discuss the subject within the Working Group. Thus a specific decision by the Ad Hoc Committee would strengthen his hand in taking up the subject. He concluded by affirming that the prevention of nuclear war is "an important subject; there is no doubt about that." Its importance, however, would not be diminished by its first being discussed in a working group.

4. Two Draft Papers

As the modalities for debating the issue of preventing nuclear war continued to be discussed in the Ad Hoc Committee, and in the corridors, two draft papers emerged, one by the Eastern European States and another by some Western States.

The Bulgarian draft, circulated on July 3rd, contained nine paragraphs.[15] The most distinctive paragraph dealt with outlawing the use of nuclear weapons: "The obligation by nuclear-weapon States not to be the first to use nuclear weapons should be welcomed and those nuclear-weapon States which have not yet assumed such an obligation should take reciprocal steps to this effect." This reflected, of course, the Soviet initiative (made in the general debate) of announcing unilaterally that it would not be the first to use nuclear weapons.

The Western draft, submitted on July 5th by the Federal Republic of Germany, the Netherlands, and Japan, contained 11 paragraphs.[16] It emphasized Article 2 of the U.N. Charter on refraining from the threat or use of force and Article 51 regarding the inherent right of individual or collective self-defense if an armed attack occurs. Perhaps the two most important paragraphs dealt with matters not reflected in the Bulgarian draft: "All States, in particular nuclear-weapon States, [should] promote the objective of the prevention of nuclear war through the preparedness for more openness and transparency, including on military budgets, and an expanded exchange of information and views on military strategy, in particular as related to nuclear weapons, with a view to enhancing both confidence and stability." Another paragraph stressed "the necessity to prevent attacks which may take place by accident, miscalculation, or communications failure, by taking steps to improve communications between Governments, particularly in

areas of tension, by the establishment of 'hot lines' and other methods
of reducing the risk of nuclear conflict such as advance notification of
ICBM launches within, as well as beyond, national boundaries, advance notification of strategic exercises, and an expanded exchange of
strategic forces data."

Neither paper explicitly dealt with a parallel dichotomy running
through SSD II and also relating to the prevention of nuclear war. The
Western States generally advocated deterrence as a prime method to
prevent nuclear war. The Eastern European States tended generally to
advocate nuclear disarmament as the method to do so.

5. "Disappointing Pace"

At the 13th meeting of the Ad Hoc Committee on July 6th[17]—
toward the beginning of the last week of SSD II—Ambassador Herder
reported on the accomplishments of Working Group III in dealing with
item 11 (implementation of the Declaration of the 1980s as the Second
Disarmament Decade and the initiatives and proposals of Member
States.) He said that the question of the prevention of nuclear war had
been discussed extensively. Various approaches were put forward, including the two specific proposals. He reported that the Group expressed the wish to continue consideration of the question with a view
to producing a consensus document. He therefore recommended that
consideration of the item be continued in a small drafting group "which
should report on the outcome of its deliberations as soon as possible."
The Chairman asked the whole Ad Hoc Committee whether it accepted the recommendation of Ambassador Herder. It was decided to
do so.

Ambassador Venkateswaran of India expressed his delegations's
"deep concern at the disappointing pace of the progress in our work."
He asserted that "new doctrines and themes are being advanced which
would have the effect of reconciling the world to an endless and catas-
trophic arms race while the main actors involved debate whether the
present time is propitious for disarmament." He then spoke about the
subject of preventing nuclear war: "It is in the field of the prevention of
nuclear war that my delegation finds the widest gap yawning between
the concern expressed by world leaders and the work we, their representatives, are carrying out here in identifying practical measures at
this session. I can find no statement made in the plenary meeting
which does not refer to the grave issue of the danger of nuclear war. No
one who has had occasion also to listen to the respective representa-

tives of the non-governmental organizations during the past weeks can be in any doubt as to the depth of popular anxiety and concern over the danger of nuclear war. And yet we still seem to be paralyzed and unable to agree even on some modest measures in this regard which could help to allay the fear that has us in its grip." He said that "the success or failure of this Special Session will in the final analysis be determined by whether or not we are able to discipline ourselves and adopt concrete and practical measures for the prevention of a nuclear catastrophe, pending the total elimination of nuclear weapons." He asked, "is it any surprise, therefore, that in answer to the clamor for an end to the menace of nuclear weapons, we hear voices raised in defense of doctrines of deterrence, in defense of the arms race itself?" He further asked, "is it not ironical that at a meeting on disarmament the build-up of armaments is being justified in the name of disarmament and the option to use nuclear weapons is being concealed in the name of preventing nuclear war?"

Soviet Ambassador Issraelyan observed that "the essential question before this session is the question of preventing nuclear war." On June 17th the Soviet Union formally proposed that special attention be given to the question of preventing nuclear war since "it was included in the agenda of life itself." His delegation expressed its dissatisfaction that only on July 2nd the Committee decided that the question should be taken up in Working Group III. So far there had been a lively discussion and documents were produced, but no agreement had been reached. He asked, "why was that not done at the very beginning of this session, as suggested by a broad group of delegations?" He agreed that consultations should continue, on this question in particular, and one more attempt should be made to reach agreement. Ambassador Arthur R. Menzies of Canada asserted that his delegation and a number of other delegations with which he worked closely have fully supported throughout all measures aimed at the prevention of all war, in particular, nuclear war.

Ambassador von Dongen of the Netherlands said that the subject of the prevention of nuclear war "has been in the minds of all representatives, irrespective of the working group or the drafting group in which they have been engaged." The prevention of nuclear holocaust "has been the backdrop against which all discussions in virtually all groups have taken place." He did not subscribe to the view of the Soviet delegation that it has not received sufficient attention. His delegation, together with the German Federal Republic, submitted a paper that very morning, "an honest attempt, motivated by great concern and by a recognition of the importance of the subject." He urged "a more realistic, a more factual, and admittedly, a more modest approach," since "the propagandistic approach adopted by some delegations is not helpful."

Ambassador Stephan Staykov of Bulgaria felt that SSD II "cannot be successful unless, in the final document, there is a text concerning the prevention of nuclear war." Ambassador D. M. Summerhayes of the U.K. indicated that his delegation supported the Western working paper. It was untrue that there was objection in some circles about further discussion of the question of the prevention of nuclear war. Ambassador Yoshio Okawa of Japan said that, representing a country which has learned by experience what a nuclear war entails, his delegation wanted to be a member of the small group discussing the prevention of nuclear war. Mr. Ferenc Gajda of Hungary felt that in the few days more that the session had at its disposal, "we should therefore concentrate our efforts on finding a proper and acceptable solution [to the problem of preventing nuclear war] and on drawing up the relevant part for inclusion in our final document, expressing the great concern we in this room and the masses outside have expressed in that respect."

Ambassador Henning Wegener of the Federal Republic of Germany felt that some earlier speakers suggested, "perhaps in a self-centered manner, that they felt more ardently than others about the prevention of nuclear war, that they are more attached than others to the Final Document, that they are more concerned than others about where we stand in our work." His delegation wanted to refute the criticism that "we have dodged the question of the prevention of nuclear war." Their joint paper tried to strive for consensus which should not be abandoned. Mr. Richard Butler of Australia felt that "the central issue" is the prevention of nuclear war and "there is perhaps no more vital issue facing humanity today." His delegation supported consensus, feeling that "the enemy of consensus is in fact advantage being sought on the basis of division." U.S. Congressman Samuel S. Stratton said that his delegation wanted "not only to prevent nuclear war but to prevent all war." There is, however, "no quick fix, no simple gimmick, and no particular slogan that in itself is going to bring an end to either conventional or nuclear war." He felt that the debate was an exercise "in which the U.S. has been rather subtly blamed for its refusal to fall for such a simple and highly unrealistic brand of wording to put into a final document." No new formula from SSD II is needed to bring about an end to war, only the basic tenets of the U.N. Charter, specifically its Article 24.

At the 14th meeting of the Ad Hoc Committee on July 7th[18] the Chairman reported at the close of the meeting at 10:30 p.m. that he had not yet received a report from the convenor of the drafting group on preventing nuclear war.

6. "Does Not Exist Any More"

It is problematic if the two draft papers could have been reconciled, certainly with time quickly running out. However, any opportunity to do so was truncated by a manoeuver which was reported in *Disarmament Times*,[19] but denied by the Eastern European delegates involved.

On July 6th a drafting group under Ambassador Herder met further to consider the issue of preventing nuclear war. Progress was considered constructive as it met into the night. The group agreed to meet the following morning, July 7th. A Dutch delegate worked overnight to synthesize several proposals. The group gathered at the appointed time, 10:00 a.m., but Chairman Herder was not present. Upon arriving just before noon, Ambassador Herder reportedly announced that "this committee no longer has official stature to continue. Working Group III does not exist any more. I was the Chairman of Working Group III. I no longer have official status to chair this meeting."

This action left some Western delegates dismayed, since they felt that real progress was made the previous evening and since the Eastern bloc was the group pressing for consideration of the issue. One Western delegate felt that Ambassador Herder's action had "destroyed" the drafting process. He commented, "It is a great pity, really, since we had done a lot of work and we were ready to do more." On the other hand, there were reports that some Eastern European States felt that the negotiations were becoming "a silly exercise." Some observers concluded that, on this issue, the Soviet Union preferred no loaf to half a loaf.

The net result is that SSD II made no statement on preventing nuclear war.

At the 15th and final meeting of the Ad Hoc Committee on the evening of July 9th,[20] the report to the plenary was presented, discussed, and adopted. The inability to reach agreement on a statement to prevent nuclear war was not explicitly mentioned; only the absence of a statement in the draft report implied the situation.

Several delegates made statements about the failure of the session (although more made them the next day in the plenary.) Indian Ambassador Venkateswaran declared that the report to be adopted "fails to come to grips with the basic reasons for the failure of this session." He said that "still worse, it does not hold out any hope or encouragement to the millions of people all over the world who have placed such store on the outcome of this session, in particular with respect to removing the threat of nuclear holocaust, which has been increasingly weighing upon them in recent years." He felt that the delegates "by adopting a report which, under the facade of high-sounding words, seeks to conceal the obduracy with which certain States have clung to their narrow security concerns, in total disregard of the anxieties and apprehensions of the vast majority of the countries and peoples of the world, we have in fact abdicated our responsibilities to the U.N. and to the international community as a whole." SSD II has "clearly failed to address ourselves to the most important and fateful issues facing mankind today." He wanted to place on record that "the minimum basis on which we should have proceeded was that of the adoption by consensus at this session of at least some urgent measures for the prevention of nuclear war and for nuclear disarmament." The report being adopted "will serve only to promote still further the growing cynicism concerning the lack of confidence in the U.N. system created to meet the concerns of the international community." Thus the Indian Government dissociated itself from the conclusions of the report. He concluded by saying that "the saddest part of it all is that if we had only dared we could have won."

7. Other Approaches

The consideration of the broader topic of the prevention of nuclear war was not confined to the Bulgarian or Western draft texts and the discussions in the drafting group of Working Group III. Other States insisted on dealing differently with this issue, especially since some had worked on it earlier.

India and Mexico on July 2nd introduced a draft resolution[21] which, in a sense, constituted a follow-up to General Assembly resolution 36/81 B on preventing nuclear war. This requested the Secretary-General to "appoint a representative group of public persons of great eminence, consisting of statesmen, scientists, physicians, jurists, religious leaders, philosophers, and other suitable qualified persons, for the purpose of advising on special measures and procedures—practical, political, and legal—designed for the collective control, management, and resolution of critical or confrontational situations which could escalate to nuclear war, in addition to those already provided for in the Charter of the U.N." France submitted a somewhat parallel proposal, which was incorporated into the paper on a World Disarmament Campaign.[22] The Indian and Mexican draft was barely considered. It was, however, included in full in the Concluding Document of SSD II.

India on July 2nd also submitted another draft resolution, including a draft convention, on the prohibition of the use of nuclear weapons.[23] It reaffirmed earlier resolutions of the General Assembly going back to 1961 that the use of nuclear weapons would be a violation of the Charter of the U.N. and a crime against humanity. The draft convention in Article 1 asks the States Parties solemnly to undertake not to use or threaten to use nuclear weapons in any circumstances. Again, while this was printed in full in the Concluding Document of SSD II, it was not seriously considered. It did, however, emerge as a draft resolution and convention at the 37th General Assembly, and was adopted.

India on July 8th—when SSD II was obviously about to fail—submitted still a third draft resolution on the prevention of nuclear war.[24] The operative paragraph calls upon States to undertake the following "urgent measures" to prevent nuclear war: 1) A convention on the complete prohibition of the use or threat of use of nuclear weapons; 2) Cessation of the testing of nuclear weapons pending the conclusion of a treaty banning the testing of nuclear weapons; 3) A complete freeze on the development, production, and deployment of nuclear weapons and their means of delivery along with a cut-off in the production of fissionable materials for weapons purposes. Submitted only the day before SSD II was scheduled to conclude, this draft received almost no attention, but again was printed in full in the Concluding Document of SSD II.

8. 37th Regular Session

The 37th regular session of the General Assembly became the venue to which the debate on preventing nuclear war was transferred. Several efforts from SSD II were continued, some successful.

A group of 19 States, many Non-Aligned, co-sponsored a draft resolution on the prevention of nuclear war. This recalled the 1981 resolution on prevention of nuclear war. The draft resolution requested the CD to undertake, " as a matter of highest priority, negotiations with a view to achieving agreement on appropriate and practical measures for the prevention of a nuclear war." It further urged that the provisional agenda for the 38th General Assembly include an item on prevention of nuclear war. This resolution was overwhelmingly adopted, with 130 favorable votes, none opposed, and 17 abstentions. The latter included all NATO States (except Greece) and Australia, Japan, and New Zealand.[25]

A more comprehensive resolution, co-sponsored by 31 States, gave even greater emphasis for the need of nuclear disarmament. It urged all States to implement the recommendations of SSD I concerning nuclear disarmament. It further called upon the CD to "concentrate its work on the substantive and priority item on its agenda, to proceed to negotiations on nuclear disarmament without further delay." It finally called upon nuclear-weapon States engaged in separate negotiations on issues of nuclear disarmament to exert the utmost effort to achieve concrete results. This was adopted 134 to none, with 12 abstentions. The latter included France, the U.K., and the U.S.A., as well as Belgium, Colombia, German Federal Republic, Italy, Japan, Lebanon, Luxembourg, Netherlands, and Turkey.[26]

Still a third resolution, introduced by Yugoslavia, urged the CD to establish an ad hoc working group on the cessations of the nuclear arms race and nuclear disarmament. This was adopted 131 to none, also with 17 abstentions, largely from NATO.[27]

Thirteen socialist States co-sponsored a draft resolution on "nuclear weapons in all aspects." This called upon the CD to negotiate a nuclear disarmament program in accordance with the Final Document of SSD I, and to establish an ad hoc working group on the cessation of the nuclear arms race and on nuclear disarmament. This draft drew more opposition. The final vote was 118 to 19, with nine abstentions. The negative votes were cast by the NATO States (except Greece), Japan, and Israel, while the abstentions were Greece, Guatemala, Lebanon, Paraguay, Philippines, Saudi Arabia, Somalia, Uruguay, and Zaire.[28]

The Indian resolution, including a draft convention, on the non-use of nuclear weapons also was introduced, this time co-sponsored by 20 States. It requested the CD on a priority basis to negotiate an international convention prohibiting "the use or threat of use of nuclear weapons under any circumstances." This was adopted 117 to 17, with eight abstentions. Again, NATO voted in the negative while Austria, Finland, Greece, Guatemala, Ireland, Israel, Japan, and Paraguay were among those which abstained.[29]

India and Mexico also submitted a draft resolution on prevention of nuclear war.[30] A key operative paragraph invited "Member States to transmit their views on the appointment by the Secretary-General of a representative group of public persons of great eminence, consisting of statesmen, scientists, physicians, jurists, religious leaders, philosophers, and other suitable qualified persons, for the purpose of advising on special measures and procedures—practical, political, and legal—designed for the collective control, management, and resolution of critical and confrontational situations which could escalate to nuclear war, in addition to those already provided in the Charter of the U.N." The sponsors decided not to press this resolution to a vote during the 37th General Assembly.

In still another initiative, also originating in SSD II, India submitted a draft resolution on "urgent measures for the prevention of nuclear war and for nuclear disarmament."[31] This contained a four-point program, beginning with a convention on the complete prohibition of the use of nuclear weapons. India later withdrew this draft resolution.

9. No First Use of Nuclear Weapons

The announcement in SSD II, in a statement read for President Brezhnev and amplified by Soviet Foreign Minister Gromyko, that the Soviet Union "assumes an obligation not to be the first to use nuclear weapons . . . effective immediately" was widely discussed.[32] Initially, many forgot that China made the same "unilateral" announcement 18 years earlier when it first detonated an atomic weapon. The Soviet announcement caused considerable debate, with 49 States discussing the issue in the general debate of the plenary and seven in the Ad Hoc Committee. Nothing came of this proposal since SSD II ended without endorsing any substantive disarmament measure.

However, in the 37th General Assembly, Soviet Foreign Minister Gromyko discussed the proposal further.[33] He began by asserting that "it would be a mistake to underestimate the rising menace of war, but it is an even greater mistake to fail to see that possibilities do exist for putting up an insurmountable barrier against war." He called the obligation "unilaterally assumed by the Soviet Union not to be the first to use nuclear weapons" an "act of historic importance and it was seen as such throughout the world." He asked: "Is it not time for our Western partners, the countries of NATO, to assess in earnest the opportunities opened up by the Soviet Union's initiative?" He concluded: "We expect them to weigh it carefully once again."

The German Democratic Republic introduced a draft resolution, co-sponsored by three other socialist States, on the "non-use of nuclear weapons and prevention of nuclear war." This considered that "the solemn declarations by two nuclear-weapon States made or reiterated at the Second Session of the General Assembly devoted to disarmament concerning their respective obligations not to be the first to use nuclear weapons offer an important avenue to decrease the danger of nuclear war" and expressed "its hope that the other nuclear-weapon States would consider making declarations with respect to not being the first to use nuclear weapons." This was adopted 112 to 19, with 15 abstentions. The negative votes were cast by NATO (except Greece which voted in favor), Australia, Israel, Japan, and New Zealand. The abstentions were Austria, Bahamas, China, Finland, Guatemala, Ivory Coast, Malawi, Malaysia, Paraguay, Philippines, Rwanda, Saudi Arabia, Singapore, Uruguay, and Zaire.[34]

Some of the reservations expressed on this draft resolution are worth noting:

O Denmark: "We value and respect declarations concerning the obligation not to be the first to use nuclear weapons. It should not be excluded that, at a given state of the process of disarmament, solemn declarations not to resort to first use of nuclear weapons may be an important confidence-building measure. But, in our opinion, arms build-up, weapons arsenals, and political conduct must be seen as a whole."[35]

O China: "The Chinese delegation has already clarified the difference between our position and the position of another nuclear State . . . We abstained . . ."[36]

O Austria: "We have some doubt as to whether declarations by the nuclear-weapons States not to be the first to use nuclear weapons, important as they may be from a political point of view as declarations of intent, are at present in themselves able to decrease the nuclear threat."[37]

O Finland: "While we strongly oppose the use of nuclear weapons as one aspect of the principle of the non-use of force, as laid down in the Charter of the U.N., we realize that the question of the non-first-use of nuclear weapons is one of the most controversial problems between the two military alliances. It is directly linked with the most sensitive part of the doctrines guiding the defense policies of many Member States of the U.N. These controversial elements . . . led my delegation to abstain."[38]

O India: "Pending the complete elimination of nuclear weapons, the best means of preventing nuclear war is through the complete prohibition of the use or threat of use of nuclear weapons in any circumstances."[39]

O Belgium: "To single out in this commitment one part of the arsenals, in this particular case, that the nuclear weapons would never be used except in response to an attack, would considerably reduce the purport of the commitment of our countries."[40]

○ U.S.A.: "Its basic idea is disarmingly simple: unilateral declarations by States that they will not be the first to use nuclear weapons. At first blush the idea also might strike most as obvious and unassailable: is not nuclear war, after all, a horror, the threat of which all men can agree must be reduced and eliminated? . . . The issue of selective prohibition of the use of nuclear weapons has appeared here in one form or another for many years. The representatives to this Committee thus understand that the superficial appeal of such resolutions is deceptive. The underlying issues are, indeed, complex and troubling, and they cry out not to be ignored . . . As the NATO Member States declared again in Bonn, Germany, in June of this year: 'None of our weapons will ever be used except in response to attack.' . . . In the light of the Charter the proposals for declarations on non-first-use of nuclear weapons are unnecessary and redundant; they divert attention from the need to address the danger of war itself; they also misdirect attention from the threat posed by the massive build-up of the strategic and intermediate-range nuclear forces of one bloc of States, which my Government has repeatedly curtailed. In present circumstances, calls by that side for unenforceable unilateral pledges are hollow . . . My Government believes that draft resolution is not only superfluous but mischievous, in that it attempts to direct attention away from the binding character of the provisions of the Charter and from the serious challenge of negotiated agreements that fairly and verifiably reduce the level and instability of both nuclear and conventional military forces."[41]

SSD II and the 37th regular session did not make any firm moves to lessen the threat of nuclear war. However, the debates were rich and the resolutions emerging from the 37th session were numerous. The problem was tossed back to the CD which only gingerly is backing into the problem of preventing nuclear war.

REFERENCES

1. Resolution 36/100.
2. Resolution 36/92 I.
3. Resolution 36/81 B.
4. A/AC.206/SR.41, pp. 4–7.
5. A/S-12/11, pp. 3–4. May 4, 1982.
6. A/S-12/11/Add. 1, pp. 6–7. June 4, 1982.
7. A/S-12/11/Add. 2, pp. 4–5. June 14, 1982.
8. A/S-12/11/Add. 4, pp. 1–3.
9. *Ibid.*, p. 2.
10. *Ibid.*, pp. 2–3.
11. A/S-12/AC.1/PV.3, pp. 3–5.
12. A/S-12/AC.1/PV.9, p. 56.

13. A/S-12/AC.1/PV.10.
14. A/S-12/AC.1/PV.12.
15. A/S-12/32, Annex III, p. 1.
16. A/S-12/32, Annex III, pp. 2–3.
17. A/S-12/AC.1/PV.13
18. A/S-12/AC.1/PV.14, p. 42.
19. Vol. V, No. 21, July 9, 1982, pp. 1–2. See follow-up, Vol. V, No. 23, November 1982, p. 3.
20. A/S-12/AC.1/PV.15
21. A/S-12/AC.1/L.2.   Also   A/S-12/32, pp. 10–11.
22. A/S-12/AC.1/40.
23. A/S-12/AC.1/L.4.   Also   A/S-12/32, pp. 13–14.
24. A/S-12/AC.1/L.6.   Also   A/S-12/32, pp. 14–16.
25. A/37/PV.98, pp. 67–68. This is resolution 37/78 I.

26. A/37/PV.98, pp. 61–62. This is resolution 37/78 F.
27. A/37/PV.98, pp. 66–67. This is resolution 37/78 G.
28. A/37/PV.98, pp. 59–60. This is resolution 37/78 C.
29. A/37/PV.101, pp. 45–46. This is resolution 37/100 C.
30. A/C.1/37/L.2 and Rev.1
31. A/C.1/37/L.5.
32. A/S-12/PV.12, pp. 22.
33. A/37/PV.98, pp. 68–70.
34. Resolution 37/78 J.
35. A/C.1/37/PV.41, pp. 74–75.
36. *Ibid.*, p. 76.
37. *Ibid.*, p. 76.
38. *Ibid.*, p. 77.
39. *Ibid.*, p. 78.
40. *Ibid.*, pp. 79–80.
41. *Ibid.*, pp. 81–82.

6.

The Nuclear Freeze

A freeze on nuclear weapons was a concept occasionally heard in the halls of the U.N. in New York and Geneva in the 1960s and 1970s. In 1981, with frustrations mounting over the Strategic Arms Limitation Treaty (SALT II), a group of U.S.A. disarmament experts and activists launched a U.S. nuclear weapons freeze campaign. This urged a bilateral, U.S./U.S.S.R. freeze on the testing, production, and deployment of all nuclear weapons and their delivery vehicles.

During 1982, the nuclear freeze grew to become the largest disarmament campaign in the U.S.A. in the atomic era, even surpassing the campaigns in the late 1950s and early 1960s.

In late 1981, the U.S. National Nuclear Freeze Campaign established an International Task Force to forge links with the equally burgeoning disarmament campaigns in Western Europe. Then, in anticipation of the Second U.N. Special Session on Disarmament, the U.S. campaign felt the necessity of internationalizing the freeze effort and bringing it to the U.N. For this purpose the International Task Force opened an office in the U.N. community and hired several representatives to acquaint members of U.N. delegations, Secretariat, press, and non-governmental organizations (NGOs) with the U.S. campaign.

This chapter tells the substantive story of this successful effort. Several nuclear freeze proposals were made to the U.N. Special Session and the nuclear freeze became a well-discussed issue. However, due to the agreement to operate by consensus, the Special Session adopted no substantive resolutions, including those on the nuclear freeze. This issue was, nevertheless, taken to the 37th regular session of the General Assembly which met only ten weeks after the Special Session adjourned. The International Task Force again set up an office, and hired staff, to encourage this effort in September/December 1982.

In December 1982, two nuclear freeze resolutions were adopted, including the Mexican/Swedish initiative which paralleled the proposals of the U.S. campaign. This was introduced, both in the special and regular sessions, by Mexican Ambassador Alfonso Garcia Robles, who in the autumn of 1982 was awarded (together with Mrs. Alva Myrdal) the Nobel Peace Prize.

The Mexican/Swedish initiative was adopted on December 13th overwhelmingly—by a vote in the plenary of 119 to 17, with five abstentions. This may have been one of the most important disarmament resolutions adopted in recent times by the U.N. General Assembly, certainly the most important of the 58 disarmament resolutions adopted in December 1982. The U.S.A. and NATO became politically isolated on this issue.

Equally significant, the U.N. vote, both in the First Committee and in the plenary, caused repercussions in some NATO States where many people and parliamentarians were ahead of their governments in demanding a nuclear freeze. Accordingly, the impending U.N. votes caused internal political debates on the nuclear freeze. As a result, there were some defections from NATO: Greece voted in favor of the freeze, and Iceland and Denmark abstained. In voting against the freeze, the Governments of Norway and the Netherlands had much explaining to make, to the U.N. and to their own constituents.

1. The General Debate

Beginning on June 8, 1982, most of the 157 Member States of the U.N. participated in the general debate of the Second U.N. Special Session. A few addresses favorably mentioned the nuclear freeze, such as the following:

○ BANGLADESH. *Chairman of the Council of Ministers Lieutenant-General Hussain Muhammad Ershad:* "A total freeze on the production, development, and research on and development of nuclear weapons and their delivery systems to be followed by the application of universal and non-discriminatory safeguards to all nuclear facilities in the world . . ."[1]

○ CANADA. *Prime Minister Pierre Elliot Trudeau:* "In seeking to arrest the arms race, the problem that continues to preoccupy me is the technological momentum that lies at its root . . . Four years ago I put before this Assembly a 'strategy of suffocation' designed to deprive the nuclear arms race of the oxygen on which it feeds . . . [This would] halt the technological momentum of the arms race by freezing at the initial or testing stage the development of new weapons systems. While I continue to believe that such a technological freeze is fundamental to controlling the arms race, I would now propose, however, that it be incorporated into a more general policy of stabilization."[2]

○ MEXICO. *Secretary for External Relations Jorge Casteneda:* "It is essential and urgent to seek an immediate halt to the nuclear-arms race, but for now we can support the so-called 'nuclear freeze' as an initial measure . . . The important thing is to accept a parity in over-all terms and move on to put a halt to the development of new weapons systems."[3]

○ INDIA. *Minister for Foreign Affairs P.V. Narasimha Rao:* "The logic of a freeze is unassailable as an earnest of subsequent cuts. Early this year, India proposed the concept of a freeze on nuclear weapons. This proposal provided for a complete stoppage of any further production of such weapons combined with a complete cut-off in the production of fissionable material for weapons purposes. These combined measures would mean that no more nuclear weapons would then be produced anywhere in the world and nuclear facilities everywhere, whether in nuclear weapon States or non-nuclear weapon States, would become peaceful and stay peaceful for all time . . ."[4]

○ IRELAND. *Prime Minister Charles J. Haughey:* "I believe that the nuclear Powers should take account of the many public calls for a freeze on nuclear weapons at least to the extent of agreeing on such a freeze or moratorium for, say, an initial two-year period. This would mean agreeing not to add to the existing number of warheads or of delivery vehicles for nuclear weapons on either side over a two-year trial period when serious negotiations such as the strategic arms reduction talks (START) are under way. Of course, if this two-year moratorium should increase trust on either side, it could be extended year by year while real and substantive disarmament measures are being worked out."[5]

○ NIGERIA. *Minister of External Affairs Ishaya Audu:* "We greet with enthusiasm the peace movements in Europe, North America, and elsewhere, the proponents of 'ground zero,' and the public at large, who have continued to dramatize the unacceptability of the nuclear weapons option. We share with them the expectation that a nuclear freeze could become immediately possible as a result of the deliberations of this Special Session."[6]

○ ROMANIA. *Minister of Foreign Affairs Stefan Andrei:* "In order to halt the arms race, we propose the freezing of military expenditures at the 1982 level and their reduction by ten to 15 per cent by 1985."[7]

○ SWEDEN. *Prime Minister Thorbjorn Falldin:* "The super-Powers must . . . reach agreement on freezing nuclear-weapon arsenals and the number of delivery vehicles. Such a freeze could constitute the starting point for negotiations on balanced and verifiable reductions of various kinds of nuclear weapons, as well as on limitations on the development and production of new types of nuclear weapons and delivery vehicles."[8]

○ U.S.S.R. *Minister of Foreign Affairs Andrei A. Gromyko:* "President Leonid Brezhnev has sent a message to the Second Special Session . . . 'In the search for measures which would actually halt the arms race, many political and public figures of various countries have recently turned to the idea of a freeze, in other words, of stopping a further build-up of nuclear potentials. The considerations advanced in this connection are not all in the same vein; still, on the whole, we believe they go in the right direction. We see in them the reflection of peoples' profound concern for their destinies.' "[9]

Some addresses in the general debate explicitly attacked the nuclear freeze concept, including the following:

○ PEOPLE'S REPUBLIC OF CHINA. *Foreign Minister Huang Hua:* "Historical experience tells us that a party which gains the upper hand in an arms race would seek to freeze the status quo and maintain its superiority while the party in an unfavorable position would try to change the status quo, catch up with the other, and redress the imbalance. Now, one super-Power stresses that an arms freeze should come first, while the other insists on priority for arms reduction."[10]

○ ITALY. *President Giovanni Spadolini:* "Proposals for 'freezing' existing ascertained imbalances can only aggravate the tension between East and West and make it more difficult to achieve specific disarmament agreements—agreements which must be based on the criteria of reciprocity."[11]

○ PORTUGAL. *Ambassador Rui Eduardo Barbosa de Medina:* "The proposals made to freeze the current situation do not, however, seem to us acceptable. They would mean maintenance of an imbalance if adequate measures to ensure a new balance were not taken. Clearly these are proposals that do not serve the interests of peace."[12]

○ UNITED KINGDOM. *Prime Minister Margaret Thatcher:* "Decisive action is needed, not just declarations or freezes."[13]

2. June 12th and Beyond

A great psychological, if not immediately political, boost to the freeze effort at the U.N. came on June 12th with the demonstration of several hundred thousand persons marching past U.N. Headquarters and a total of 750,000 persons gathering in Central Park. The first of two official slogans of the June 12th rally was a "call for a freeze and reduction of all nuclear weapons."

While, politically, the walls of the "glass house on the East River" appeared too thick for delegates to hear the demonstrations, some of the statesmen acknowledged the pleas of the public if not their politics. A few examples follow:

○ CANADA. *Prime Minister Pierre Elliot Trudeau:* "The Warsaw Pact countries . . . would be ill-advised to assume that public demonstrations in the West will weaken our negotiating position. True, hundreds of thousands of demonstrators in Western Europe, in Canada, and here in New York last week have taken pains to express the extent to which a renewed arms race is fundamentally repugnant to their values. In many ways, I suppose most of us in this Assembly agree with them . . ."[14]

○ GERMAN FEDERAL REPUBLIC. *Chancellor Helmut Schmidt:* "Not only here in New York, but in many cities in many countries all over the world we have been witnessing during these days and weeks of spring 1982 gatherings of young and older people who are voicing their fear of a terrible and excessive arms build-up and an overkill that surpass all understanding. Today it is not only idealistic pacifists and starry-eyed Utopians who are protesting against such concepts. Doubts are more and more urgently being raised as to the wisdom of the strategic thinkers, the diplomats, and the statesmen and as to their capability finally of breaking out of the vicious circle of armament and still more armament . . . We should not underestimate the great and positive moral force that emerges in the movement for effective disarmament. We should not simply push aside those who support that movement, dismissing them as amateurs who lack sufficient insight. Instead, and on the contrary, the driving force that has become apparent in the unrest of many of our fellow citizens must be regarded as a motivation and a moral obligation for us."[15]

○ India. *Prime Minister Indira Gandhi made a statement trans-*

mitted to the Assembly: "Never has a feeling so deeply affected people, across divisions of class, political ideology, and even of international frontiers. It may not yet encompass the whole of the human race, but its numbers are increasing . . ."[16]

○ JAPAN. *Prime Minister Zenko Suzuki:* "In anticipation of this Special Session, voices for the elimination of nuclear weapons have risen in Japan like a floodtide. Many people from all walks of life in Japan, who greatly outnumber those who came here from Japan on the occasion of the First Special Session, are now visiting here, and many of them are present in this Assembly Hall in order to convey their earnest wish to the United Nations . . ."[17]

○ NETHERLANDS. *Prime Minister Andreas A. M. van Agt:* "Here at the U.N. we are on stage: everything we say and do or fail to achieve at this session will be watched by millions of our citizens, whose alarm at the dangers threatening them is not only understandable but often justified and legitimate. In a number of Western countries, my own included, this grave concern has inspired the growth of massive peace movements. If the peoples in other countries, where the liberty of expression is severely circumscribed, were free to organize disarmament rallies, I have no doubt that the turn-out would be as great as it was in New York or Amsterdam . . ."[18]

○ SWEDEN. *Prime Minister Thorbjorn Falldin:* "The call for disarmament is growing in strength. Behind this call stands a strong and world-wide peace movement. This opinion is a genuine expression of the anxiety people feel about war of a magnitude never experienced before . . ."[19]

○ U.S.S.R. *Foreign Minister Andrei A. Gromyko:* "The situation in the world causes legitimate concern among peoples. It has found its expression in parliamentary debates, discussions in international forums, and in the upsurge of a mass anti-war movement for which the Soviet people has profound esteem . . ."[20]

3. NGO Statements

The first month of the five-week SSD II witnessed much talk and activity about the nuclear freeze. Many NGO meetings were held explaining or advocating the freeze, some attended by diplomats. *Disarmament Times*, the NGO-sponsored newspaper at SSD II, published numerous articles and editorials on the freeze. Of the 77 addresses given to SSD II by NGOs and peace and disarmament research institutions, 30 positively endorsed the freeze. A few samples follow:

Top: Demonstrators marching past U.N. Headquarters on June 12th
Bottom Left: Demonstrators near U.N. Headquarters on June 12th
(Jennifer Warburg Photo)
Bottom Right: Civil disobedience near Permanent Mission of the
U.S.A. on June 14th

Top: Demonstrators with Japanese Buddhist monk (Jennifer War-
burg Photo)
Bottom: Civil disobedience in front of Permanent Mission of the
U.S.S.R. on June 14th (Jennifer Warburg Photo)

Top: Demonstrators in Central Park on June 12th (Jennifer Warburg Photo)

Bottom: Civil disobedience in front of Permanent Mission of the U.S.A. on June 14th (Jennifer Warburg Photo)

Top: Representatives of the Children's Walk for Life, with Assistant
Secretary-General (for Disarmament) Jan Martenson
Bottom: World peace march at U.N. Headquarters. In wheel chairs
left to right: Lord Philip Noel-Baker of the U.K. and the Ven.
Nichidatsu Fujii of Japan

○ ACTION RECONCILIATION/SERVICE FOR PEACE, *Federal German Republic*. *Bishop Kurt Scharf:* "Working for the cause of peace today means . . . fourthly . . . which would be the first step . . . freezing the production, testing, and deployment of nuclear weapons now . . ."[21]

○ CAMPAIGN FOR NUCLEAR DISARMAMENT, *United Kingdom*. *Ms. Joan Ruddock:* "It is our fervent hope that, as a minimum, a bilateral freeze on nuclear weapons between the U.S. and Soviet Union can be achieved."[22].

○ GANDHI PEACE FOUNDATION, *India*. *Sri Radhakrishna:* "In the short term, I believe certain priorities could be identified, and we urge the Special Session to agree to the following . . . , (b) to freeze the manufacture, testing, and deployment of nuclear weapons and their delivery systems . . ."[23]

○ HIROSHIMA PEACE CULTURE FOUNDATION, *Japan*. *Mr. Takeshi Araki, Mayor of Hiroshima:* "On behalf of the citizens of Hiroshima, I wish to call in particular for the immediate and complete banning of nuclear tests and the freezing of all nuclear weapon stocks, which should ultimately be eliminated."[24]

○ INSTITUTE OF WORLD ECONOMICS AND INTERNATIONAL RELATIONS, *U.S.S.R. Academy of Sciences*. *Dr. Oleg Bykov:* "Logic dictates above all the urgency of freezing the strategic arms of the U.S.S.R. and the U.S.A. for the duration of the current talks. That important measure would facilitate progress towards radical nuclear arms limitation and reduction."[25]

○ INTERCHURCH PEACE COUNCIL, *the Netherlands*. *Mr. Wim Bartels:* "The link with the rapidly growing American peace movement is getting stronger and we are working out the complementary functions of the European peace campaign and the freeze campaign in the U.S., which we firmly support."[26]

○ INTERNATIONAL ASSOCIATION FOR RELIGIOUS FREEDOM. *President Nikkyo Niwano:* "As a first step on the path towards a total disarmament and new international security, we make the following requests of the U.N. and of national governments: . . . thirdly, the initiation of negotiations for the freezing of production of fissionable material for weapon purposes."[27]

○ ISRAELI INSTITUTE FOR THE STUDY OF INTERNATIONAL AFFAIRS. *Prof. Mieczyslaw Maneli:* "At this stage of the evolution of mankind and of the international community, we can achieve only a series of short-term, partial, and intermediate goals: specifically, the freezing of the nuclear armaments race . . ."[28]

○ RUSSIAN ORTHODOX CHURCH, *U.S.S.R. Patriarch Pimen:* "We call upon you to rid our earth of the blight of nuclear weapons and, as a step towards that goal, to impose an immediate freeze and total ban on those weapons."[29]

○ PARLIAMENTARIANS FOR WORLD ORDER. *Mr. Douglas Roche:* "We call upon the nuclear Powers to seek a temporary freeze by all nations on the testing, production, and deployment of nuclear weapons and delivery systems, pending a genuine reduction in nuclear arsenals. Such a freeze is a concrete, practical step which can be taken now, without delay."[30]

○ WOMEN FOR PEACE, *Norway. Ms. Eva Nordland:* "On the global level we want an immediate freeze: a total halt in the testing, production, and deployment of nuclear weapons."[31]

○ PUGWASH CONFERENCES ON SCIENCE AND WORLD AFFAIRS. *Prof. Bernard Feld:* "To reverse the present arms race we must first stop racing. This call for a 'standstill freeze' on current nuclear armaments is an effective way of initiating the essential process of nuclear disarmament. Such a freeze should also include the development of new weapon technologies, a major factor in fueling the runaway competition in modern weapons and systems of mass destruction."[32]

4. Four Proposals

In this favorable climate, diplomats prepared for submission several freeze resolutions, even though they realized opposition to any freeze action by the U.N. was an article of faith among the members of NATO. Since SSD II was running behind schedule, the four proposals were not submitted until the last week of SSD II, in July. The sponsors of each gave an address in introducing the text. The essence of the four is as follows:

○ INDIA. Calls upon all nuclear-weapon States to agree to a freeze on nuclear weapons, which would, inter alia, provide for a simultaneous total stoppage of any further production of nuclear weapons and a complete cutoff in the production of fissionable materials for weapons purposes."[33]

○ IRELAND. "The U.S.S.R. and the U.S.A. should agree on a limited, but renewable, moratorium on the introduction of any further strategic nuclear weapons or delivery vehicles. The initial agreement should be for a period of two years, during which time negotiations on the reduction of strategic nuclear weapons and their delivery vehicles should be pursued vigorously."[34]

○ MEXICO AND SWEDEN. Mexican Ambassador Alfonso Garcia Robles introduced the text which is identical to that of the resolution adopted by the 37th General Assembly given above, except that the clause was omitted limiting its duration unless other nuclear States joined.[35] See Table 7.

○ INDIA. On the penultimate day of the anticipated closing of SSD II, India submitted a draft resolution on the prevention of nuclear war, one clause of which called for "a complete freeze on the development, production, and deployment of nuclear weapons and their means of delivery along with a cut-off in the production of fissionable materials for weapons puposes."[36]

The Irish proposal and the three draft resolutions for a nuclear freeze were not, in the end, put to a vote because the whole SSD II ended in deadlock. However, some States vowed to take their issues, including the nuclear freeze, to the 37th regular session of the General Assembly, beginning in mid-September 1982, where resolutions could be voted upon and the unanimity rule did not apply.

5. 37th General Assembly

During the general debate in the General Assembly, late in September and early in October, many statements were made about disarmament, some including the nuclear freeze. When the First or Disarmament Committee began its work in mid-October, many more States mentioned the nuclear freeze. The Mexican-Swedish draft was circulated on October 19th. Mexican Ambassador Alfonso Garcia Robles made an explanatory address about the resolution on November 19th. He emphasized the existing nuclear parity between the super-Powers, citing several authorities, including the Independent (Palme) Commission on Disarmament and Security Problems (of which he was a member) and Prof. Hans Bethe. He quoted the latter's testimony before the U.S. Senate Foreign Relations Committee in May 1982 that "our strategic forces are, if anything, superior to those of the Soviet Union [and] the greatest threat to our national security and to that of our allies is the grotesque size and the continuing growth of the nuclear arsenals of both sides." Garcia Robles also discussed the verifiability of the freeze, quoting Dr. Herbert Scoville that "verification can no longer be legitimately invoked as an excuse not to proceed to an agreement on a freeze and on reductions."[37]

Ambassador Garcia Robles indicated that the draft as introduced by Mexico, Sweden, Ecuador, and Colombia was identical to that sub-

TABLE 7
THE TEXT OF THE ADOPTED FREEZE RESOLUTION

Resolution 37/100 B. Nuclear Arms Freeze*

The General Assembly

Recalling that, in the Final Document of the Tenth Special Session of the General Assembly, in 1978, it expressed deep concern over the threat of the very survival of mankind posed by the existence of nuclear weapons and the continuing arms race,

Recalling also that, on the same occasion, it pointed out that existing arsenals of nuclear weapons were more than sufficient to destroy all life on earth and stressed that mankind was therefore confronted with a choice: halt the arms race and proceed to disarmament, or face annihilation,

Noting that the conditions prevailing today are a source of even more serious concern than those existing in 1978 because of several factors such as the deterioration of the international situation, the increase in the accuracy, speed and destructive power of nuclear weapons, the promotion of illusory doctrines of "limited" or "winnable" nuclear war and the many false alarms which have occurred owing to the malfunctioning of computers,

Believing that it is a matter of the utmost urgency to stop any further increase in the awesome arsenals of the two major nuclear-weapon States, which already have ample retaliatory power and a frightening overkill capacity,

Believing also that it is equally urgent to activate negotiations for the substantial reduction and qualitative limitation of existing nuclear arms,

Considering that a nuclear arms freeze, while not an end in itself, would constitute the most effective first step for the achievement of the above-mentioned two objectives, since it would provide a favorable environment for the conduct of the reduction negotiations while, at the same time, preventing the continued increase and qualitative improvement of existing nuclear weaponry during the period when the negotiations would take place,

Firmly convinced that at present the conditions are most propitious for such a freeze, since the Union of Soviet Socialist Republics and the United States of America are now equivalent in nuclear military power and it seems evident that there exists between them an overall rough parity,

1. *Urges* the Union of Soviet Socialist Republics and the United States of America, as the two major nuclear-weapon States, to proclaim, either through simultaneous unilateral declarations or through a joint declaration, an immediate nuclear arms freeze which would be a first step towards the comprehensive program of disarmament and whose structure and scope would be the following:

(a) It would embrace:

(i) A comprehensive test ban on nuclear weapons and of their delivery vehicles;

---

*Operational paragraph 1 (c) was not in the draft presented to the Special Session

(ii) The complete cessation of the manufacture of nuclear weapons and of their delivery vehicles;

(iii) A ban on all further deployment of nuclear weapons and of their delivery vehicles;

(iv) The complete cessation of the production of fissionable material for weapons purposes;

(b) It would be subject to all relevant measures and procedures of verification which have already been agreed by the parties in the case of the SALT I and SALT II treaties, as well as those agreed upon in principle by them during the preparatory trilateral negotiations on the comprehensive test ban held at Geneva;

(c) It would be of an original five-year duration, subject to prolongation in case other nuclear-weapon States join in such a freeze, as the General Assembly expects them to do;

2. *Requests* the above-mentioned two major nuclear-weapon States to submit a report to the General Assembly, prior to the opening of its thirty-eighth session, on the implementation of the present resolution;

3. *Decides* to include in the provisional agenda of its thirty-eighth session an item entitled "Implementation of resolution 37/100 B on a nuclear arms freeze."

---

mitted to SSD II except for one additional subparagraph in the first operative clause: "it would be of an original five-year duration, subject to prolongation in case other nuclear-weapon States join in such a freeze, as the General Assembly expects them to do." This was inserted to ensure Soviet support for the resolution.

The First Committee on November 23 voted on the freeze resolution.[38] It prevailed by a vote of 103 in favor, 17 against, and six abstaining. The negative votes were cast by the NATO States and a few of their close allies. Of NATO members, the only defections were Greece (which voted in favor) and Denmark and Iceland (which abstained).

6. Explanations of Vote

As is often the custom, a number of States before and after the vote gave the reasons why they voted as they did, both for the record but especially for a restive public back home. (Obviously, those voting against the resolution, or abstaining, had more explaining to do.) Some examples:

○ AUSTRIA: ". . . Austria is not in a position to make an assessment as to whether at present there exists an equilibrium between the great Powers in the field of armaments when all armament systems are taken into account . . . Austria decided to cast a positive vote, because of the exceptional dangers posed by nuclear weapons and because a possibly existing disequilibrium could also be balanced by measures taken in the field of other types of weapons systems."[39]

○ CANADA: "Freezes and moratoriums have had an unhappy history since the Second World War. It is in the nature of a freeze, of course, that it is non-binding and therefore just as it can be unilaterally assumed it can be unilaterally abandoned . . . What is undeniable is that a freeze proposal, particularly, a comprehensive one, as this is, prejudges all the complex technical, scientific, political, legal, and even economic issues, as well as the military issues . . . I would like to refer to the well-known Canadian provisions on certain types of freezes, for example, a negotiated freeze of technology, a negotiated freeze of the production of fissionable weapons material, so it is not the word 'freeze' that frightens us or the notion of a freeze that troubles us. It is the particular type of freeze proposal with which we have to deal, and while we sympathize with the objectives and the honesty of purpose of the proponents, we are unable to support it."[40]

○ DENMARK: ". . . A freeze might legitimize the recent massive growth in the nuclear weaponry of the Soviet Union and leave intact the resulting imbalance. Seen from a European point of view, the Soviet build-up of SS-20s gives rise to particular alarm. We find that a freeze should not be the point of departure for, but the logical result of, the negotiations in Geneva . . . These considerations, weighed against the strong concern of the Danish public over the continuing nuclear arms race, led the Danish Government to abstain . . . However, my government would like to emphasize that our vote today on these proposals does not imply any change in the Danish Government's firm commitments to both elements in NATO's double-track decision of December 1979 or in Denmark's foreign and security policy."[41]

○ GERMAN FEDERAL REPUBLIC: ". . . The following arguments can be advanced against the freeze philosophy and can show its serious flaws. A freeze could be justified only if the participants in a freeze decision would at that time fully enjoy and preserve their right to security; in other words, if there was a genuine balance, both in the global context and at relevant sub-global levels . . . Secondly, proponents of the freeze assert that there is parity between the U.S. and the Soviet Union. This claim of parity is constantly repeated but rarely substantiated . . . The Soviet Union claimed parity in 1978 and still pretends that it exists now . . . hundreds of Soviet nuclear warheads later. That is a logical impossibility . . . Instead of codification of existing balances, we need an effective reduction through balance and verifiable agreements . . ."[42]

○ NETHERLANDS: "At this juncture a freeze of the development, production, and/or deployment of nuclear weapons and their delivery vehicles would legitimize the recent massive growth in missile weaponry of the Soviet Union and leave intact the resulting imbalance. Thus the West would be prevented from remedying the vulnerabilities which now exist . . . A 'freeze' under today's conditions would be equivalent to a consolidation of certain destabilizing aspects of the present East-West relationship . . . We hold that negotiations of a general agreement freezing nuclear forces at current levels is probably not practicable . . . Unilateral restraint alone cannot produce a safer world . . . A freeze now would lead not to a safer world but to a less stable situation, and thus increase rather than decrease the chances of a nuclear war."[43]

○ NORWAY: "From the conceptual point of view, there are at least three important problems connected to the general idea of a freeze. First, a freeze would, by definition, keep the balance of power frozen in the state it is from the moment the freeze enters into effect. It would thus also freeze present imbalances . . . A freeze on nuclear forces in Europe at this stage would only benefit one of the parties to the ongoing negotiations on these weapons. A second problem is that a freeze could, in certain instances, stand in the way of a real reduction of nuclear arms . . . A third problem related to a freeze concerns verification . . . We cannot support the . . . parts of the present freeze proposal dealing with the testing of delivery vehicles and with the production and deployment aspects, as they would run counter to the positions taken by NATO countries, including Norway, both as to the INF and the START talks. In the opinion of the Norwegian Government a freeze including these elements would seriously prejudge the outcome of the present INF negotiations in Geneva and detract from what must be our principal objective, that is, significant reductions of existing nuclear arms in the ongoing negotiations."[44]

○ PAKISTAN: "We believe that the threat from nuclear weapons is all-pervasive, and that efforts to eliminate the threat can be made at more than one level . . ."[45]

○ U.S.S.R.: "The Soviet Union, in principle, takes a positive attitude to the idea of a freeze on nuclear weapons and stockpiles as a first step towards reducing these stockpiles, which should be followed up by real and tangible nuclear disarmament . . . All the nuclear powers must participate in a freeze . . . The Soviet delegation does not oppose the fact that the first appeal for a freeze was addressed only to the Soviet Union and the U.S.A. We also proceed from the premise that the freeze proposal should be limited to a certain time frame and that the question of its continuation has to be settled taking into account the actions of other nuclear States. As for verification of a freeze, this question requires further agreement through talks between the parties to it . . ."[46]

    ○ U.S.A.: "With regard to [the resolution], we share many sentiments and objectives contained in its preambular part. At the same time, other, disturbing words are to be found there. '. . . illusory doctrines of "limited" or "winnable" nuclear war' are said to be promoted by unnamed persons or States. It is true that Soviet spokesmen—and even some resolutions before this Committee—have asserted, however falsely, that the U.S. promulgates such doctrines. One must ask whether the authors of this resolution have accepted these totally unfounded claims . . . Members of the Committee will surely want to analyze carefully the merits of endorsing a freeze which would be impossible to define or verify—and in any event be unfair and unbalanced. What are urgently needed are negotiated agreements for reductions and increased stability, not a hopeless effort to lock in a dangerous and unacceptable status quo. The U.S. trusts the good sense of this Committee not to dismiss and undermine the START and INF negotiations by supporting resolutions calling for a nuclear freeze."[47]

With the nuclear freeze resolution being overwhelmingly endorsed by the First Committee, the vote in the plenary of the General Assembly was just a formality, with the co-sponsors hoping to pick up some additional favorable votes from smaller States not present for the vote in the First Committee. When, on December 13th, the resolution came before the plenary, it was adopted 119 to 17, with five abstentions.[48] The voting pattern is given below in Table 8, with the States listed in the political/geographical groupings in the U.N. system.

7. The Indian Resolution

As in SSD II, so in the regular session, India also introduced its initial draft resolution confined to the freeze. This again advocated a multilateral freeze: "calls upon all nuclear-weapon States to agree to a freeze on nuclear weapons, which would, inter alia, provide for a simultaneous stoppage of any further production of nuclear weapons and a complete cut-off in the production of fissionable material for weapons purposes." This draft omitted mention of testing and deployment. The Indian draft, put to a vote in the First Committee, received 105 positive votes to 16 negative votes, with six abstentions.[49] Japan, which voted against the Mexican-Swedish draft, abstained on the In-

TABLE 8
VOTING PATTERN ON THE FREEZE RESOLUTION

STATES IN FAVOR (119)

African (43)

Algeria*
Angola*
Benin*
Botswana*
Burundi*
Cen. Afr. Rep.*
Chad*
Comoros*
Congo*
Djibouti*
Egypt*
Equat. Guinea*
Ethiopia*
Gabon*
Ghana*
Guinea*
Guinea-Bissau*
Kenya*
Lesotho*
Liberia*
Libyan Arab Jam.*
Madagascar*
Malawi*
Mali*
Mauritania*
Mauritius*
Mozambique*
Niger*
Nigeria*
Rwanda*
Sao Tome & Principe*
Senegal*
Sierra Leone*
Sudan*
Swaziland*

Togo*
Tunisia*
Uganda*
Un. Rep. Cameroon*
Un. Rep. Tanzania*
Upper Volta*
Zaire*
Zambia*

Asian & Pacific (33)

Afghanistan*
Bahrain*
Bangladesh*
Bhutan*
Burma
Cyprus*
Dem. Yemen*
Fiji
India*
Indonesia*
Iran*
Iraq*
Jordan*
Kuwait*
Laos*
Lebanon*
Malaysia*
Maldives*
Mongolia
Nepal*
Oman*
Pakistan*
Papua New Guinea
Qatar*
Saudia Arabia*
Singapore*

Solomon Islands
Sri Lanka*
Syrian Arab Rep.*
United Arab.
   Emir.*
Vanuatu
Viet Nam*
Yemen*

Western European
& Other States (6)

Austria
Finland
Greece N
Ireland
Malta*
Sweden

Eastern European (10)

Bulgaria W
Byelorussian SSR
Czechoslovakia W
German Democratic
   Republic W
Hungary W
Poland W
Romania W
Ukranian SSR
U.S.S.R. W
Yugoslavia*

Latin American (27)

Argentina*
Bahamas
Barbados

---

*—Member of Non-Aligned caucus
N—Member of NATO
W—Member of Warsaw Pact

TABLE 8
VOTING PATTERN ON THE FREEZE RESOLUTION

STATES IN FAVOR (119) *(Cont'd)*

Bolivia*	El Salvador	Panama*
Brazil	Grenada*	Paraguay
Chile	Guyana*	Peru*
Colombia	Haiti	St. Lucia*
Costa Rica	Honduras	Suriname*
Cuba*	Jamaica*	Trinidad & Tobago*
Dominican Rep.	Mexico	Uruguay
Ecuador*	Nicaragua*	Venezuela

STATES AGAINST (17)

Asian & Pacific (2)   *Western European & Other States (15)*

Israel	Australia	New Zealand
Japan	Belgium N	Norway N
	Canada N	Portugal N
	France N	Spain N
	German Fed. Rep. N	Turkey N
	Italy N	United Kingdom N
	Luxembourg N	U.S.A. N
	Netherlands N	

STATES ABSTAINING (5)

African (1)   *Asian & Pacific (1)*

Somalia*   Philippines

Latin American (1)   *Western European (2)*

Guatemala   Denmark N
                                        Iceland N

STATES ABSENT AT VOTE (16)

African (7)   *Asian & Pacific (4)*

Cape Verde*	Seychelles*	China
Gambia*	South Africa	Dem. Kampuchea
Ivory Coast*	Zimbabwe*	Samoa
Morocco*		Thailand

Eastern European (1)	*Latin American (4)*
Albania	Dominica
	St. Vincent & Grenada
	Antigua & Barbuda
	Belize*

dian one. China, which decided to absent itself politically during the votes on the Mexican-Swedish draft, abstained on the Indian draft. In an explanation of vote, China asserted that "in general, to demand a freeze on nuclear weapons to stop the nuclear arms race is understandable." However, it added that "an indiscriminate demand that all nuclear States should freeze nuclear weapons obviously can be only to the advantage of the nuclear Powers, thus legalizing their nuclear superiority over other countries and making their nuclear threat and blackmail legitimate, perpetrated, and permanent."[50] In the plenary, the Indian resolution was adopted 122 to 16, with six abstentions.[51] While no Irish proposal was submitted to the 37th General Assembly, Ireland made a detailed case for a freeze.

8. Parliamentary Reverberations

The Mexican-Swedish freeze resolution was the most important of the 58 disarmanent-related resolutions adopted by the 37th General Assembly in December 1982.

If this resolution created some attention in a usually blasé General Assembly, it created even more of a stir in certain countries where a strong constituency for disarmament watched its diplomats twist on the issue. Parliamentary manoeuvering, supported by peace activists, on the freeze was reported from at least the following States:

○ DENMARK. The right-wing Government opposed the freeze, but the Radical Liberal Party, the Socialist People's Party, and the Socialist Democratic Party threatened to bring down the Government if it opposed the U.N. resolution. Thus Denmark abstained.[52]

○ ICELAND. In Parliament, freeze supporters initiated a successful effort for the country to abstain in the U.N. vote. There was some support in Parliament for an affirmative vote at the U.N. despite the country's membership in NATO.[53]

○ NETHERLANDS. After the Netherlands voted against the freeze in the U.N.'s First Committee, a parliamentary debate urging the Netherlands to abstain in the U.N. plenary lost 72 to 69. Two Christian

Democrats voted with the Government only to save the Christian Democratic Foreign Minister from defeat. The Dutch Ambassador to the U.N. told the General Assembly that, since the vote on the freeze resolution was taken in the First Committee, "an intensive thorough debate has been held in the Second Chamber of our Parliament on the concept of a nuclear arms freeze." He added that "in that lively debate in our most important democratic institution, the fear was expressed that our vote against the freeze draft resolution could be misinterpreted." He wanted to make the additional statement that "voting against a freeze draft resolution would convey the wrong impression that my Government and the people of the Netherlands as a whole are not of the opinion that there are more than enough nuclear weapons, or that we are not worried about the ongoing nuclear arms race." He declared that "although an agreed freeze could at a later stage in the disarmament process contribute to curbing the nuclear arms race, at this moment it is neither the boldest nor the quickest way of tackling the nuclear threat."[54]

o NORWAY. In Parliament, the issue was debated after the Government voted negatively in the First Committee. The governing Conservative Party was against the freeze resolution, but the Labor Party, the Radical Liberal Party, and the Socialist Left Party advocated abstention, with the Christian People's Party and the Center Party not taking a position. In the end, the freeze supporters did not want to cause a governmental crisis on this issue, since U.N. votes have been seen as a traditional governmental prerogative.[55]

9. Next Steps?

The resolutions of the General Assembly are only declaratory or advisory, and are often ignored. In itself, the adopted freeze resolution will not compel the U.S.A. or the U.S.S.R. to issue a unilateral declaration to freeze its weapons, let alone seriously negotiate a comprehensive bilateral freeze. Yet the overwhelming vote on the resolution adds much world pressure on the White House and the Kremlin to consider a freeze seriously.

U.N. Secretary-General Javier Perez de Cuellar in his first annual report to the General Assembly in 1982 put his finger on the chronic problem at the U.N. "There is a tendency in the U.N. for Governments to act as though the passage of a resolution absolved them from further responsibility for the subject in question. Nothing could be further from the intention of the Charter . . . In other words the best resolution in the world will have little practical effect unless Governments of Member States follow it up with the appropriate support and action."[56]

The freeze is already being discussed in the Committee on Disarmament at Geneva and will be discussed in the 38th General Assembly in September/December 1983.

In the meantime, various forms of the nuclear freeze are being discussed by many peace campaigns in Western Europe. The major peace groups in the U.K. have supported the freeze. The new national campaign in Denmark, Stop Nuclear Missiles, has included the freeze in its 14-point program. The leaders of the Greens in the German Federal Republic support the freeze. The No to Nuclear Weapons organization in Norway is pro-freeze. Peace movements in Sweden and the Low Countries are pro-freeze. Indeed, the freeze is closely intertwined with the struggle from the northern tip of Norway to Sicily against the emplacement of Cruise and Pershing II missiles.

While the European campaigns are making their own connections between the nuclear freeze and the Euromissiles, the Third National Conference of the U.S. Nuclear Weapons Freeze Campaign on February 6, 1983 made the following policy decision: "With regard to intermediate-range missiles in Europe, the Campaign recognizes the urgent need to stop new, destabilizing weapons on either side that would increase the risk of nuclear war and undermine the prospects for a comprehensive, bilateral freeze. Accordingly, the Campaign opposes the deployment of cruise and Pershing II missiles in Europe which will introduce a new, qualitatively different and greater danger of nuclear war in the European theater. In addition, the Campaign favors substantial reductions in Soviet intermediate-range missiles."[57]

REFERENCES

1. A/S-12/PV.17, p. 13.
2. A/S-12/PV.18, pp. 31–32.
3. A/S-12/PV.4, pp. 8–10.
4. A/S-12/PV.9, p. 82.
5. A/S-12/PV.8, p. 12.
6. A/S-12/PV.13, pp. 58–60.
7. A/S-12/PV.22, p. 38.
8. A/S-12/PV.2, p. 67.
9. A/S-12/PV.12, p. 27.
10. A/S-12/PV.8, p. 36.

11. A/S-12/PV.12, p. 12.
12. A/S-12/PV.5, p. 66.
13. A/S-12/PV.24, p. 7.
14. A/S-12/PV.18, pp. 29–30.
15. A/S-12/PV.10, pp. 58–62.
16. A/S-12/PV.9, p. 91.
17. A/S-12/PV.5, p. 37.
18. A/S-12/PV.13, pp. 33–35.
19. A/S-12/PV.2, pp. 59–60.
20. A/S-12/PV.12, p. 47.

21. A/S-12/AC.1/PV.5, p. 7.
22. *Ibid.*, p. 22.
23. A/S-12/AC.1/PV.8, p. 36.
24. A/S-12/AC.1/PV.5, p. 48.
25. A/S-12/AC.1/PV.8, p. 67.
26. A/S-12/AC.1/PV.5, p. 57.
27. *Ibid.*, p. 62.
28. A/S-12/AC.1/PV.8/Add.1,   pp. 3–5.
29. A/S-12/AC.1/PV.6, pp. 27–30.
30. *Ibid.*, pp. 53–55.
31. *Ibid.*, p. 102.
32. A/S-12/AC.1/PV.7, p. 77.
33. A/S-12/AC.1/L.1 and A/S-12/32, p. 10.
34. A/S-12/AC.1/46/Rev.1.
35. A/S-12/AC.1/L.3 and A/S-12/32, pp. 11–12.
36. A/S-12/AC.1/L.6 and A/S-12/32, pp. 14–16.
37. A/C.1/37/PV.38, pp. 31–32.
38. A/C.1/37/PV.40, p. 33.
39. *Ibid.*, p. 41.
40. *Ibid.*, pp. 42–45.
41. *Ibid.*, pp. 34–35.
42. *Ibid.*, pp. 12–17.
43. *Ibid.*, pp. 28–32.
44. *Ibid.*, pp. 26–27.
45. *Ibid.*, p. 32.
46. *Ibid.*, pp. 36–41.
47. A/C.1/37/PV.36, pp. 6–17.
48. A/37/PV.101, p. 44. It is resolution 37/100 B.
49. A/C.1/37/PV.40, p. 22.
50. *Ibid.*, pp. 23–25.
51. A/37/PV.101, p. 43. It is resolution 37/100 A.
52. *Disarmament Campaigns*, Jan. 1983, p. 19.
53. *Disarmament Times*, Vol. V, No. 24. December 1983. p. 2.
54. A/37/PV.101, pp. 56–57.
55. *Frys,* edited by Magne Barth. Oslo: Pax Forlag. 1983. 148 pp.
56. A/37/1. September 1982. 4 pp.
57. The draft of this chapter was published by WCRP and the Douglas Inquiry as a 24-page pamphlet in March 1983 under the title, "The Nuclear Freeze Goes International: The United Nations Breakthrough." Also previous material was published by the author in the WCRP Report: "Freeze or Burn: The Nuclear Freeze at the Second Special Session." 1982. 18 pp.

7.

World Disarmament Campaign

The World Disarmament Campaign (WDC) began in a sense with a speech by U.N. Secretary-General Kurt Waldheim on the first day of the First U.N. Special Session on disarmament (SSD I) in 1978 and was inaugurated on the first day of the Second Special Session (SSD II) in 1982. The intervening four years did not automatically produce a WDC and, on several occasions along the way, the establishment of the Campaign appeared in jeopardy.

1. Origins

Secretary-General Kurt Waldheim in his opening statement to SSD I, on May 23, 1978, proposed to expand greatly funds devoted to disarmament research and education. In part he stated: "There is a need to intensify and broaden the scope of national progress of information and study concerning disarmament. We should recall the high investment which is devoted to research and development in the military field. No other area of human activity receives a similar input of scientific resources; nothing remotely comparable is devoted to research on how the arms race can be contained and reversed. This encourages constant competition and change in military technology which too often affects the over-all relations between States." Then Mr. Waldheim made his specific proposal: "I would, therefore, suggest that we devote to national and international disarmament efforts one million dollars to every thousand million currently spent on arms. This would constitute a valuable step in correcting the huge imbalance in our priorities." He further explained: "It should serve at least as a moral and political objective to be implemented by each country within the framework of its national, regional, or international disarmament potential. Some may wish to strengthen their own disarmament education or information activities; some may wish to increase their research capabilities; others may wish to further the work of international organizations. I do not offer any rigid prescription here, only a purpose and a goal."[1]

While this proposal of using one-tenth of one per cent of arms expenditures for disarmament research and education touched a responsive chord among NGOs and some delegates, there was, however, no enthusiasm to implement the proposal, and it did not appear in the omnibus Final Document of SSD I.

One of the proposals of the Secretary-General which was approved by SSD I was the creation of an Advisory Board on disarmament. What became known as the Advisory Board on Disarmament Studies, composed of 30 persons from as many countries, held its fourth and fifth sessions in 1980. A member of the Board, Mexican Ambassador Alfonso Garcia Robles—with materials submitted by some NGOs—suggested that the earlier proposal of the Secretary-General for a fund for disarmament research and education be the basis for a study. The Board in its report of possible studies included one "on the conduct and financing of a world-wide disarmament campaign." The Board was unable, however, to single out this among the studies to be undertaken by the General Assembly.[2]

It fell upon Ambassador Garcia Robles to draft and introduce a resolution in the 35th session of the U.N. General Assembly in 1980 on a WDC. This draft resolution was co-sponsored by nine other countries, mostly Non-Aligned. Although most U.N. disarmament studies cost several hundred thousand dollars, Ambassador Garcia Robles realized that the General Assembly was in no mood to authorize an expensive study and thus he proposed that one on this subject be authorized for $35,000—"equivalent to what is spent in two seconds—two seconds—for the world arms race." The Advisory Committee on Administrative and Budgetary Questions (ACABQ) cut the budget for the study to $17,500. The plenary of the General Assembly voted to adopt the resolution, 128 to none, with 17 abstentions. The latter were mostly members of NATO.[3]

2. The U.N. Study

Early in 1981 the Secretary-General appointed a group of experts to undertake the study. Since the resolution suggested that preference be given to members of the U.N. Secretariat, four persons came from the latter while three were junior diplomats. The experts sent a questionnaire to selected NGOs and research institutes. A group of NGOs sponsored a consultation in June 1981 on a WDC attended by some of the experts. In September 1981 the latter presented a 19-page report to the Secretary-General who released it to the 36th General Assembly.[4]

The general purpose of the WDC was stated as "to mobilize world public opinion on behalf of disarmament." The Campaign would "address the priorities for disarmament laid down by the Final Document" of SSD I. It would be "carried out in all regions of the world in a balanced, factual, and objective manner." It would be designed to "increase understanding of the growing threat of the arms race" and should explain to the public "the benefits of effective disarmament measures in eliminating the dangers of war so as to ensure the survival of mankind."

The specific objectives of the Campaign would be "to inform, to educate, and to generate public understanding and support for disarmament." Operational guidelines were suggested. Although the Campaign would be universal, certain constituencies would receive particular and sustained attention: elected representatives, parliamentarians, and public officials; the media; non-governmental organizations; educational communities; peace research institutes. Also the Campaign would pursue a wide range of activities, although "methods suitable for one country or group may not be appropriate for another." The U.N. system would have a role in the Campaign, but so would Member States of the U.N. and NGOs.

The report was weak in discussing structure, but it suggested that the Campaign should have "the over-all guidance and coordination" of the U.N. Secretary-General. While "every effort" would be made to carry out activities within existing U.N. resources, it was recognized that "the size and scope of the Campaign would depend on the availability of resources." Thus a trust fund might be established by means of voluntary contributions from Member States and other sources, including a traditional U.N. pledging conference.

3. 36th General Assembly

The 36th General Assembly in 1981 studied the report. A number of speakers discussed it during the general debate in the First Committee. Ambassador Garcia Robles again introduced a draft resolution, which was co-sponsored by eight other States. There were enough reservations, especially by some Western States—and especially the U.S.A.—that only a minimal resolution was suggested. Even this was later modified, with the operative verb about the report being changed from "adopts" to "commends." The resolution was adopted 143 to none, with two abstentions. The latter were the U.S.A. and Israel.[5]

U.S. Ambassador Kenneth Adelman in the First Committee reflected his objections, calling the Campaign a "well-meaning but fundamentally flawed approach to disarmament." He felt that it "blurs the vital distinction between open and closed societies." As a consequence, the Campaign would "inevitably come to focus only on public opinion in the free societies of the world; its effect on public opinion in closed societies would be zero."[6]

The resolution asked Member States to transmit to the Secretary-General their suggestions and comments on the Campaign and the study. Also the resolution ambiguously asked the Secretary-General to transmit the study and opinions of governments to SSD II "in order that the Assembly may take the decisions it considers advisable for the solemn launching of the Campaign, including a pledging conference to take place at the initial stage of the Special Session."

4. The Prep Comm

The Prep Comm early placed the WDC on the provisional agenda of SSD II, as a sub-item under the larger item on "measures to mobilize world public opinion in favor of disarmament." The final session of the Prep Comm, in April/May 1982, just a few weeks before SSD II was scheduled to begin, plainly did not know how to deal with the WDC. It asked the U.N. Centre for Disarmament to provide an "outline" of the Campaign, since it wanted material beyond that contained in the expert study. This 10-page "Outline of a Program" for the WDC was presented to the Prep Comm on May 12th—the last week of the last session of the Prep Comm—for discussion.[7]

This new paper contained sections on the concept of the Campaign, program activities, conclusions, and budgetary estimates. The section on program included 1) improving U.N. means of communication with the world public, media, and NGOs; 2) establishing systematic cooperation with international NGOs that can stimulate public opinion; 3) special events, such as Disarmament Week; and 4) a publicity program for the Campaign itself. In each of the specific program activities, there was a time-frame (year) and source of the budget, either from the regular U.N. budget or from a voluntary fund. No over-all amount was indicated.

At the final meeting of the Prep Comm, Chairman Olu Adeniji made a statement on the WDC which reflected the consensus of Member States. He said that the President of the Second Special Session "should launch the World Disarmament Campaign at the opening meeting of the session, following a formal decision to the effect." He also recommended that the President should "carry out the consultations he deemed appropriate in connection with the best modalities of pledging contributions to the Campaign." The Chairman also noted that the U.N. Centre for Disarmament presented a tentative outline of some of the elements of the WDC at the request of the Committee. The latter "took note of the outline" and recommended that the Special Session request the Secretary-General to submit a program for consideration and adoption by the Special Session.[8]

5. Launching of WDC

At the opening of SSD II on June seventh, the report of the Prep Comm was adopted without a vote. President Ismat Kittani then pointed out that the report included steps to be taken in connection with the launching of the WDC. He then read the recommendations and asked if, in endorsing the report, the plenary also approved this particular recommendation. There was no negative response and he ruled that it was "so decided."

Then President Kittani declared: "I therefore now have the honor and pleasure solemnly to declare that, as the first substantive step taken by this Second Special Session of the General Assembly, devoted to disarmament, the World Disarmament Campaign has been officially opened." He earlier indicated that, as requested, he conducted consultations about the best modalities of pledging contributions to the WDC. He concluded that "it appears from these exchanges that, while some delegations prefer to wait until the discussion of the Secretary-General's report before making commitments, others would like to avail themselves of the opportunity of the general debate, during which they would be making pledges." He added that "either of the suggested alternatives are feasible and both procedures have their merit."[9]

6. Negotiations

Negotiations on the WDC were delayed because of the difficulty in organizing the real work of SSD II. On June 17th it was finally agreed that Working Group III under the chairmanship of Ambassador

Gerhard Herder of the German Democratic Republic would consider, among others, agenda item 13 on "measures to mobilize world public opinion in favor of disarmament," of which the WDC was one of three sub-items. However, the Group first discussed the fellowships on disarmament program.[10] Thus only on June 23rd was the Group able to begin discussion on the WDC.

When a vacuum occurs diplomats have little difficulty filling it with rhetoric. Thus with Working Group III having a relatively light agenda (compared with the other two Groups), delegates spent hours debating the WDC. They had both concealed and open agendas. The U.S.A., and some other Western States, wanted to pursue its criticism—first raised in the 36th General Assembly—that the Campaign might not obtain free access to Eastern European States. Also, the West was uneasy about voluntary funding. Some preferred to take funds from the regular U.N. budget, by "redistributing" it, rather than making additional contributions through the regular budget or a voluntary fund. A feud between the role of the Department of Public Information in the Campaign vis-a-vis the U.N. Centre for Disarmament found some Member States backing their favorite U.N. bureaucracy. A number of Member States insisted that their own initiative relating to the Campaign be included. Some NGOs, never allowed to be present at meetings of the Group, made signals that they wanted to be more than consumers of the Campaign and desired some kind of consultative status.

After some discussion, the Working Group realized that it had to get down to drafting a paper. Canada contributed an early draft as did the U.S.A. The latter re-emphasized two earlier objections to the Campaign: such a Campaign "blurs the distinction between open and closed societies" and "'mobilizing world public opinion'—as opposed to supplying facts and expert views—is an activity singularly unsuited to this Organization, which is after all an assemblage of Governments." However, the paper indicated that the U.S.A would no longer oppose the creation of a Campaign: "Now that a decision has been taken to launch such a Campaign and to adopt in due course specific plans for such a Campaign, the U.S. delegation believes that it is mandatory to ensure that a balanced and universally applicable, and fiscally responsible, program is in fact executed."[11]

A number of Member States submitted initiatives which they wanted to become part of the Campaign. These included the following:

○ Mongolia: Continue to observe disarmament week each year.[12]

○ Bulgaria: Worldwide action for collecting signatures in support of measures to prevent nuclear war.[13]

○ Japan: Collect documentation on the effect of the bombing of Hiroshima and Nagasaki as a warning to the dangers of the arms race.[14]

○ Sierre Leone: Some U.N. Information Centers be strengthened especially in the developing areas to inform on the dangers of the arms race.[15]

○ Egypt: Measures to enhance the activities of the U.N. Information Centers relating to disarmament.[16]

○ Romania: Organize a world conference on the role of mass media in promoting peace.[17]

○ France: Creation of a Universal Council of Conscience.[18]

During SSD II, *Disarmament Times* ran a number of stories about the WDC, including negotiations in the Working Group and two editorials.[19] Some independent observers felt that this emphasis by *Disarmament Times* may have helped make the Campaign one of only two concrete initiatives which in the end were adopted by SSD II.

At the beginning of the last week of SSD II, the members of the Working Group were still debating issues to be inserted, or deleted, from the emerging paper. Certain compromises reached tentatively were overthrown. In an effort to rescue this most promising result of SSD II, Chairman Adeniji of the Ad Hoc Committee appointed a 15-member drafting group to attempt to remove the many remaining brackets from the text. He appointed Ambassador Constantin Ene of Romania as chairman. Finally on July 8th or the penultimate day before SSD II was scheduled to conclude, the group succeeded in obtaining a unanimous report, due largely to the guidance of the chairman.

The final paper[20] contains 22 paragraphs. Its introduction indicated that the "operational guidelines and modalities" given in the two reports of the Secretary-General[21] should be taken into account. The Objectives consist of three primary purposes: to inform, to educate, and to generate public understanding and support for the objectives of the U.N. in the field of arms limitation and disarmament. Moreover, the Campaign should be "carried out in all regions of the world in a balanced, factual, and objective manner." The universality of the Campaign should be guaranteed. The U.N. system, Member States "with respect for their sovereign rights," and "in particular non-governmental organizations" all have their roles to play.

As for the Contents of the Campaign, emphasis was placed on the role of the U.N. Information Centers, UNDP offices, and other appropriate U.N. offices. Dissemination "of false and tendentious information" should be avoided. Regarding Modalities, the U.N. should coordinate the Campaign, with the U.N. Centre for Disarmament providing "the central guidance" within the U.N. system and maintaining liaison with the governmental and non-governmental organizations and research institutes. Also, "within the Campaign," the Department of Public Information "should play its role as assigned by the General Assembly in utilizing its expertise and resources in public information to ensure its maximum effectiveness." It should also "set out appropriate tasks for UNESCO in its field of competence." The paper requested the Secretary-General to submit to the 37th General Assembly "the specifics" of a program for the WDC, "taking into account the views expressed by Member States" during SSD II. Then the paper listed specific proposals for inclusion in the WDC made by delegations. The Secretary-General was requested to submit to each regular session of the General Assembly" for its review a report on the implementation of the WDC, during the preceding year." It also asked that the Secretary-General convey to the General Assembly the relevant views of the Advisory Board on Disarmament Studies, "taking into account the tasks the General Assembly may further entrust to it." This is an open-ended proposal to breathe new life into an Advisory Board, the usefulness of which has been questioned. There is a final section on Financial Implications, inviting the Secretary-General both to explore the possibility of deploying existing U.N. resources in the regular budget of the U.N. and for Member States to supplement such resources with voluntary contributions, which are also solicited from NGOs, foundations/trusts, and other private sources.[22] The unabridged paper on the Campaign is given in Appendix C.

7. Pledges to the Voluntary Fund

Since no pledging conference could be agreed upon for the voluntary fund for the WDC, delegates had the choice of announcing a contribution in the general debate or in meetings of the Ad Hoc Committee, or could wait until the discussion of the new report on the program of the WDC by the Secretary-General. It is not known how intensive were any further consultations of the President of SSD II on eliciting contributions. Table 9 gives the contributions to the WDC, both at the end of SSD II and at the end of the 37th General Assembly.

8. 37th General Assembly

In November 1982, the Secretary-General submitted the report requested by SSD II giving the outline of the program of WDC.[23] This occurred in the middle of the work of the First or Disarmament Committee of the 37th regular session of the General Assembly. A few

TABLE 9
CONTRIBUTIONS TO THE WORLD DISARMAMENT
CAMPAIGN IN JULY AND DECEMBER 1982[24]

From Governments
    #Bangladesh—Announced, no amount
    ##Bulgaria—20,000 lev or $20,000*
    ##Byelorussian SSR—100,000 rubles or $125,000*
    #Finland—250,000 markaas or $46,000
    ##Hungary—250,000 forints or $6,250*
    #India—1,000,000 rupees or $103,000
    ##Iraq—$10,000
    #Mexico—$50,000
    ##Mongolia—3,000 tugriks or $1,000*
    #Sweden—500,000 kronor or $67,000
    ##Ukrainian SSR—200,000 rubles or $250,000*
    ##U.S.S.R.—1,500,000 rubles or $1,875,000*
From Non-Governmental Organizations
    #Friends World Committee for Consultation—$5,000
From Individuals—$615.00

Grand Total: $2,558,865, of which $281,615 was in currency to be spent anywhere.**

    #—Contribution announced during SSD II
  ##—Contribution announced later in 1982
    *—Contribution in non-convertible currency, with dollar amounts very approximate
  **—At press time (April 1983), the following additional contributions had been received during 1983: Canada C$70,000 (or approximately $56,980), German Democratic Republic 100,000 marks ($41,350), Romania 300,000 lei ($27,272), and World Council of Churches $5,000.

States had mentioned the Campaign in the general debate in the plenary and more mentioned it in the general debate in the First Committee.

The Secretary-General's new report contained an initial section on the general framework of the Campaign, based on the text approved at SSD II. Then there was a section on program of activities for 1983. The report admitted that the Campaign would have to be implemented "on the basis of a long-term strategy," with its success dependent upon "the extent of the active and material support of Member States in cooperation [with] non-governmental organizations." The specific activities proposed for 1983 were selected using three criteria: their immediate impact, their multiplier effect, and their ability to be carried out without extensive preparation. Plans for 1984 and beyond would be formulated later, in light of experiences during 1983. It was revealed that the Centre held informal discussions on the WDC with several agencies of the U.N., particularly the Department of Public Information. Also the report indicated that "a number of activities within the framework of the Campaign have been carried out in 1982 after its launching."

The proposed program was divided into five areas of activity.

1. U.N. Information Materials. Materials would be produced in an appropriate format and in sufficient quantities and languages to meet Campaign needs. Some 12 publications were listed, from the ongoing "Disarmament Yearbook" to a U.N. newsletter on disarmament activities. Eight possible audio-visual materials were also listed, from a calendar of posters in the 1981 international competition to a wall sheet to raise consciousness among young people.

2. Interpersonal Communication, Seminars, and Training. This is an area where "greatest horizontal expansion of contact between the U.N. and NGOs is necessary." Correspondence would be expanded beyond the more than 1,000 NGOs, research institutions, and individuals which are on the Centre's Register. Regional seminars for NGOs and the media, begun in 1981, would be continued. Eight possibilities were listed.

3. Special Events. Disarmament Week (October 24–31 each year) would be used for special events. These would be organized at U.N. Headquarters, at U.N. Information Centres, and other U.N. field offices in cooperation with States and NGOs.

4. Publicity Program. A number of activities are envisaged, such as the active participation of well-known personalities in the arts, sciences, sports, and public affairs in the Campaign.

5. U.N. Information Centres and other U.N. field offices would be encouraged to stimulate local activities in support of the Campaign.

The Secretary-General's report also included the financial aspects of the program. Apart from funds already available in the regular budget for the biennium of the U.N., additional costs for activities, excluding staff requirements, are estimated to be $760,000, with $440,000 of that amount requested by the Department of Public Information. To the time the report was issued (early November 1982) still only about $300,000 was pledged to the voluntary fund, and some of this was in local currencies. Funding for the balance would need to be found from various sources, such as further voluntary contributions by Member States, NGOs, foundations, trusts, and other private sources. Also there was the hope for the redeployment of resources within the regular U.N. budget. The Secretary-General promised to submit a separate report on this possibility. Additional staff for the Centre for Disarmament would include two in New York, one in Geneva, and two general service employees.

NGOs meeting toward the end of SSD II felt the need both to continue the NGO momentum and associate themselves with the one tangible outcome of SSD II—the WDC. Accordingly, the Ad Hoc NGO Liaison Group, convening at U.N. Headquarters in September 1982, took up the request of some NGOs that it organize a NGO Consultation for the WDC on November 8–10, also in New York.

When four visas among the 85 persons invited were denied, the participants on the opening day of the Consultation cancelled it and turned the meeting into an Informal NGO Seminar on Disarmament. Nevertheless it gave most consideration to the WDC. Its "Report on Findings" contained a significant section on the WDC.[25] It declared that "NGO participation in the decision-making process of the WDC should be recognized officially by the U.N." It also asserted that the active cooperation of NGOs would be "vital to the success" of the WDC and thus the U.N. Centre for Disarmament should invite the participation of NGOs whenever appropriate. It was further agreed that: 1) NGOs should undertake to link and expand their work to fulfill the objectives of the WDC; 2) NGOs should ask the U.N. Centre to hold consultations with NGOs from all regions on the implementation and development of the Campaign at regular intervals; and 3) NGOs should ask the U.N. General Assembly to make provisions for the inclusion of distinguished persons from the NGO community in the Secretary-General's Advisory Board on Disarmament Studies, since the latter, reconstituted, would have some responsibility for the Campaign.

The Seminar voted that the Ad Hoc Group organize a future consultation, possibly in a developing country. Further it was suggested that this be persued within the framework of the WDC with "a clearly established status with the U.N. and with an absolute guarantee that all participants be granted visas to enter the host country of the meeting."

With the background of the new report by the Secretary-General on program, the First Committee discussed the campaign and three resolutions were introduced and adopted. The principal one, introduced by Ambassador Alfonso Garcia Robles, was co-sponsored by India, Romania, Sri Lanka, Sweden, and Yugoslavia. Its six operative clauses included the following: 1) Approved the "general framework" of the WDC in A/37/548*, including the submission of an annual report to the General Assembly on the implementation of the Campaign during the preceding year, and the transmission to the Assembly of the relevant views of the Advisory Board on Disarmament Studies; 2) Approved the proposed program of activities for 1983; 3) Reiterated its invitation to Member States to "supplement available U.N. resources with voluntary contributions;" 4) Decided that there should be a pledging conference of Member States at each regular session of the General Assembly; 5) Declared again that voluntary contributions made by NGOs, foundations, trusts, and other private sources would also be welcome; and 6) Decided to include the item of a WDC on the provisional agenda of the 38th General Assembly.

This resolution was adopted by consensus.[26] Two other resolutions were also submitted.

A second resolution on the WDC was introduced by four socialist States. This emphasized launching a world-wide action to collect signatures in support of measures to prevent nuclear war. It also urged the "better flow of information" on disarmament and "to avoid dissemination of false and tendentious information." This dubious resolution was adopted, but with a relatively low number of votes.[27]

A final resolution on the WDC was an initiative of the U.S.A. This called upon Member States to "facilitate the flow of a broad range of accurate information on disarmament matters, both governmental and non-governmental, to and among their citizens," to further the WDC. This was adopted without a vote in the plenary.[28]

9. "Accurate" Information

In the course of the adoption of the U.S.-sponsored resolution on the WDC, an incident occurred which may symbolize some of its future problems.

Ambassador Adelman was principal sponsor, and perhaps author, of this U.S. draft resolution. He negotiated the draft during meetings of the First Committee and hoped that he had unanimous agreement—a victory for one of the few U.S.-initiated disarmament resolutions in recent history. However, just before the Chairman—Ambassador James V. Gbeho of Ghana—was ready to ask for a vote, Soviet Ambassador Viktor Issraelyan raised his hand and revealed that his country would go along with the consensus with only "a very slight amendment." This was the addition of an adjective to modify the noun, "information," in the phrase, "broad range of information." The Soviet Ambassador in his intervention suggested a Russian adjective which, he thought, meant in English either "truthful" or "authentic." He asked Ambassador Adelman if he would accept that one modifying adjective.

This addition is, of course, a longtime request by totalitarian States, in other U.N. forums, which the U.S.A., under both Republican and Democratic administrations has long recognized and regularly opposed. Ambassador Adelman quickly responded: "In keeping with the wonderful spirit of cooperation prevailing right now . . . the word, 'truthful,' would, I think, be very helpful." He thus publicly indicated to the Soviet representative that he would accept this proposal. As it was time for lunch, Ambassador Adelman impatiently urged the Chairman to call for the vote, since he saw "no reason for having lunch right now in the midst of our debate." Adelman badly wanted his resolution unanimously adopted before lunch! However, the Chairman brusquely replied, "Powerful as the delegations of the U.S.S.R. and the U.S.A. are, there are other parties who are being asked to make a judgment on this." He adjourned the meeting.[29]

After lunch, the First Committee reconvened and the modifying adjective was finally agreed upon: "accurate" information, a suggestion of the representative from Nigeria. But the Irish delegate perceived the important surrender of the U.S. delegate and refused to countenance it. He said that "any qualification of the word, 'information,' is . . . inappropriate." The Irish insisted that the Committee not adopt the resolution by consensus, but take a vote. In the roll call, Ireland and Brazil abstained. Afterwards, Sweden, Canada, and the Netherlands all expressed their reservations in effect at Adelman's easy acquiescence to the blandishments of Ambassador Issraelyan.[30]

Several weeks later in the plenary of the General Assembly, the draft resolution received the consensus that the U.S.A. was so badly seeking. Yet an important, universal principle was sacrificed. Who can decide what is "accurate" or "authentic" or "truthful" information in disarmament? Only the forces of the market, or freedom of expression, or the test of history can make that determination, even though totalitarian governments always seek the opportunity to do so.

REFERENCES

1. *Building the Future Order*, by Kurt Waldheim. New York: The Free Press. 1980. 262 pp. pp. 71–72.

2. A/35/575.

3. For a discussion of the resolution, see A/C.1/35/PV.40, pp. 16–20 and PV.43, pp. 66–70. The final vote is in A/35/PV.94, pp. 52–53. The adopted resolution is 35/152 I.

4. A/36/458. 19 pp.

5. For a discussion of the resolution, see A/C.1/36/PV.3, 9, 10, 13, 14, 17, 19, 22, 23, 24, 30, 38, and 41. The final vote is in A/C.1/36/PV.30, pp. 12–16. The adopted resolution is 36/92C.

6. A/C.1/36/PV.38, pp. 52–56.

7. A/S-12/27. 10 pp.

8. A/S-12/1, paragraph 53, page 16.

9. A/S-12/PV.1 pp. 47-48.

10. Assessment of the U.N. program of fellowships on disarmament since its inception in 1979. A/S-12/8. 10 pp. April 1982.

11. A/S-12/AC.1/51. 3 pp. June 29, 1982.

12. A/S-12/AC.1/26.

13. A/S-12/AC.1/31 and General Assembly resolution 36/92 J.

14. A/S-12/AC.1/44.

15. A/S-12/AC.1/47.

16. A/S-12/AC.1/63.

17. A/S-12/AC.1/24, p. 7.

18. A/S-12/AC.1/40.

19. "To Break the WDC Stalemate," by Homer A. Jack and Caroline Krebs, *Disarmament Times*, Vol. V, No. 16, June

30th, 1982. "On Keeping WDC Alive and Well," by Alan Geyer and Jozef Goldblat, *Disarmament Times*, Vol. V, No. 19, July 7, 1982.

20. A/S-12/32. Annex V, pp. 1–4.

21. A/36/458 and A/S-12/27.

22. For detailed accounts of the evolution of the WDC, see three WCRP memoranda by the author: "Toward A World Disarmament Campaign." March 1981. 11 pp. "Mobilizing World Public Opinion for Disarmament: The Future of the World Disarmament Campaign." Feb. 1982. 11 pp. "The Final Meetings of the Preparatory Committee." June 1982. 17 pp. pp. 6–8.

23. A/37/548.* 11 pp.

24. Compiled from information released by the U.N. Centre on Disarmament.

25. "Informal NGO Seminar on Disarmament: Report on Findings." New York: NGO Committee on Disarmament. November 1982. 15 pp.

26. 37/100 I.

27. 37/100 H.

28. 37/100 J.

29. A/C.1/37/PV.42, pp. 68–72.

30. A/C.1/37/PV.43, pp. 38–56.

31. Several weeks after the 37th General Assembly was adjourned, U.S. President Ronald Reagan nominated Ambassador Adelman to become Director of the U.S. Arms Control and Disarmament Agency.

8.

Disarmament Machinery

The institutions dealing with disarmament issues are generally designated in U.N. circles as "disarmament machinery." The improvement of these institutions has long been a preoccupation of the U.N. A whole section of the Final Document of SSD I is related to machinery. Also item 12 of the final agenda of SSD II was entitled, "Enhancing the effectiveness of machinery in the field of disarmament and strengthening of the role of the U.N. in the field, including the possible convening of a World Disarmament Conference." Also "machinery" was an important section both of the assessment of SSD I and of the Comprehensive Program of Disarmament.

In preparation for SSD II, delegates had before them a study by experts on Institutional Arrangements Relating to the Process of Disarmament.[1] This grew out of a General Assembly resolution in 1979.[2] The study was completed in September 1981. Its purpose was to make a comprehensive review of the present institutional requirements and future estimated needs in the U.N. management of disarmament affairs, outlining possible functions, structure, and institutional framework for future needs. This study did not, however, break new ground, since the experts agreed to work by consensus and thus decided not to "express an opinion on the deliberative and negotiating bodies in the light of the political nature of such an assessment." As a matter of fact, the group also did not make any specific recommendations for changes in the structure of the U.N. Centre for Disarmament, also because it would step on sensitive political toes.

The whole question of how much time and value should be given to discussing disarmament machinery has always been a controversy within the U.N. This debate arose again in the Ad Hoc Committee of SSD II when it discussed, briefly, agenda item 12 on machinery. Soviet Ambassador Vladimir V. Shustov reiterated the Soviet position on machinery as follows: "Despite the great significance of organizational questions in the disarmament field, success in disarmament negotiations depends in the last analysis on the political will of States." He felt that "it is, after all, no secret to anyone that the true reasons for the lack of progress which can be observed now in solving crucial disarmament problems are to be found not in the organization of the work of the relevant U.N. machinery, but in the lack of desire on the part of certain militarily major States to put a halt to the arms race and in their aspirations to continue on a course of piling up weapons."[3] This longtime position of the Soviet Union was perhaps more insistent than usual because the socialist States were trying to prevent the U.N. Centre for Disarmament from being upgraded into a Department and slipping out from under the supervision of the Under-Secretary-General for Political and Security Council Affairs—traditionally a "Soviet post" in the U.N. Secretariat.

However, Ambassador Celso Antonio de Souza e Silva of Brazil made a similar observation to that of the Soviets: "There is little point in enlarging the existing machinery of the Secretariat or in creating new agencies or in assigning new additional tasks to administrative organs that can do only what Governments collectively ask them to do." He concluded that "whatever the shortcomings, the present structure cannot be blamed for the lack of results."[4] Ambassador Julio C. Carasales of Argentina observed that "it would be quite paradoxical if the only achievements recorded as a result of this Special Session on disarmament were procedural and bureaucratic." He declared that "this is not what world public opinion expects of us."[5] Ambassador A. P. Venkateswaran of India also said that "what has really held up the disarmament process, in our view, is not any lack of machinery, but a conspicuous absence of political will, particularly on the part of the major actors."[6]

Some of the dimensions of the debate on disarmament machinery will be discussed below, except the World Disarmament Campaign which is discussed in Chapter 7. The delegates to SSD II found many opportunities to discuss machinery and also a number of States submitted formal proposals which were published in the Concluding Document.[7] Of the more than 50 specific proposals submitted, more than one-third dealt with machinery and these came from both large and small States.

1. The First Committee

The First Committee of the General Assembly is the principal deliberative body for disarmament affairs in the U.N. system. It is, together with the Disarmament Commission, the most inclusive organ—comprising all Member States. It meets for a longer time than the DC, usually for more than two months. Since SSD I was held, and at the behest of its Final Document, the First Committee almost exclusively devoted its attention to disarmament and international security issues. Despite this concentration by what some call the Disarmament Committee, it has been continuously criticized for its organization of work. During the 37th General Assembly, for example, the First Committee dealt with 22 agenda items on disarmament (not including international security) and adopted a record number of 58 resolutions. Yet resolutions do not disarmament make!

There have been many proposals to rationalize the work of the First Committee so that its decisions can be more focused and not repetitive. Austria, for example, emphasized the "proliferation of sometimes repetitive and overlapping resolutions and a debate that sometimes lacks focus and structure." It also urged that time allotted to the general debate in the First Committee "be used as effectively as possible."[8] The draft assessment of SSD I—riddled with brackets—mentioned ways of avoiding "a multiplicity of U.N. resolutions," with "a more efficient use of the time available to the deliberative bodies." Another proposal urged that the "working methods and procedures of the First Committee need to be improved substantially." Still a third suggestion was that the Bureau of the First Committee or a special ad hoc group formed by the Chairman should "attempt to harmonize similar drafts on the same subject and repetitive initiatives should be limited to a minimum."[9] These criticisms are increasingly apt, since in recent years some States appear to want credit for initiating or co-sponsoring any resolution more than have one good resolution—not theirs, but a compromise—adopted.

2. The Disarmament Commission

The Disarmament Commission (DC) was established in 1952 as an organ of the General Assembly, but fell into disuse some years before SSD I. The Final Document revived DC to "consider and make recommendations on various problems in the field of disarmament and to follow up the relevant decisions and recommendations" of SSD I. The DC was also a subsidiary organ of the General Assembly, and a deliberative—and not negotiating—body, composed, as the First Committee, of all Member States of the U.N.

The DC submitted a special report to SSD II, covering the years 1979 through 1982.[10] This included sections on organization of work

and a discussion of the work itself. The Commission made the minimum recommendation to SSD II: "The members of the Commission
are of the opinion that the Commission should continue to work on the
basis of the relevant provisions of the Final Document [of SSD I], and
decisions and recommendations which the Assembly may wish to
adopt at its Second Special Session."

The annual sessions of the DC since its re-establishment have not
been notable, and questions arose as to its utility and function. Ireland
in the Ad Hoc Committee admitted that the DC "has not fared so well
under the new arrangements agreed on in 1978." Ambassador Noel
Dorr felt that the DC "does not seem fully to have developed a role of
its own as distinct from that of the First Committee and the question as
to which items it should address has not been satisfactorily settled."[11]
Ambassador Arthur R. Menzies of Canada stated that the DC has been
"unable to focus on a sufficiently limited number of subjects in the
short time available to it each year" and it should focus on "substantive
and in-depth deliberations on the most pressing issues."[12]

Various proposals have been made to strengthen the work of the
DC and, in a sense, to "save" it. In the bracketed material in the draft
assessment, one proposal was that there be "an organic link" between
the First Committee and the DC. Another proposal was that the DC
play "a more active role in preparing the ground for the subsequent
negotiation of concrete disarmament agreements." Also it should carry
out in-depth considerations of various experts' studies made on disarmament.[13] The draft CPD proposed that the DC assist the General
Assembly in the review and appraisal of the implementation of the
CPD, especially in the interval between comtemplated review conferences.[14]

3. Committee on Disarmament

One of the specific positive results of the recommendations in the
Final Document of SSD I was the establishment of the Committee on
Disarmament (CD) as a continuation of the Conference of the Committee on Disarmament (CCD). Meeting also in Geneva, it was composed
of 40 Member States and, soon after SSD I, achieved the participation
of France and China and thus of all five known nuclear weapon States.
Still, CD achieved almost no results as the principal disarmament
negotiating body and thus has repeatedly been criticized for its organization of work. Also it has been criticized for failure to rotate or expand
its membership.

The CD made a special report to SSD II.[15] This consisted of a description of the organization of work of the Committee from January 1979 through April 1982. The report also discussed the substantive work of the Committee. Appendices included the draft CPD and a list of documents issued by CD.

In the discussion of machinery in the Ad Hoc Committee, many complaints and proposals were made about the CD. Greece, for example, complained that the CD "is not and must not be a closed club." It added that "there cannot be two categories of States, the privileged and the non-privileged, or the principal ones and the secondary ones."[16] While CD no longer has two co-chairmen (from the U.S.A. and the U.S.S.R. when it was the ENDC and CCD), there is still difficulty for a majority of members to establish certain working groups despite pressure from the General Assembly to do so. The debate did not explicitly state what some Member States insist is reality: that the CD, while paid for by the General Assembly and staffed by the U.N. Secretariat, is a quasi-independent organization not directly responsible to the General Assembly—or at least not taking orders from it.

Some of these criticisms are reflected in the assessment of SSD I and in the CPD. The draft assessment asserted that "some major Powers have proved unwilling to entrust the CD with the task of multilateral negotiations and are reluctant to bring to the Committee concrete proposals and initiatives, particularly with respect to issues relating to nuclear weapons." Attempts have been made, it was stated, "to restrict the Committee's work within narrow limits and sufficient information regarding restricted negotiations conducted outside the Committee has not been made available soas to contribute to the success of multilateral negotiations." This is the real meaning of the oft-used phrase in U.N. circles of the U.N. playing "a central role" in disarmament affairs. Too many States feel that the U.N. is playing a peripheral role as long as bilateral disarmament negotiations do not report directly and frequently to multilateral bodies. Also the draft assessment suggested that "in order to function more effectively and produce concrete results, the CD must function as a negotiating body and not as a forum for debate." Indeed, the negotiating potentialities of such a forum—first established in 1962!—"have yet to be fully explored." Also some felt that "debates having a general character should be left as a prerogative of the deliberative bodies."[17]

The most that SSD II could do was, in the Concluding Document, stress "the need for strengthening the central role of the U.N. in the field of disarmament and the implementation of the security system provided for in the Charter of the U.N. in accordance with the Final Document and to enhance the effectiveness of the CD as the single multilateral negotiating body."[18]

SSD II did ask the CD to report to the 37th General Assembly about the problem of expanding its membership "consistent with the need to enhance its effectiveness." This need was made plain during SSD II with a number of States lining up to become new members of CD: Afghanistan, Austria, Bangladesh, Finland, Ireland, Senegal, Turkey, and Viet Nam. At SSD II itself no solution to the problem of a "limited expansion" was politically possible to achieve. Indeed, at the session of CD in August/September 1982, soon after SSD II concluded, an answer to this question could also not be found.

The 37th General Assembly discussed this matter at some length, with some States still advocating their candidacy for membership, even suggesting a rotation of CD's 40 members. All the General Assembly could do was, in an omnibus resolution on institutional arrangements—adopted without a vote—request the CD to report to the 38th or 1983 General Assembly "on the review of the membership of the Committee."[19] This same resolution also commended to the CD the proposal that it consider "designating itself as a conference" rather than as a committee. This is apparently a public relations effort to make the CD appear to be a more permanent institution.

4. Disarmament Fellowships

On the initiative of Nigeria, the Final Document of SSD I contained a paragraph that "in order to promote expertise in disarmament in more Member States, particularly in the developing countries, the General Assembly decides to establish a program of fellowships on disarmament."[20] A fellowship program began in 1979 and a three-year report of this effort was produced for SSD II.[21]

The primary objective of the program is to "promote expertise in disarmament . . . to enable the holders of fellowships to derive from their training the knowledge and professional competence that will help increase their ability to deal with problems of disarmament." Fellowships are awarded to persons who might soon be entrusted to positions of responsibility in the field of diplomacy and disarmament, not for academic pursuit leading to degrees. A selection panel screens candidates, ensuring the needs of developing countries and over-all geographical balance. There have been two nominations for every fellow selected; in the years 1979–81, a total of 59 persons received fellowships.

Fellows are engaged for a six-month period, beginning at the CD in Geneva in mid-summer and ending in early December at U.N. Headquarters in New York at the conclusion of the consideration of disarmament items in the General Assembly. The group of fellows visits several European capitals to discuss disarmament, notably Stockholm, Bonn, East Berlin, and Budapest at the invitation of governments. (In the future they may also visit Tokyo, Hiroshima, and Nagasaki.) In addition to observing the procedures of disarmament bodies and the U.N., the fellows listen to lectures, attend seminars, and write papers. The budget for this program, including travel and subsistance to the fellows, has been $250,000 each year.

SSD II was not unmindful of this fellowship program. The draft assessment asserted that the fellowship program "has become one of the more concrete results" of SSD I."[22] SSD II had no great difficulty in agreeing to continue and indeed increase the number of fellowships from 20 to 25. This was one of two proposals which met the required consensus of the session. The one-page statement on the fellowship program is found in Annex IV of the Concluding Document[23] and notes the cooperation of certain governments in its work. It is reproduced in full in Appendix D below.

Since SSD II chose not to activate a financial committee, it made no appropriations for the two entities it unanimously endorsed, including the fellowship program. Thus both had to be financed by action of the 37th General Assembly.

At that General Assembly, a resolution initiated by Nigeria continued the expanded fellowship program, recalling that SSD II decided to increase the number to 25. The resolution also requested more adequate staffing for "the expanded structure of the program."[24]

This resolution was adopted without a vote, although a few delegates had misgivings about the increase in budget in a year when attempts were strong for zero growth in the whole U.N. budget. For example, the U.S. delegate, Mr. Gordon C. Luce, after the vote in the plenary, made in part the following statement: "We are concerned about the financial implications of an extended fellowship program. We of course support the noble objectives of educating a group of internationally selected individuals about the vital issues of disarmament and security. We are also aware that the draft resolution now includes the language 'bearing in mind the savings that can be made within existing budgetary appropriations.' Nevertheless, we cannot ignore the financial implications of increasing the program from 20 to 25 fellows. We would have preferred that any increase in the budget for this program would have been financed by offsetting reductions within existing resources. However, as the report on disarmament fellowships makes clear, total additional costs required for 1983 amount to over $134,000. This amount is excessive and in our view does not adequately represent and take into account the savings possible within existing resources."[25] Mr. Luce also revealed that the report on the ongoing work program of the U.N.[26] contained a list of activities included in the 1982–83 U.N. regular budget which "might be considered of low priority." He stated that Annex II of that report included the disarmament fellowship program and suggested a reduction in the number of fellows from 20 to ten each year. He concluded by warning: "We shall be closely monitoring the financial implications of various resolutions in the future, especially those concerning subjects deemed of low priority by the U.N. itself."

5. U.N. Institute for Disarmament Research

The proposal for the establishment of the U.N. Institute for Disarmament Research (UNIDIR) was an initiative of France at SSD I in the form of a working paper.[27] The 33rd General Assembly in 1978 began the process of creating UNIDIR[28] and it was established in Geneva on October 1, 1980 after extensive discussions in the Advisory Board on Disarmament Studies and adoption of another General Assembly resolution.[29] It was agreed that UNIDIR would fall within the framework of the U.N. Institute for Training and Research (UNITAR) for an interim arrangement until SSD II was held. It had a 17-member Advisory Council, with voluntary funding in its initial phase principally from France.

Thus UNIDIR's future was part of the machinery agenda of SSD II. The draft assessment suggested that "the growing importance of the [disarmament] studies should also lead to decisions concerning UNIDIR, an institution for independent research, especially as far as long-term problems are concerned." This proposal asked that UNIDIR be given sufficient status, with the means necessary to fulfill its task.[30]

No decision could be taken during SSD II on the future of UNIDIR, but this was pursued during the 37th session of the General Assembly. Norway, in its omnibus draft resolution on institutional arrangements, devoted a section to UNIDIR. This decided that the

Institution function autonomously, working in close relationship with the Department for Disarmament Affairs, ensure participation on an equitable political and geographical basis, and continue to undertake independent research. The Advisory Board on Disarmament Studies would function as the Board of Trustees of UNIDIR, with its headquarters remaining in Geneva and its activities funded by voluntary contributions from States and private organizations. The whole resolution on machinery was adopted without a vote.[31]

6. Advisory Board on Disarmament Studies

The Final Document of SSD I contained the following proposal: "The Secretary-General is requested to set up an advisory board of eminent persons, selected on the basis of their personal expertise and taking into account the principle of equitable geographical representation, to advise him on various aspects of studies to be made under the auspices of the U.N. in the field of disarmament and arms limitation, including a program of such studies."[32]

In 1979 a Board of 30 eminent persons was appointed by Secretary-General Kurt Waldheim and began to meet. It discussed individual disarmament studies and a comprehensive program of studies. It helped establish the U.N. Institute for Disarmament Research. As the Board's mandate began to expire at the end of 1981, time was devoted to discuss any future mandate, including the possibility of being an advisory board for the Secretary-General in the whole field of disarmament, not confined to studies.[33] A report of the Board was submitted to SSD II.[34]

The draft assessment of SSD I asserted that "the performance of the Advisory Board on Disarmament needs to be assessed on the basis of a cost/benefit analysis and its role should be precisely defined." (In its three years of existence, the Board spent a large amount of money for its slender accomplishments.) The assessment added that, in order for the Board to ensure better coordination and avoid duplication, it might serve as a Governing Council to the UNIDIR.[35]

SSD II made no statement on continuing the Board, and its mandate, but this problem was discussed by the 37th General Assembly. The Secretary-General submitted a note to the General Assembly, listing certain functions for a continued mandate.[36] These included the following: 1) To advise the Secretary-General on various aspects of studies and research in the area of arms limitation and disarmament,

2) To serve as the Advisory Council of the UNIDIR, 3) To advise the Secretary-General on the implementation of the World Disarmament Campaign, and 4) To provide the Secretary-General with advice on other matters on disarmament at his specific invitation.

The omnibus resolution on institutional arrangements and machinery, initiated by Norway, contained the briefest sub-section continuing the mandate of the Board: "Requests the Secretary-General to revive the Advisory Board on Disarmament Studies in line with his note of 28 October . . . and to entrust it with the functions listed therein."[37] This whole resolution was adopted without a vote, but there was no great enthusiasm evident about continuing this particular piece of disarmament machinery.

The original concept of an Advisory Board implied, to some, the appointment by the Secretary-General of eminent persons who would not necessarily be diplomats. Yet the 30 persons appointed came largely from the diplomatic community. For this reason, and others, two proposals were made at SSD II to create a different kind of panel. India and Mexico submitted a draft resolution on removing the dangers of nuclear war. One of its operative paragraphs requested the Secretary-General to appoint "a representative group of public persons of great eminence, consisting of statesmen, scientists, physicians, jurists, religious leaders, philosophers, and other suitably qualified persons, for the purpose of advising on special measures and procedures—practical, political, and legal—designed for the collective control, management, and resolution of critical or confrontational situations which could escalate to nuclear war, in addition to those already provided for in the Charter of the U.N."[38] Nothing came of this draft resolution and it was not put to a vote in the 37th General Assembly.

France, under the prodding of one of its leading statesmen, Edgar Faure—who was present at SSD II—proposed the creation of a "Universal Conscience Council." This would provide "general information on the various aspects of the problems relating to disarmament and arms control, international security, and the link between disarmament and development." It would encourage "intellectual movement," since disarmament cannot succeed by "emotional reactions alone." While disarmament is "desired by the heart, [it] must be achieved by the use of reason." Thus the Council would consist of eminent persons representing the "main categories of the spiritual life of mankind, and science, culture, art, and philosophy, former Heads of State or Government who are unanimously respected and no longer involved in national political activities, and eminent persons representing the principal religious faiths and lay philosophies of a humanist and social nature."[39] Nothing also came of this proposal.

7. Centre for Disarmament

The Disarmament Affairs Division of the U.N. Secretariat became the U.N. Centre for Disarmament on January 1, 1977, partly as a result of the study on the Review of the Role of the U.N. in the Field of Disarmament.[40] SSD I in the Final Document asserted that "in order to enable the U.N. to continue to fulfill its role in the field of disarmament and to carry out the additional tasks assigned to it by this Special Session, the U.N. Centre for Disarmament should be adequately strengthened and its research and information functions accordingly extended."[41]

The experts' study on Institutional Arrangements Relating to the Process of Disarmament dealt at length with some of the functions of the U.N. Centre, especially relating to deliberation and negotiation, implementation and verification, information, studies, and training. Among the recommendations made unanimously by the experts was that 1) The responsibility vested in the Secretary-General for coordinating the various activities undertaken in disarmament by the various bodies in the U.N. system should be clearly reaffirmed and 2) The Centre should be strengthened with an appropriate number of additional staff.[42]

When SSD II convened, it also had the draft assessment of SSD I. This contained four paragraphs on the U.N. Centre, some divergent, and all in brackets:

"[158. The U.N. Centre for Disarmament has provided valuable support to the activities in the field of disarmament as envisaged at the First Special Session. It has helped members of the U.N. by providing information on disarmament, supporting research and studies on various aspects of disarmament, and providing the necessary secretariat services whenever required. The dramatic increase in activities related to disarmament, however, has not been matched by an increase in the limited resources available to the U.N. Centre for Disarmament. Therefore, its further strengthening and status should properly reflect the central role and primary responsibility of the U.N. in the field of disarmament.]

"[159. In spite of the wide-ranging difficulties and the limited means available to it, the U.N. Disarmament Centre has been successful during the last four years in accomplishing the additional tasks entrusted to it at the First Special Session.

"[160. To discharge the further additional responsibilities during the period to follow the Second Special Session, this organ should be strengthened substantially.]

"[161. First, its present status within the U.N. Secretariat should be upgraded. Secondly, its staff as well as its financial means should be increased. Thirdly, the Centre should be enabled to act as the main monitoring unit responsible for the continuation of all other U.N. institutions with an interest in matters of disarmament.]"[43]

The draft CPD also contained two paragraphs about the Centre, also in brackets:

"[11. The U.N. machinery for disarmament should be appropriately strengthened in order to enable the U.N. to carry out its role in contributing to and carrying out a review of the implementation of the CPD. In particular, the Centre for Disarmament should be provided with the resources and personnel necessary to strengthen its functions relating to (a) support and assistance to multilateral negotiations, (b) dissemination and coordination of information relating to disarmament matters, and (c) research studies with respect to specific areas of disarmament.]

"[12. In order to expand and strengthen the U.N. disarmament machinery, as has been done up to now, in a gradual manner, the next step should be to change the existing 'U.N. Centre for Disarmament' into a 'Department for Disarmament Affairs,' to be headed by an Under-Secretary-General. The Department would report directly to the Secretary-General and would be at the same level as the other Departments, such as the Department of Political and Security Council Affairs and the Department of International Economic and Social Affairs."][44]

This last proposal was freighted with politics, since any increase in the status of the Centre would mean that its Director, an Under-Secretary-General, would report directly to the U.N. Secretary-General and not through the Under-Secretary-General in charge of the Department of Political and Security Council Affairs. The latter has traditionally been a Soviet national (although technically an international civil servant). Much of the discussion about the Centre reflected this political situation, with the socialist States trying to maintain the status quo—and able to do so more easily in U.N. bodies that operated by consensus.

In the brief time allocated by the Ad Hoc Committee of SSD II for oral statements on disarmament machinery, several States discussed the U.N. Centre. Japan urged that the experimental team within the Centre on reference and data processing be strengthened so that a disarmament information data bank could be created.[45] Ireland called for an increased status of the Centre within the Secretariat, and establishing it as a department directed by an Under-Secretary-General.[46] Canada and Norway made the same suggestions.[47] On the other hand, Soviet Ambassador Shustov asserted that "there is no need to raise the question of a radical restructuring of the Centre, inter alia, by the establishment within the Secretariat of a separate department on disarmament, as is sometimes proposed." There is an "extremely important advantage" in having it as an integral part of the Department of Political and Security Council affairs since it ensures "a linkage between disarmament and international security." Indeed, "an artificial separation of the functions of the Secretariat in serving disarmament negotiations from its activities designed to promote the efforts of States to strengthen international security would only be detrimental to this cause." He concluded that "to disrupt the present machinery for servicing disarmament negotiations would be unjustified and would, to a significant extent, divert attention from substantive questions of disarmament and lead to useless organizational changes which would only result in misleading public opinion."[48]

SSD II was unable to resolve any structural or financial problems relating to the Centre and these were referred to the 37th General Assembly. Here, an omnibus resolution, initiated by Norway, did address itself directly to an increased status for the Centre. The subsection of the resolution was as terse as it was important: "Requests the Secretary-General to transform the Centre for Disarmament appropriately strengthened with the existing over-all resources of the U.N. into a Department for Disarmament Affairs, headed by an Under-Secretary-General and which will be so organized as to reflect fully the principle of equitable geographical distribution."[49] This was adopted without a vote, since the socialist group realized that, had there been a vote, the change would in any case have been overwhelmingly adopted.

8. New Institution

For years forward-looking proposals have been made for the creation of some kind of new disarmament institution within the U.N.

system, to coordinate and raise to a higher level all aspects of disarmament. The problem of verification has especially been cited as a new role for the U.N. if substantial disarmament agreements are negotiated. During SSD I two such proposals were submitted formally and discussed. The Netherlands proposed the establishment of an International Disarmament Organization to implement disarmament agreements. Sri Lanka proposed the creation of a World Disarmament Authority or Institution to have "over-all competence in the field of disarmament." Neither was endorsed by the Final Document of SSD I, but both were listed for further study.

In the preparations for SSD II, and during it, the need for further bodies was also discussed. Dutch Prime Minister Andreas A. M. van Agt in the plenary made a reformulation of the earlier proposal during SSD I for the establishment of an International Disarmament Organization. It could be defined as "the operational framework for the implementation of international arms control and disarmament treaties with important functions in the field of verification and for the handling of complaints." Further, it would prepare review conferences and serve as an information clearing house. He urged that, as a first step, the U.N. Secretary-General be asked to seek the views of Governments on the establishment of such an organization.[50]

Mrs. Inga Thorsson of Sweden recalled in the Ad Hoc Committee of SSD II that her country "has for many years argued in favor of the establishment of an independent disarmament body within the U.N. system." She felt that "it is now time to decide, at least in principle, that such an independent body within the U.N. framework shall be established."[57] The formal Swedish proposal for modification of the composite draft on the assessment of SSD I before SSD II was as follows: "The General Assembly decided in principle to establish a U.N. Disarmament Agency. The Secretary-General shall submit a concrete proposal to the 38th session regarding the practical implementation, organization, and staffing of such an agency, bearing in mind, inter alia, that the agency should have sufficient resources, that it should have an independent position within the U.N. system, that it should have a governing body elected by the General Assembly and adequate regular funding to be able to undertake the work requested by Member States, and that it should report directly to the Assembly."[52]

Italy submitted a working paper entitled, "Institution of an International Body for the Verification of Disarmament Agreements." This began by calling attention to the fact that "there exists no organ or authority at the international level entrusted with the specific task of ensuring compliance with the obligations and commitments assumed in disarmament agreements and of directly enforcing procedures aimed at verifying any allegation of non-compliance." The paper suggested that such a service could be created in successive stages, the first being an ad hoc section within the U.N. Centre for Disarmament. Among its duties would be to act as a permanent secretariat to the various consultative committees of experts envisaged by existing and future disarmament agreements. Later the entity could become a Centre for the Verification of Disarmament Agreements and, still later, an independent agency.[53]

A third proposal came from France, which at SSD I first raised the possibility of the creation of an International Satellite Monitoring Agency. SSD I did not adopt this proposal, but the 33rd or 1978 General Assembly adopted a resolution asking the Secretary-General to undertake an experts study of the technical, legal, and financial implications of establishing such an agency. This study was completed in 1981.[54] (See Chapter 9 on Disarmament Studies.) The Minister for Foreign Affairs of France, speaking in the general debate at SSD II, reiterated France's determination to pursue efforts to promote this proposal. France in a note verbale to SSD II asked that it take note of this study and its conclusions. It further requested that the Secretary-General report on practical arrangements for implementating the conclusions of the satellite study.[55]

The Swedish proposal found its way in the draft assessment. Another paragraph in brackets noted that "new responsibilities could be given to the international community, for instance, in the verification area or in the implementation of the relationship between disarmament and development. Such tasks call for corresponding innovations in the institutional framework."[56] In the draft CPD, both the International Disarmament Organization and the U.N. Disarmament Agency appeared in paragraphs, well bracketed. Also several proposals were included on the Satellite Monitoring Agency and the International Verification Agency.[57]

The 37th General Assembly discussed further the International Satellite Monitoring Agency in a resolution introduced by France. This took note of the study, asked that it be published, and requested the Secretary-General to report to the 38th General Assembly in 1983 "on the practical modalities for implementing its conclusions." This was adopted by a vote of 126 to nine, with 11 abstentions. All Warsaw Pact States, except Romania, voted against the resolution, while those abstaining included a number of other socialist countries—and the U.S.A.[58]

9. The Future

Several proposals were made to deal with future evaluations of progress in disarmament, including a future Special Session. These include review conferences of the CPD, a Third Special Session, and a World Disarmament Conference.

The draft CPD suggested another Special Session of the General Assembly to review the implementation of the CPD. Such reviews would not only assess the implementation of disarmament measures, but elaborate in concrete terms future disarmament measures in future stages.[59]

The draft implementation or assessment concluded with the following suggestion: "A decision should be taken at the Second Special Session on the holding, in June 1987, of a Third Special Session . . . which would, among other things, review the implementation of the measures included in the first stage" of the CPD.[60]

The Concluding Document of SSD II asserted in its last paragraph: "The Third Special Session of the General Assembly devoted to disarmament should be held at a date to be decided by the General Assembly at its 38th session."[61]

The socialist States have advocated a World Disarmament Conference since 1971, but earlier it was a Non-Aligned initiative. The U.S.A. and China vetoed in effect the convening of a Conference when it was proposed by the Soviet Union in 1971. However, an Ad Hoc Committee on the World Disarmament Conference was established by the General Assembly and this has kept the concept alive. The Ad Hoc Committee presented a special report to SSD II. This covered its work during the period between SSD I and SSD II. The report also reflected its conclusions and recommendations made from 1978 through 1982, including those relating to its mandate. Most important, it quoted the positions of the five nuclear weapon States on convening a Conference, with the Soviet Union the only one showing any enthusaism.[62]

The conclusions of the Ad Hoc Committee, made in 1981, were reiterated in 1982: 1) "No consensus with respect to the convening of a World Disarmament Conference under the present conditions has yet been reached among the nuclear-weapon States whose participation in such a conference has been deemed essential by most States Members of the Organization;" 2) The general Assembly "may wish to decide that after its Second Special Session a World Disarmament Conference would take place as soon as the necessary consensus on its convening has been reached;" 3) The General Assembly "may wish to renew the mandate of its Ad Hoc Committee and request it to continue to maintain close contact with the representatives of the nuclear-weapon States . . ."[63]

The 37th General Assembly took no action on future special sessions or review conferences, but did renew the mandate of the Ad Hoc Committee for the World Disarmament Conference. The resolution, adopted without a vote, continued the work of the Committee.[64]

A World Disarmament Conference appears, at this time, a futile exercise. The continuation of the Ad Hoc Committee is, and has been, a wasteful use of human and financial resources. If the socialist States want to continue to advocate the convening of a World Disarmament Conference, they should re-examine its role, especially in light of the existence—if not success—of the 40-nation CD and other disarmament negotiating bodies and a potential CPD.

REFERENCES

1. A/36/392. 77 pp., including an annex on replies of States.
2. 35/87 E.
3. A/S-12/AC.1/PV.11, pp. 32–36.
4. *Ibid.*, pp. 37–42.
5. *Ibid.*, pp. 73–80.
6. *Ibid.*, pp. 62–65.
7. A/S-12/32, Annex II, 18 pp.
8. A/S-12/AC.1/PV.11, p. 22.
9. A/S-12/1, p. 45.
10. A/S-12/3. 25 pp.
11. A/S-12/AC.1/PV.11, p. 16.
12. *Ibid.*, pp. 28–30.
13. A/S-12/1, p. 46.
14. A/S-12/32, Annex I, p. 47.
15. A/S-12/2. 145 pp.
16. A/S-12/AC.1/PV.11, p. 7.
17. A/S-12/1, pp. 46–47.
18. A/S-12/32, pp. 23–24.
19. 37/99 K.
20. Paragraph 108.
21. A/S-12/8. 10 pp.
22. A/S-12/1, p. 48.
23. A/S-12/32, Annex IV, p. 1.
24. 37/100 G.
25. A/37/PV.101, pp. 61–62.
26. A/36/658.
27. A/S-10/AC.1/8.
28. 33/71 K.
29. 34/83 M.
30. A/S-12/1, p. 49.
31. 37/99 K (part IV).
32. S/10/2, paragraph 124.
33. For one description of the work of the Board, see the *1981 U.N. Disarmament Yearbook*. pp. 341–50.
34. A/36/654.
35. A/S-12/1, p. 48.
36. A/37/550. 3 pp.
37. 37/99 K (Section III).
38. A/S-12/AC.1/L.2, reprinted in A/S-12/32, pp. 10–11.
39. A/S-12/AC.1/40. See also *Disarmament Times*, Vol. V, No. 18, p. 4.
40. A/31/36.
41. S/10/2, paragraph 123.
42. A/36/392, p. 30.
43. A/S-12/12/1, pp. 47–48.
44. A/S-12/32, Annex I, p. 48.
45. A/S-12/AC.1/PV.11, p. 12.
46. *Ibid.*, p. 17.
47. *Ibid.*, pp. 28–30 and p. 82.
48. *Ibid.*, pp. 33–35.
49. 37/99 K (section V).
50. A/S-12/PV.13, pp. 51–52. Also A/S-12/22.

51. A/S-12/AC.1/PV.9, pp. 44–45.
52. A/S-12/AC.1/39.
53. A/S-12/AC.1/19 and Rev. 1. 5 pp.
54. A/AC.206/14. 120 pp.
55. A/S-12/AC.1/55.
56. A/S-12/1, pp. 48–49.
57. A/S-12/32, pp. 49, 51.

58. 37/78 K.
59. A/S-12/32, Annex I, p. 47.
60. A/S-12/1, p. 54.
61. A/S-12/32, p. 24.
62. A/S-12/4. 10 pp.
63. *Ibid.*, pp. 9–10.
64. 37/97.

9.

Studies and Documentation

A veritable library of disarmament materials was prepared or otherwise available for SSD II. Some of this material was the result of a series of studies by experts, authorized by the General Assembly since SSD I. (Many of the studies made before SSD I are still useful.) Others of these studies were commmissioned by the Prep Comm, but these did not reach the number authorized for preparations for SSD I.

The documentation also includes the deluge of reports, records, and working papers resulting from the 18 months of the work of the Prep Comm and from the five weeks duration of SSD II itself. Also some miscellaneous materials were available and useful. Since SSD II was truncated, this listing extends to documents of the 37th regular session of the General Assembly. Finally, this chapter includes an incomplete list of articles on SSD II, written before, during, and after this world event. Also the availability of some of this material will be explored.

1. U.N. Expert Studies

1. *Comprehensive Nuclear Test Ban*. May 1980. A/35/257. This was made by consultant-experts based on General Assembly decision 34/422 of December 1979. The contents: 1) Background summary; 2) Negotiations leading to the partial test ban treaty; 3) Treaty on the Non-Proliferation of Nuclear Weapons; 4) Deliberations and negotiations (1963–1979); 5) Trilateral negotiations on a comprehensive test ban; 6) Major unresolved issues and; 7) Conclusions. There are five appendices. In a foreword, U.N. Secretary-General Kurt Waldheim wrote, "In my first statement to the Conference of the Committee on Disarmament, in 1972, I stated the belief that all the technical and

scientific aspects of the problem had been so fully explored that only a political decision was necessary in order to achieve agreement. I still hold that belief. The problem can and should be solved now."

2. *Comprehensive Study on Nuclear Weapons.* A/35/392. September 1980. 177 pp. This was made by a group of experts based on General Assembly resolution 33/91 D of December 1978. The contents: 1) Introduction; 2) Factual information on present nuclear arsenals; 3) Trends in the technological development of nuclear-weapon systems; 4) Effects of the use of nuclear weapons; 5) The doctrines of deterrence and other theories concerning nuclear weapons; 6) Security implications of the continued quantitative increase and qualitative improvement of nuclear-weapon systems; 7) Implications of the treaties, agreements, and negotiations related to nuclear disarmament; and 8) Conclusion: "The perpetual menace to human society."

This study has been widely quoted and published. It has been issued by the U.N. in the Study Series 1 as Sales No. E.81.I.11. and published commercially by Autumn Press. (Boston). 1981. 232 pp. See also a summary in Fact Sheet No. 17. 12 pp.

3. *Implementation of the Declaration on the Denuclearization of Africa.* (An alternative title: South Africa's Plan and Capability in the Nuclear Field). September 1980. A/35/402. 42 pp. This study by appropriate experts was based on General Assembly resolution 34/76 B of December 1979. The Contents: 1) Introduction: context of the study; 2) Nuclear energy profile of South Africa; 3) South Africa's nuclear weapon capability; 4) South Africa's nuclear weapon calculations; 5) Two indicators of a possible South African nuclear weapon capability; 6) Recent initiatives in the nuclear field involving South Africa; and 7) Conclusions. One of the latter: "There is no doubt that South Africa has the technical capability to make nuclear weapons and the necessary means of delivery."

Fact Sheet No. 15. 8 pp. Study Series 2. 40 pp. Sales No. E.81.I.10.

4. *Study on all Aspects of Regional Disarmament.* October 1980. A/35/416. 64 pp. This study by qualified governmental experts was based on General Assembly resolution 33/91 E of December 1978. The contents: 1) Introduction; 2) Past experience and present endeavors; 3) Regional approach to disarmament; 4) Survey of conceivable measures; and 5) Conclusions. The latter includes the statement: "Given the political will, there is a vast and, to a large extent, unexplored potential for progress in disarmament if the global approach is

supplemented with determined and systematic efforts at the level of the different regions."

Fact Sheet No. 16. 12 pp. Study series 3. 59 pp. Sales No. E.81.IX.2.

In accepting this study, the General Assembly in resolution 35/156 D requested Member States to comment on the study. The latter is found in A/36/343 and Add.1 and in A/S-12/16. 11 pp.

5. *The Implications of Establishing an International Satellite Monitoring Agency*. August 1981. A/AC.206/14. 120 pp. This was undertaken by a group of governmental experts based on General Assembly resolution 33/71 J of December 1978 and 34/83 E of December 1979. The contents: 1) Introduction; 2) Conclusions; 3) Technical implications; 4) Legal implications; and 5) Financial implications. Also there are six annexes. The conclusions reflected no technical, legal, or financial obstacles. As regards the latter, the Agency would "cost the international community each year well under one per cent of the total annual expenditure on armaments."

The 37th General Assembly in resolution 37/78 K requested the Secretary-General to report to the 38th General Assembly on the practical modalities for implementing the conclusions of the study with respect to the institutional aspects.

Fact Sheet No. 25. August 1982. 12 pp.

6A. *The Relationship Between Disarmament and Development*. October 1981. A/36/356. 195 pp. This was made by governmental experts based on General Assembly resolution 32/88 A. The experts were chaired by Mrs. Inga Thorsson, then Under-Secretary of State for Disarmament in the Government of Sweden. This was one of the largest studies ever undertaken by the U.N. on disarmament. The contents: 1) Introduction; 2) The framework and scope of the relationship between disarmament and development; 3) Present-day utilization of resources for military purposes; 4) Economic and social effects of a continuing arms race and of the implementation of disarmament measures; 5) Conversion and redeployment of resources released from military purposes through disarmament measures to economic and social development purposes; 6) Possible institutional measures for the international reallocation of resources from armaments to development; and 7) Summary, conclusions, and recommendations. There are three appendixes, including a list of 40 commissioned research reports received by the Group of Governmental Experts. The first conclusion of the report: "The world can either continue to pursue the arms race with characteristic vigor or move consciously and with deliberate speed toward a more stable and balanced social and economic development within a more sustainable international economic and political order. It cannot do both."

This study has been interpreted in a popular book: *Safe and Sound: Disarmament and Development in the Eighties*, by Clyde Sanger. Ottawa: Deneau publishers. 122 pp. 1982.

Fact Sheet No. 21, 12 pp. February 1982.

Study Series 5. 189 pp. Sales No. E.82.IX.1.

6B. *Relationship Between Disarmament and Development: Report of the Secretary-General*.

May 1982. A/S-12/13. 39 pp. /Add.1. 9 pp. /Add. 2. 7 pp. /Add.3. 2 pp. and /Add.4. 3 pp.

This report, based on General Assembly resolution 39/92 G of December 1981, invited Member States to respond to the study.

7A. *Institutional Arrangements Relating to the Process of Disarmament*. September 1981. A/36/392. 77 pp. This report by governmental experts is based on General Assembly resolution 34/87 E of December 1979. The contents: 1) Introduction; 2) Present institutional arrangements in the U.N. relating to the process of disarmament; 3) Views on present institutional arrangements and future estimated needs in the U.N. relating to the process of disarmament; and 4) Conclusions and recommendations.

7B. *Enhancement of the Effectiveness of Machinery in the Field of Disarmament* and *Strengthening of the Role of the U.N. in this Field* . . . May 1982. A/S-12/12. 31 pp. /Add.1. June 1982. 6 pp. /Add.2. June 1982. 10 pp. /Add.3. June 1982. 4pp.

This is based on General Assembly resolution 36/97 D of December 1981, which accepted the report on Institutional Arrangements and requested Member States to send their comments to the Secretary-General. Contents: 1) Introduction; and 2) Replies received from Governments.

8. *Israeli Nuclear Disarmament*. September 1981. A/36/431. 27 pp. This experts report was authorized by General Assembly resolution 34/89 of December 1979. The contents: 1) Introduction; 2) Israel's nuclear development; 3) Israel's nuclear-weapon potential; 4) Factors affecting Israel's nuclear policy; 5) International reports concerning Israeli nuclear armament; and 6) Conclusions. Among the conclusions: "On the basis of the available authoritative information, the Group of Experts is unable to conclude definitely whether or not Israel is at present in the possession of nuclear weapons."

Study Series 6. 22 pp. Sales No. E.82.IX.2.

9A. *World Disarmament Campaign.* September 1981. A/36/458. 19 pp. The General Assembly in resolution 35/152 I of December 1980 requested the Secretary-General to appoint a small group of experts to make this study. The contents: 1) Introduction; 2) General Purpose; 3) Specific objectives; 4) Operational guidelines; 5) Constituencies; 6) Activities; 7) Direction and finance; and 8) Summary.

9B. *World Disarmament Campaign; Report of the Secretary-General.* May 1982. A/S-12/14. 17 pp. /Add.1. June 1982. 6 pp. /Add.2. June 1982. 6 pp. The General Assembly, in resolution, 36/92 C of December 1981, expressed appreciation for the report and invited Member States to transmit their comments. (This was not a study by U.N. experts.)

9C. *Outline of a Program for the World Disarmament Campaign.* June 1982. A/S-12/27. 10 pp. This report is based on the request of the Prep Comm in paragraph 53 of its report to SSD II asking the Secretary-General to submit a detailed outline of a program for the Campaign. The contents: 1) Preface; 2) Introduction; 3) Concept; 4) Program of activities; and 5) Conclusion. (This was not a study by U.N. experts.)

9D. *World Disarmament Campaign.* November 1982. A/37/548.* 11 pp. SSD II, in Annex V or the Concluding Document, requested the Secretary-General to present a report on the specifics of a Campaign. Contents: 1) Introduction; 2) General framework; 3) Program of activities for 1982; and 4) Financial aspects of the proposed program.

Fact Sheet No. 28. 24 pp. February 1983.

10. *Confidence-Building Measures.* October 1981. A/36/474. 47 pp. This was made by governmental experts based on General Assembly resolution 34/87 B of December 1979. The nine chapters are 1) Introduction; 2) General considerations; 3) The concept of confidence-building measures; 4) Evolution of confidence-building measures; 5) Principles; 6) Approach; 7) Illustrative list of measures which may contribute to building confidence; 8) Role of the U.N.; and 9) Conclusions and recommendations.

Fact Sheet No. 20. 12 pp. January 1982.

Study Series 7. 42 pp. Sales No. E.82.IX.3.

11. *Study on the Relationship Between Disarmament and International Security.* November 1981. A/36/597. 63 pp. This was made by a group of experts based on paragraph 97 of the Final Document of SSD I and General Assembly resolutions 33/91 I of December 1978 and 35/156 E of December 1980. The contents: 1) The Detrimental conse-

quences of the arms race; 2) Analysis of the interrelationship of disarmament and international security; 3) The process of disarmament and international security; 4) Détente and international cooperation as means of strengthening international security and disarmament; 5) The relationship between specific disarmament measures and international security; 6) Disarmament, international security, and the role of the U.N. in the maintenance of peace and in the implementation of the system of international legal order and security as provided for in the charter of the U.N.; and 7) Conclusions.

Fact Sheet No. 22. 12 pp. March 1982.

Study Series 8. 55 pp. Sales No. E.82.IX.4.

In accepting this study, the General Assembly in resolution 36/97 L of December 1981, invited Member States to respond to the study. This appeared in A/S-12/16. 11 pp. and /Add.1.

12A and 12B. *Chemical and Bacteriological (Biological) Weapons.* Two studies were made: A/36/613 issued in November 1981 in 56 pages and A/37/259 issued in November 1982 in 109 pages.

The first study was made by qualified experts based on General Assembly resolution 35/144 C of December 1980. The contents include: 1) Introduction; 2) Organization of work and record of proceedings; 3) Background to the problem of the alleged use of chemical weapons and sources of information on the subject; 4) General observations on chemical weapons and sources of information on the subject; 5) Evaluation of written submissions; 6) The question of mycotoxins; 7) On-site collection and examination of evidence; and 8) Conclusions. There are also five annexes. The final paragraph of the Conclusions is as follows; "In the opinion of the Group, this report is inconclusive. Any investigation designed to lead to definitive conclusions regarding the alleged use of chemical weapons and to an assessment of the extent of the damage caused by such chemical weapons would require timely access to the areas of alleged use of chemical warfare agents in order to establish the true facts. Such an exercise has so far not been possible."

The General Assembly in resolution 36/96 B of December 1981 continued the work of this Group and it submitted a second report. The contents include: 1) Introduction; 2) Organization of work and records of proceedings; 3) Sources of information on the subject of the alleged use of chemical weapons; 4) Evaluation of written submissions; 5) On-site collection and examination of evidence; 6) Samples obtained during on-site visits; and 7) Conclusions. There are six annexes. The final concluding paragraph: "While the Group could not state that these allegations had been proved, nevertheless it could not disregard the circumstantial evidence suggestive of the possible use of some sort of toxic chemical substance in some instances."

The General Assembly in resolution 37/98 E of December 1982 took note of the report and did not renew the mandate of the Group. However, in resolution 37/98 D it requested the Secretary-General to compile and maintain lists of qualified experts whose services could be made available at short notice to undertake such investigations. Also the resolution requested the Secretary-General to obtain the assistance of consultant experts to devise procedures to investigate violations of the Geneva Protocol.

13. *Reduction of Military Budgets*. May 1982. A/S-12/7. 111 pp. This study is based on General Assembly resolution 35/142 B of December 1980. Also it comes after many earlier studies, made since 1973, by the U.N. on this subject. The first such study after SSD I was A/35/479 in 57 pages plus appendixes. It was based on General Assembly resolution 33/67 of December 1978 and appeared in October 1980. It is also in study series 4, in 197 pages, Sales No. E.81.I.9.

The contents of the 1982 study: 1) Introduction; 2) Reporting by States; 3) Intertemporal and international comparisons of military expenditures; and 4) Problems of verification. Four working papers are also included.

14. *Economic and Social Consequences of the Arms Race and of Military Expenditures*. September 1982. A/37/386. 74 pp. This study was made by a group of consultant experts based on General Assembly resolution 35/141 of December 1980. It brings up to date two previous studies of the same title: the 1978 edition, 90 pp., available as U.N. Publication Sales No. E.78.IX.1. The 1962 edition is available in the volume "Basic Problems of Disarmament," published by the U.N. in 1970. Sales No. E.70.I.14 and 17.

The five chapters of the 1982 study are 1) Dynamics of the arms race; 2) Resources and the arms race; 3) Military outlays and socio-economic development; 4) International consequences of the arms race; and 5) Conclusions and recommendations.

The new study will also be published as a result of resolution 37/70. Fact Sheet No. 27. 16 pp. January 1983.

2. Preparatory Papers

1. *Disarmament Resolutions Adopted by the General Assembly*. April 1981. A/AC.206/3. 185 pp.

This is a paper, requested by the Prep Comm, and made by the U.N. Secretariat. It covers the period of 1978–81 and supplements an earlier paper prepared for SSD I: A/AC.187/29 and Corr.1 and /Add.1. 202 pp. and 60 pp. The contents: 1) Introduction; 2) Final Document of the First Special Session; 3) Disarmament resolutions adopted by the General Assembly at its 33rd to 35th sessions; 4) Decisions on disarmament; 5) Resolutions on international security questions; and 6) Other disarmament-related resolutions.

2. *A Comprehensive Study of Official Proposals or Declarations Made or Decisions Taken by the General Assembly on the Procedure of Unilateral or Negotiated Moratoria as a Provisional Measure for the Prohibition of Nuclear-Weapon Tests, as well as their Application by Any State.* April 1981. A/AC.206/4. 5 pp.

This is a background paper, requested by the Prep Comm, and made by the U.N. Secretariat. It covers the period 1977–80 and supplements an earlier paper on the subject prepared for SSD I: A/AC.187/69.

The contents: 1) Introduction; and 2) Proposals, declarations, and decisions.

3. *A Comprehensive Study of the Origin, Development, and Present Status of the Various Alternatives Proposed for the Prohibition of the Use of Nuclear Weapons.* April 1981. A/AC.206/5. 20 pp. This is a background paper, requested by the Prep Comm, and made by the U.N. Secretariat. It covers the period 1977–80 and supplements an earlier paper on the same subject for SSD I: A/AC.187/71.

The contents include: 1) In the context of the non-use of force in international relations; 2) In relation to a convention on the non-use of nuclear weapons; 3) In terms of security guarantees to non-nuclear-weapon States; and 4) In the context of nuclear-weapon-free zones.

4. *The Human and Material Resources Available to the U.N. Secretariat for its Work on Disarmament and the Organization of that Work.* April 1981. A/AC.206/6. 12 pp. This is a background paper, requested by the Prep Comm, and made by the U.N. Secretariat. It covers the period November 1977/April 1981 and supplements an earlier paper on the subject prepared for SSD I: A/AC.187/74 and Corr. 1.

The contents include: 1) Introduction; 2) U.N. Centre for Disarmament; 3) Financial resources; 4) Coordination; and 5) Summary of changes.

5. *A Synthesis of the Arguments Adduced For and Against each of the Four Proposals for the Creation of Nuclear-Weapon-Free Zones that have been included in the Agenda of the General Assembly . . .*

May 1981. A/AC.126/7 and /Add.1. 61 pp. This is a working paper, requested by the Prep Comm, and made by the U.N. Secretariat. It covers the period 1977–80 and supplements an earlier paper on the subject prepared for SSD I: A/AC.187/70.

The contents: 1) Introduction; 2) Proposal for a nuclear-weapon-free zone in Africa; 3) Proposal for a nuclear-weapon-free zone in the Middle East; 4) Proposal for a nuclear-weapon-free zone in South Asia; and 5) Proposal for the establishment of a zone of peace in the Indian Ocean. There are two annexes, including an index to the debates on the subject in the General Assembly.

6. *A Summary of Studies in the Field of Disarmament Prepared by the Secretary-General with the Assistance of Experts During the period 1977–1980 at the Request of the General Assembly.* May 1981. A/AC.206/9. 37 pp. This is a working paper, requested by the Prep Comm, and made by the U.N. Secretariat. It covers the period 1977–80. The contents include seven studies.

7. *A Comparative Study of the Scope Originally Proposed or Aimed at in Draft Multilateral Disarmament Treaties of a Universal Character . . . June 1981.* A/AC.206/10 and Corr. 1. 10 pp. This is a paper, requested by the Prep Comm, and made by the U.N. Secretariat. It covers the period 1978–81 and supplements the earlier paper prepared for SSD I: A/AC.187/68. This deals exclusively with the convention signed on inhumane and indiscriminate weapons.

8. *List of Disarmament and Related Proposals Officially Submitted to the U.N. September 1981.* A/AC.206/15. 83 pp. This is a background paper, requested by the Prep Comm, and made by the U.N. Secretariat. It covers the period September 1977 through 1980 and supplements an earlier paper on the subject prepared for SSD I: A/AC.187/75.

The contents include: 1) Introduction, 2) A concise list of proposals made from September 1977 to August 1978; 3) An annotated list of proposals made after the First Special Session. It includes an annex on bilateral and multilateral agreements completed.

9. *Brief Synopsis of Disarmament and Arms Limitation Negotiations Since 1978—Including Their Results—Carried out within the Framework of the U.N., on a Regional Basis or Bilaterally . . . September 1981.* A/AC.206/16. 17 pp. This is a working paper, requested by the Prep Comm, and made by the U.N. Secretariat. It covers the period 1978–81 and supplements an earlier paper on the subject prepared for SSD I: A/AC.187/67.

The contents include: 1) Introduction; 2) Disarmament and arms limitation negotiations within the framework of the U.N. or linked to it; 3) Regional disarmament and arms limitation negotiations and other multilateral talks; 4) Bilateral disarmament and arms limitation negotiations; and 5) Trilateral negotations on a comprehensive test ban.

3. Documents of the Prep Comm

1. *Interim Report to the 36th General Assembly*. October 1981. A/36/49. 9 pp.

2. (Final report to SSD II) *Report of the Preparatory Committee of the Second Special Session of the General Assembly Devoted to Disarmament*. June 1982. A/S-12/1. 58 pp.

3. *Summary Records of Official Meetings*. December 9, 1980 through May 14, 1982. A/AC.206/SR.1-42. 324 pages total.

4. *Views of the Member States on the Preparations for the Second Special Session*. April 1982. A/AC.206/19 and Add.1 and 2. 39 pp.

5. *List of Communications Concerning Disarmament Received from Non-Governmental Organizations and Research Institutions*. A/AC.206/INF/1 1 p. /Add.1., /Add.2–4.

6. *Views of Member States on the Agenda and other Relevant Questions Relating to the Second Special Session; Report of the Secretary-General*. April 1981. A/AC.206/2 and /Add.1–7. 59 pp. plus.

7. *Public Information Activities in Connection with the Second Special Session; Working Paper Prepared by the Secretariat*. October 1981. A/AC.206/18. 5 pp.

4. Reports of Disarmament Bodies

1A. *Special Report of the Committee on Disarmament*. May 1982. A/S-12/2 or CD/292. 145 pp. This special report, requested by the General Assembly in resolution 36/92 F of December 1981, supplemented other annual reports made for 1979, 1980, and 1981 in CD/53, CD/139, and CD/228. The contents: 1) Introduction; 2) Organization of work of the Committee; and 3) Substantive work of the Committee. The two appendices consist of 1) Draft CPD, and 2) List of documents issued since January 1979.

1B. *Report of the Committee on Disarmament*. October 1982. A/37/27 or CD/335. 128 pp. The contents of this annual report: 1) Introduction; 2) Organization of work of the Committee; and 3) Substantive work of the Committee during its 1982 session. Its appendices include: 1) Consolidated list of participants in the work of the Committee; 2) List and text of documents issued by the Committee; and 3) Index of statements by country and subject and verbatim records of the Committee in 1982. (The last two are published in separate volumes of CD/335.)

2. *Report of the Disarmament Commission.* June 1982. A/S-12/3. 25 pp. The General Assembly, in resolution 36/92 B of December 1981, requested the Disarmament Commission to submit a report to SSD II, especially since the Commission was revived by SSD I. The contents: 1) Introduction; 2) Organization of work of the Commission; 3) Work of the Commission at its substantive sessions from 1979 to 1982; and 4) Conclusions and recommendations to the General Assembly at its Second Special Session. Annexes include: list of documents issued, background paper on proposed principles in the field of freezing and reduction of military expenditures, and guidelines for the study on conventional disarmament.

3. *Report of the Ad Hoc Committee on the Indian Ocean.* June 1982. A/S-12/5. 17 pp. The General Assembly, in resolution 36/90 of December 1981 asked the Ad Hoc Committee to submit a report to SSD II. The contents: 1) Introduction; 2) Work of the Ad Hoc Committee; and 3) Conclusions and recommendations.

4. *Report of the Ad Hoc Committee on the World Disarmament Conference.* April 1982. A/S-12/4. 10 pp. The General Assembly, in resolution 36/91 of December 1981, requested the Ad Hoc Committee on the World Disarmament Conference, to submit a report to SSD II. Contents: 1) Introduction; 2) Work of the Committee between the Tenth Special Session of the General Assembly and its Second Special Session devoted to disarmament; and 3) Conclusions and recommendations made from 1978 to 1982 by the Ad Hoc Committee, including those relating to its mandate.

5. Reports of the Secretariat

1. *Program of Research and Studies in Disarmament: Report of the Secretary-General.* November 1981. A/36/654. 10 pp. The contents: 1) Introduction; and 2) Work of the Advisory Board on Disarmament Studies in 1981. An annex lists members of the board.

2. *Public Information Activities Concerning Disarmament Since the Tenth Special Session . . .* April 1982. A/AC.206/21. 17 pp. The

contents: 1) Introduction; 2) Centre for Disarmament; and 3) Department of Public Information.

3. *Protection of Nature from the Pernicious Effects of the Arms Race*. April 1982. A/S-12/9. 12 pp. Undertaken by the U.N. Environment Program persuant to General Assembly resolution 35/8 of October 1980 and 36/7 of October 1981. The Contents: 1) Introduction; 2) Views of Governments; 3) Summary of the studies transmitted to governments; 4) High-level expert group meetings; and 5) Recommendations.

4. *Assessment of the U.N. Program of Fellowships on Disarmament Since Its Inception in 1979*. April 1982. A/S-12/8. 10 pp. The General Assembly, in resolution 36/92 A of December 1981, requested the Secretary-General to submit a report containing this assessment. The contents: 1) Introduction; 2) Guidelines and mandate; 3) Program content (1979–81); 4) Distribution of fellowships; 5) Concrete results of fellowship program; 6) Budgetary requirements for the program; and 7) Conclusions.

5. *Prevention of Nuclear War*. May 1982. A/S-12/11. 14 pp. /Add.1. June 1982. 7 pp. /Add.2. June 1982. 8 pp. /Add.3. June 1982. 3 pp. /Add.4. June 1982. 3 pp. This report, based on General Assembly resolution 36/81 B of December 1981, is composed of replies of Member States.

6. *World-wide Action for Collecting Signatures in Support of Measures to Prevent Nuclear War, to Curb the Arms Race, and for Disarmament*. A/S-12/15. May 1982. 14 pp. /Add.1. June 1982. 3 pp. This report was based on General Assembly resolution 36/92 J of December 1981. The contents: 1) Introduction; and 2) Replies from Governments.

7. *Disarmament Week: Report of the Secretary-General*. October 1982. A/37/455. 11 pp. Contents: 1) Introduction; and 2) Replies received from Governments.

8. *Advisory Board on Disarment Studies*. October 1982. A/37/550. 3 pp. This was submitted by the Secretary-General in anticipation of the decision of the 37th General Assembly to act on the future of the Board, since it did not meet after the autumn of 1981.

9. *Status of Multilateral Disarmament Agreements*. November 1982. A/37/560. 72 pp. This compilation was made as a result of General Assembly resolution 36/92 H of December 1981 which requested the Secretary-General to prepare for each regular session of the General Assembly a composite table of signatories of and parties to disarmament agreements. This contains a useful list of dates of signatories and deposits by parties as of July 31, 1982, for nine multilateral

treaties. Also this contained a composite table of signatories and parties.

6. Documents of SSD II

1. *Concluding Document*. July 9, 1982. A/S-12/32. 24 pp. Also there are six annexes: 1) Text for the draft Comprehensive Program of Disarmament; 2) List of proposals by Member States; 3) U.N. program of fellowships on disarmament; 4) World Disarmament Campaign; 5) List of NGOs which addressed SSD II; and 6) List of research institutions which addressed SSD II. (Also Fact Sheet No. 26. 24 pp.)

2. *Provisional Verbatim Record of Plenary Meetings*. A/S-12/PV. 1-29.

3. *Index to Statements on Disarmament at the Plenary Meetings of the Twelfth Special Session*. New York: U.N. Centre for Disarmament. June/July 1982. 52 pp.

4. *Verbatim Record of Meetings of the Ad Hoc Committee*. A/S-12/AC.1/PV.1-15.

5. *Index to Statements on Disarmament at the Meetings of the Ad Hoc Committee of the Twelfth Special Session*. New York: U.N. Centre for Disarmament. July 1982. n.p.

6. *Miscellaneous Documents, including Proposals of Member States*. A/S-12/AC.1/1-68. For consecutive listing, see Concluding Document, pp. 5–9. For a listing of proposals, see Concluding Document, Annex II.

7. *Draft resolutions*. A/S-12/AC.1/L.1–6. For texts, see Concluding Document, pp. 10–16.

8. *Working Group Documents*. A/S-12/AC.1/WG I, WG II, WG III.

9. *Resolutions and Decisions Adopted by the General Assembly during Its Twelfth Special Session*. July 1982. A/S-12/6*. 10 pp. Also GA/6633.

10. Miscellaneous Documents:
   a. *List of Delegations*. ST/SG/SER.C/L. 576 and /Add.1 and /Add. 2.
   b. *Communications Received (from NGOs) Relating to Disarmament*. A/INF/S-12/2, 21 pp. /Add.1. October 1982. 36 pp.
   c. *Agenda*. A/S-12/10.
   d. *Annotated Provisional Agenda*. A/S-12/10, Add.1. 16 pp.
   e. *Report of the Credentials Committee*. A/S-12/28. 5 pp.

7. Miscellaneous Materials

1. *United Nations Disarmament Yearbook*.
   Vol. III. 1978. Sales No. E.79.IX.3. 535 pp.
   Vol. IV. 1979. Sales No. E.80.IX.7. 481 pp.
   Vol. V. 1980. Sales No. E.81.IX.4. 493 pp.
   Vol. VI. 1981. Sales No. E.82.IX.7. 458 pp.
2. *Status of Multilateral Arms Regulation and Disarmament Agreements*. *Special Supplement to 1977 Yearbook*. 144 pp. Sales No. E.78.IX.2.
3. *Final Document of Special Session of the General Assembly on Disarmament 1978*. February 1981. DPI/679. 28 pp.
4. *Disarmament: A Periodic Review by the U.N.*
   Vol. 1, No. 1. May 1978. Sales No. E.78.IX.3.
   Vol. V, No. 2. November 1982. Sales No. E.83.IX.1.
5. *Repertory of Disarmament Research*. Geneva: U.N. Institute for Disarmament Research. 1982. 449pp. Sales No. GV.E.82.0.2.

8. Availability

All U.N. documents, including those of SSD II, are published in all six official languages of the U.N.: Arabic, Chinese, English, French, Russian, and Spanish. Every attempt is now being made by the U.N. to issue these documents simultaneously. In addition, the governments of the German Federal Republic and of Japan translate some U.N. documents into German and Japanese, but these are not available through the U.N. system.

U.N. documents are made automatically available to 327 depository libraries in 125 countries. About one-half of these libraries receive all mimeographed records by surface mail, in the language they request. The other half of the libraries receive only the official records—which are printed and bound, but often delayed by one or more years. Those libraries receiving the official records do not normally receive the mimeographed materials, including provisional records of meetings.

Most U.N. mimeographed documents are not available for purchase, but of course can be photocopied. A number of disarmament studies and other documents are available for sale, especially if a sales number is shown. To order these documents, write directly to U.N. Publications, United Nations, A-3315, New York, N.Y. 10017, U.S.A. The smaller Fact Sheets are available without cost from the Department for Disarmament Affairs, United Nations, New York, N.Y. 10017, U.S.A.

Increasingly, U.N. information is being computerized. There are indices available of the general debate in the plenary of SSD II and of the Ad Hoc Committee.

9. Selected List of Articles

Bartels, Wim. "Save the Humans! Disappointment and Hope at the UN Special Session." *IFOR Report*. Oct. 1982. pp. 12–13.

Brown, Jock. "Peace Phoenix Rises from U.N. Ashes." *Sequoia: The Church at Work*. August 1982. pp. 1,6.

Cagan, Leslie. "June 12th: A Look Back, A Look Ahead." *The Mobilizer*. Sept. 1982. p. 1, 9–10.

Camp, Kay. "Opportunity Lost: Disarmament Session—A Disappointment." *Philadelphia Inquirer*. July 16, 1982. pp. 11-A.

Caulfield-James, B. "Disarmament at the United Nations." *America*. Volume 147, pp. 91–92. August 21/28, 1982.

Corradini, Alessandro. "National Arms Policies and the Message of the 1978 and 1983 Special Sessions on Disarmament." *Disarmament*. Nov. 1982. pp. 61–71.

Dahlitz, Julie. "The Second Special Session Devoted to Disarmament." In *Nuclear Arms Control*. Melbourne: McPhee Gribble. 238 pp. 1983. pp. 198–209. Also in *Disarmament*. Nov. 1982. pp. 49–59.

Epstein, William. "The Freeze: A Hot Issue at the United Nations." *Bulletin of the Atomic Scientists*. Volume 38, pp. 50–52. October 1982.

Gandhi Marg. "Disarmament and Human Survival." Special issue of *Gandhi Marg* for SSD II. New Delhi: Gandhi Peace Foundation. May 1982. 444 pp.

Hudson, Richard. "The Thick Glass Walls on the East River." *Global Report*. August/September 1982. pp. 1–4. Also in *Transnational Perspectives*, Vol. 8, No. 3. 1982.

Jack, Homer A. "The UN Special Session: Two Years After. *Arms Control Today*. June 1980.

———. "Citizen's Guide to the Second Special Session." *Disarmament Times*. November 1981, 4 pp.

———. "The Politics and Hopes for the Second Special Session. *Review of International Affairs*. December 5, 1981. pp. 21–22.

———. "Mapping Plans for UN Disarmament Session. *Sane World*. December 1981. pp. 1, 4.

————. "The Second U.N. Special Session on Disarmament." *Arms Control Today*. February 1982. pp. 4–5.

————. "Politics and Hopes in UN." *Maryknoll*. April 1982. pp. 16–19.

————. "Both Sides of U.N. Plaza. *Friends Journal*. July 1/15 1982. pp. 14–16.

————. "Report on the U.N. Special Session." *Sane World*. October 1982. p. 3.

————. "A Political Postmortem." *Review of International Affairs*, Oct. 5, 1982. pp. 7–9.

————. "Non-Governmental Organizations and Public Opinion at SSOD II." *Disarmament*, Nov. 1982. Vol. 4, No. 2. pp. 73–83.

————. "Overcoming the Failure of the Second Special Session on Disarmament." *Bulletin of Peace Proposals*. Vol. 13, No. 3. 1982. pp. 177–87.

————. "Disarmament Resolutions: Pressure of a Ritual?" *Transnational Perspectives*. Vol. 8, No. 1. 1982. pp. 18–20.

Jaffe, Susan. "Why the Second Session Flopped." *Nation*. September 4, 1982. pp. 174–76.

Joyce, James Avery. "Who Killed SSD II?" *World Citizen*. Fall 1982. pp. 2–3.

————. "Who Killed the Special Session on Disarmament?" *Christian Century*. Oct. 20, 1982. pp. 1050–52.

Judd, Frank. "The United Nations Second Special Session on Disarmament." July 1982. 3 pp. (mimeographed).

Keys, Donald. "U.N. Special Session Ends—A Disheartening Failure." *World Federalist*. September 1982. pp. 1, 8.

Mattern, Douglas. "Requiem for a Not So Special Session." *The Bulletin of the Atomic* Scientists. Nov. 1982. pp. 58–59.

O'Hara, J. A. "Of Many Things." *America*. Volume 146, p. 468. June 19, 1982.

————. "The Global Peace Crusade." *Macleans*. Volume 95, pp. 28–29. June 28, 1982.

Olson, James M. "The UN Special Session: What Lessons?" *Unitarian Universalist World*. August 15, 1982. p. 2.

Paine, C. "The Freeze and the U.N." *Bulletin of the Atomic Scientists*. Volume 38, pp. 10–15. June 1982.

Pollak, R. "Covering the Unthinkable." *The Nation*. Vol. 234. pp. 516–23. May 1, 1982.

Quaker Office at the United Nations. "Second Special Session on Disarmament. *In and Around the U.N*. New York: Quaker Office at the United Nations. June/July 1982. pp. 1–2.

Reissen, Mary Beth. "Peacemakers and the Second Special Session."
Bulletin Pax Christi. August 15, 1982. pp. 9–12.

Roche, Douglas. "A Summary of the U.N. Second Special Session on
Disarmament." House of Commons, Ottawa. July 1982. 30 pp.
(Mimeographed).

Schwarzbart, Elias M. "Inside the UN: Disarmament Futility." *Freedom*. September–October 1982. p. 35.

Segall, Jeffrey. "A UN Second Assembly." *Reconciliation Quarterly*.
June 1982. pp. 35–37.

Warburg, Jennifer and Doug Lowe. *You Can't Hug With Nuclear
Arms!* Dobbs Ferry, N.Y.: Morgan Press. 1982. n.p.

"Disarmament Forum That Won't Produce any Results." *Business
Week*. May 17, 1982. p. 46.

"Malgré la Décevante Session Spéciale de l'ONU." *Mutations*. No. 58.
August 1982. pp. 1–9.

"Perspective." *U.N. Monthly Chronicle*. Vol. 19, pp. 49–64. June
1982.

"War of Words Over Who's For Peace." *U.S. News and World Report*.
Vol. 92, p. 6. June 28, 1982.

"Second Special Session of the General Assembly Devoted to Disarmament." *Disarmament*, Nov. 1982. Vol. V, No. 1. 96 pp. Sales No.
E.83.IX.1.

Disarmament Times in six issues published during 1981 and 24 issues
during 1982 devoted many articles to SSD II which are not listed
above.

10. Documents of the 37th General Assembly

1. *Provisional Verbatim Records of the Plenary*. A/37/PV.1-115.
General Debate: /PV.5–34.
Voting on First Committee Disarmament Resolutions: /PV.98
and 101.

2. *Provisional Verbatim Records of the First Committee*.
A/C.1/37/PV.1–45.

3. *Draft Resolutions (and Statements of Financial Implications):*
A/C.1/37/L.1–76.

4. *Reports of the First Committee to the Plenary:* A/37/652–73.

5. *Annotated Preliminary List of Items to Be Included in the Provisional Agenda of the 37th Regular Session of the General Assembly*.
June 1982. A/37/100. 378 pp. plus annexes.

6, *Preliminary List of Items*. February 1982. A/37/50/ and Rev. 1.

7. *Resolutions and Decisions Adopted by the General Assembly*

during the First Part of its Thirty-Seventh Session. January 1983.
GA/6787. 588 pp.
   8. *Membership of the First Committee*. A/C.1/37/4. 23 pp. /Add.
1. 2 pp.
   9. *Program of Work and Time-Table*. A/C.1/37/2*. 1 p.
   10. *Reports of the Fifth Committee to the Plenary*. A/37/730–35.

11. Authorized Future Studies

   1. *All Aspects of the Conventional Arms Race and on Disarmament Relating to Conventional Weapons and Armed Forces*.
   General Assembly resolution 36/97 A of December 1981 authorized this experts' study, to be completed late in 1983. Denmark, its initiator, had a difficult time obtaining approval, but persevered in the Disarmament Commission and in the 35th General Assembly (35/156 A). There were 26 abstentions to the 1981 resolution, mostly from the socialist States (except Romania) and India.
   2. *Constructing Price Indices and Purchasing-Power Priorities for Military Expenditures*. General Assembly resolution 37/95 B of December 1982 authorized this study by qualified experts. The resolution was adopted 96 to 13, with nine abstentions. The socialist States voted against the resolution, with such States as Brazil, China, and India abstaining.
   3. *Review and Supplement to the Comprehensive Study of the Question of Nuclear-Weapon Free Zones*. General Assembly resolution 37/99 F of December 1982 authorized this study, to update the 1975 Comprehensive Study of the Question of Nuclear-Weapon Free Zones in All its Aspects. (97 pp. Sales No. E.76.I.7.) The resolution was adopted 141 to one, with two abstentions. India voted against the resolution and Guyana and the U.S.A. abstained.
   The costs of this study may be typical. The proposal is to appoint 15 qualified governmental experts (nominated by governments) who would meet in two sessions totalling three weeks in 1983 and a similar time in 1984, all at U.N. Headquarters. Interpretation would be in six languages. Pre-session, in-session, and post-session documentation in all six languages would total 220 pages in 1983 and 250 pages in 1984. The total costs would be $135,000 each year for meeting servicing (interpretation in six languages) and $382,800 for documentation in 1983 and $574,300 in 1984. In addition, the related travel costs and daily subsistence allowance for the experts would be $89,600 each year. Finally, an outside consultant would be hired for a total of five

months, totalling $30,000, including travel costs. Some of the above costs might be absorbed within existing U.N. budgetary resources, but the total outlay for the two-year study could amount to $1,441,300.[1]

4. *Objective Information on Military Capabilities*. General Assembly resolution 37/99 G of December 1982 authorized preliminary investigations for a future study. This resolution was adopted 121 to no negative votes, with 17 abstentions. The latter included socialist States and India.

5. *A Comprehensive Study on the Scope, Role and Direction of the Military Use of Research and Development*. General Assembly resolution 37/99 J of December 1982 authorized this investigation. This resolution was adopted with 137 affirmative votes, no negative votes, and eight abstentions. The latter included the U.K., U.S.A., and other Western States.

The proposal is to appoint 15 qualified governmental experts who would hold two, two-week sessions in 1983 and two, two-week and one, one-week sessions in 1984, all at U.N. Headquarters. The interpretation would be in six languages. Documentation in all six languages would be 475 pages in 1983 and 1,150 pages in 1984. The costs for interpretation during the meetings would be $180,000 in 1983 and $225,000 in 1984. The costs of documentation would be $454,500 in 1983 and $1,003,200 in 1984. The related travel costs and daily subsistence allowance for the experts would be $102,000 in 1983 and $141,000 in 1984. An outside consultant would be hired for seven months for $46,200, including travel costs. Some of these costs might be absorbed within existing U.N. budgetary resources, but the total outlay could amount to $2,151,900.[2]

REFERENCES

1. A/C.1/37/L.72.   2. A/C.1/37/L.74.

10.

The Role of NGOs

The first U.N. Special Session on Disarmament (SSD I) in 1978 in many ways constituted a watershed in the activities of non-governmental organizations—NGOs*—in the field of disarmament in the U.N. system. Probably the 1932–34 Disarmament Conference at Geneva was a comparable event in the League of Nations period. NGOs in other fields at the U.N. are also active, especially in the fields of human rights, development, and anti-apartheid. NGOs in the field of disarmament, however, have never been given the status NGOs through the U.N. Charter have been given in the economic and social field.

The prominent role NGOs played at SSD I might have led to an increase in their status with the U.N. in the following years. This did not happen. However, with preparations for SSD II, NGO activities took a quantum leap. This chapter deals with the role of NGOs in disarmament in the entire U.N. system from the conclusion of SSD I in July 1978 through the conclusion of SSD II in July 1982 and some months beyond.[1] It includes the formal, if implicit, role—largely inside U.N. Headquarters—and the informal role, outside and worldwide.

1. Beyond SSD I

The penultimate paragraph of the Final Document of SSD I[2] acknowledged that "spokesmen [sic] of 25 non-governmental organiza-

---

*An NGO is an organization, but the word is also used for an individual—a representative of an organization. In this chapter, NGO will be used at times both for an organization and for an observer. Also it will include peace and disarmament research institutions.

tions and six research institutes also made valuable contributions to the proceedings of the session." Paragraph 123 of the Document also asked that "the [U.N.] Centre [for Disarmament] should also increase contacts with non-governmental organizations and research institutions in view of the valuable role they play in the field of disarmament. This role could be encouraged also in other ways that may be considered as appropriate."

The 33rd regular session of the General Assembly in September/December 1978 began to try to implement the Final Document. It adopted one resolution[3] which requested the U.N. Centre "to increase contacts with non-governmental organizations and research institutions, in accordance with paragraph 123 of the Final Document, and, after appropriate consultations, to report to the General Assembly at its 34th session on other ways of encouraging the role of such organizations and institutions in the field of disarmament." Nothing substantial resulted from this and other efforts to build upon paragraph 123.

In 1980 the U.N. Centre placed a NGO liaison officer on its staff. It compiled a mailing list of organizations and institutions concerned with disarmament and sent them regular materials, especially of an informational nature. The Centre, together with the Division of Public Information, increased the output of informational material on disarmament, especially a series of Fact Sheets.[4]

In this post-SSD I period, NGOs continued to observe the work of the First Committee in successive regular sessions of the General Assembly, although playing no designated role. They also observed the work of the reorganized Disarmament Commission (DC) and their written statements, submitted in quantities for use by delegates, were placed on an index which was an official U.N. document and circulated.[5] NGOs continued to observe the work of such subsidiary organs as the Ad Hoc Committees on the World Disarmament Conference and on the Indian Ocean.

In September 1978 the first session of the Preparatory Committee was held for the U.N. Conference on Prohibitions or Restrictions of Use of Certain Conventional Weapons which may be Deemed to be Excessively Injurious or to have Indiscriminate Effects. A small number of NGOs were present, as at the four sessions of the diplomatic conference on this topic held between 1974 and 1977. NGOs also observed at Geneva the sessions of this U.N. conference—a plenipotentiary body—convened under U.N. auspices.

The enlarged Committee on Disarmament (CD) at Geneva in 1979 opened its plenary meetings, unlike its predecessors which began in

1962 with the Eighteen-Nation Disarmament Committee (ENDC).
NGOs, the public, and the press were invited to attend. This may have
been an advance, but NGOs had to sit in the balcony—and not on the
floor where, previously, a limited number of NGOs from States Members of the Conference could sit after obtaining daily passes. Also
according to the 42nd rule of procedure, communications "from NGOs
and persons" to CD were listed and circulated to delegations.[6]

The Second Review Conference of the States parties to the Non-
Proliferation Treaty—technically not a U.N. conference—was open to
observation by NGOs during its meetings in Geneva in August/Sep-
tember 1980 as was the First Review Conference in 1975. *Disarmament Times* was published as a service to the Conference. A small
number of NGOs regularly attended. However, no additional prerogatives were accorded NGOs.

The General Assembly in 1979 and 1980 reviewed the first Disarmament Decade (the 1970s) and then made plans for the second. The
Declaration of the 1980s as the Second Disarmament Decade expressly
mentioned NGOs: "In the course of the decade of the 1980s, herefore,
governmental and non-governmental information organs of Member
States and those of the U.N. and the specialized agencies, as well as
non-governmental organizations, should, as appropriate, undertake
further programs of information relating to the danger of the armaments race. . ."[7] Another sentence in the same paragraph read: "The
U.N., in particular the Centre for Disarmament, should intensify and
coordinate its program of publications, audio-visual materials, cooperation with non-governmental organizations and relations with the
media." The Program did not, however, give any additional role to
NGOs, such as suggesting their substantive input on disarmament
issues into the U.N. system.

In this post-SSD I period, the NGO committees on disarmament at
Geneva and New York conferred on how better they might cooperate
in dealing with the U.N. and Member States on procedural and substantive issues. The Government of Sweden supplied travel funds so
that representatives of the two groups could meet occasionally to develop closer liaison. The result was the development, at a meeting in
April 1981 held at U.N. Headquarters, of an Ad Hoc NGO Liaison
Group, composed of the officers of both disarmament committees. The
Group discussed its limited mandate and presented a statement on
substantive issues and modalities for the participation of NGOs in SSD
II to U.N. Secretary-General Kurt Waldheim.

2. Preparations for SSD II

The NGO role in the preparation for SSD II was delineated at the very first meeting on December 4, 1980 at the short organizational session of its Prep Comm. The Chairman, Ambassador Olu Adeniji of Nigeria, asserted: "The Committee might follow the practice of the First Special Session on disarmament, which had decided that such representatives [of non-governmental organizations] should be present at meetings of the Committee and that they should provide the Secretariat with lists of communications received from non-governmental organizations that were conducting research in the field of disarmament."[8]

A small number of NGOs observed that organizational session and the three subsequent substantive sessions of the Prep Comm. The statements, pamphlets, and other communications which NGOs and institutions submitted to the Secretariat for use by the delegates to the Prep Comm were indexed.[9] Often NGOs brought multiple copies of these materials, usually in English, to an alcove off the principal Conference Room and they were made available for members of delegations.

The Ad Hoc NGO Liaison Group met in advance of the first substantive session of the Prep Comm and asked for three changes in the role previously accorded to NGOs: 1) to welcome oral interventions by NGOs at various sessions of the Prep Comm and its subsidiary bodies, 2) to circulate written statements by NGOs relating specifically to the agenda (but no general disarmament statements) to delegations with a U.N. cover sheet and document number, and 3) to allow NGOs to attend subsidiary organs of the Prep Comm including working groups.

At the first substantive session of the Prep Comm in May 1981, Ambassador Adeniji stated: "The Bureau's recommendation was that non-governmental organizations should be allowed to make oral statements at one meeting during the October session of the Preparatory Committee. With regard to the representation of the non-governmental organizations, the Bureau felt that the matter would be decided by the non-governmental organizations and their decision would be conveyed to the Chairman of the Committee."[10] The two additional proposals of the Ad Hoc NGO Group were not acted upon.

In this period NGOs urged the Prep Comm to make additional studies for SSD II. Among three recommended by NGOs were ones on unilateral disarmament and a multilateral freeze. No Member State took up these suggestions.

The Ad Hoc Group met at Geneva in August 1981 to discuss how to select those NGOs wishing to make oral statements to the Prep Comm. The Group reiterated its dislike of having to screen other NGOs, but expressed an understanding of why the Prep Comm (or Secretariat) refused to accept a screening role. The Group notified 500 NGOs and 75 institutions of the opportunity to make both oral and written statements to the October meeting of the Prep Comm. A number of requests were made to speak and the Ad Hoc Group submitted a list of eight NGOs and three institutions. They were heard at a plenary meeting on October 9, 1981. (For a list of the organizations and institutions making statements see Appendix E below). Their statements were printed in the verbatim report of the meeting.[11]

NGOs held consultations with individual delegates, and groups of delegates, on substantive issues of SSD II at the three substantive sessions of the Prep Comm. Also they informed delegates of the crescendo of NGO activity around the world for disarmament, especially related to SSD II. They issued special inventories of seminars, meetings, and demonstrations and also projections of parallel NGO activities during SSD II itself.[12]

3. At SSD II

The Prep Comm early suggested a role for NGOs at SSD II itself: "The Committee recommends that non-governmental organizations concerned with disarmament and peace and disarmament research institutions should be accorded the same facilities at the Second Special Session of the General Assembly devoted to disarmament as those which they had received at the First Special Session. However, in view of the importance of world public opinion for progress in disarmament, it is expected that even a greater spectrum of non-governmental organizations and their leaders will participate in the Second Special Session of the General Assembly devoted to disarmament."[13] This delineation was not accidental, but the result of detailed negotiations between the Prep Comm and the Ad Hoc NGO Liaison Group.[14]

The role of NGOs in delivering oral statements is given in Chapter 11.

Religious Leaders

There was some discussion about inviting religious leaders to SSD II. The possibility was first initiated in the Prep Comm by delegates from Nigeria and Mexico.[15] The World Conference on Religion and

Peace proposed that the Prep Comm, or its Chairman, issue a special invitation to "new groups" to participate in SSD II, including religious leaders, parliamentarians, Nobel peace laureates, as well as other NGOs.[16] In the end, the Prep Comm asked for an opinion from the U.N. Legal Office. When the latter reported that there was no precedent, no special action was taken, other than including the phrase of expecting "a greater spectrum" of NGOs.

Coordination

Given the statement delineating the NGO role, the U.N. Secretariat began to plan for modalities in receiving NGOs. A joint task force was established, headed by Mr. Jay H. Long of the Office of the Under-Secretary-General for Political and General Assembly Affairs, and including the U.N. Centre for Disarmament, the Department of Public Information, Security and Safety Services, and other relevant entities. This task force met occasionally and tried to coordinate invitations to NGOs, advance registrations, and security. Ms. Ingrid Lehmann was liaison officer between the U.N. Centre and NGOs.

More than 3,000 NGOs registered to observe SSD II, many doing so in advance. Of this number, almost one-half was from Japan. The second largest number was from the U.S.A., but all continents were represented.

Visas[17]

NGOS coming to U.N Headquarters from overseas have only occasionally faced obstacles in obtaining U.S. visas. However, the NGO Committee on Disarmament (at U.N. Headquarters) tried to prevent any problems with visas by discussing the matter with both the U.N. and U.S.A. authorities in April/May 1982. Despite some implicit commitments, hundreds of NGOs coming to SSD II had their visas delayed and 318 had their visas denied. The latter included 268 Japanese nationals, and citizens from other countries in Asia, Europe, and North America. Protests were immediately lodged by NGOs, some governments, the press, and through a suit in Federal Court against U.S. Secretary of State Alexander Haig and U.S. Attorney-General William French Smith. Both the suit and a subsequent appeal were lost.

The legal action did reveal the policy of the U.S. Government: "The Attorney-General's rationale is not just that they [the NGOs denied visas] are communists, but that they are Soviet straws. Particularly in these times of manoeuvering between the U.S. and the Soviet Union concerning initiation of negotiations on disarmament, it can hardly be argued that it was irrational or unfounded for the Attorney-General to conclude that entry of these Soviet-dominated individuals to participate in, among other things, unsponsored political activities respecting disarmament is not in the best interests of the U.S at this particular time." The U.S. brief also revealed the lack of pressure on the U.S.A. by the U.N.: "Had the applicant visa aliens a genuine right under the Headquarters Agreement [between the U.N. and the U.S.A.], it would have been manifested by a request for entry by the Secretary-General of the U.N. persuant to Section 14 of the Headquarters Agreement. However, no such request was ever made."

The New York Times in condemning the U.S. action editorialized: "America sends the world a proud message about freedom of speech and association. And it need not apologize for its position on arms negotiations. Yet Government officials behave as if they are ashamed of both. They should be ashamed only of themselves."[18] This denial of visas was not the finest hour, during SSD II, of either the U.S.A. or the U.N. Indeed, the latter issued no public protest on the matter. However, at the request of the NGO Committee on Disarmament (at U.N. Headquarters), the Committee on Relations with the Host Country of the General Assembly did discuss the NGO visa question in November 1982.

Seating

Arrangements were made for hundreds of NGOs to sit in the General Assembly Hall and listen to the general debate and other plenary meetings. Of the seats reserved for this purpose, they were filled only on opening day and for the addresses of the most prominent Heads of State or Government. The meetings of the Ad Hoc Committee were also open to NGOs, but only dozens attended. The meetings of the Working and Contact Groups were closed.

Literature

NGO literature on disarmament was solicited by the U.N. Centre and special tables were set up in the basement of the General Assembly building where quantities could be made available to delegates. The Secretariat issued a list of "Communications Received Relating to Disarmament." The first list, published in the fourth week of SSD II, contained the titles, names, and addresses of 165 NGOs and research institutions, and a supplementary document contains almost an equal number of entries.[19]

Briefings

Daily briefings for NGOs were held each morning at U.N. Headquarters. Mr. Prvoslav Davinic of the U.N. Centre gave a daily account of what happened in the session. Briefings were also given by many Eastern European, Western, and Third World diplomats on Disarmament and Security Issues, and others such as Frank Blackaby of SIPRI, Olof Palme of the Independent Commission on Disarmament and Security Issues, and Jay H. Long of the U.N. Secretariat. Several hundred NGOs attended these briefings regularly. The briefings were chaired by Ms. Sally Shelley of the Department of Public Information.

Lobbying

Attempts to influence policy were undertaken by some NGOs, individually and in groups. Two persons worked for the National Weapons Freeze Campaign of the U.S.A. for more than two months to acquaint delegates with the U.S. campaign and urge its echo in SSD II.[20] The Friends World Committee for Consultation maintained a five-person team during the entire SSD II. A small group of NGOs, under the guidance of Ms. Sheila Oakes of the National Peace Council of the U.K., met regularly and tried to influence delegates on selected issues, especially the nuclear freeze and the World Disarmament Campaign. Also this group issued a statement at the conclusion of SSD II at a press conference. The statement asserted that "the obvious failure of this session has caused us such deep concern that it has been difficult to find words properly to express our sense of outrage."[21] Lord Philip Noel-Baker's presence at this press conference was one of his last public appearances before his death in October 1982.

Attempts at lobbying were severely handicapped by alleged security problems at U.N. Headquarters during SSD II. NGOs were unable to talk to delegates on the floor of the General Assembly Hall or in the Delegates' Lounge—as they were able to do during SSD I.

Disarmament Times

First published in 1978 before SSD I, *Disarmament Times* appeared to be a valuable tool to unify the entire SSD II community: delegates, Secretariat, NGOs, and the press. Twenty issues of *Disarmament Times* were published during the five-week period. It was mailed to subscribers on every continent and several thousand were distributed gratis at U.N. Headquarters. Mr. Richard Hudson continued as editor, assisted by a full-time staff of reporters, a Publications

Committee, and an Editorial Advisory Board. Published by the NGO
Committee on Disarmament (at U.N. Headquarters), the newspaper
was financed by special funds raised for this purpose: $55,000.

4. Parallel Activities

The Ad Hoc NGO Liaison Group discussed whether or not to
sponsor a continuing NGO conference parallel to SSD II. Some U.N.
world meetings in the 1970s have had successful NGO "counter" or
"shadow" conferences. However, it was decided not to divert the focus
from the diplomatic deliberations by sponsoring a parallel NGO conference. Instead, it was decided to encourage as many parallel activities
by individual NGOs or groups of NGOs as possible—a practice encouraged also at SSD I. To sustain these possibilities, the NGO Committee on Disarmament (at U.N. Headquarters) employed a
coordinator, Dr. Willard Reid, for a six-month period to stimulate
parallel activities and try to list if not coordinate them.

Early Demonstrations
A great number of disarmament demonstrations were held in the
autumn of 1981 and early in 1982, especially in Western Europe. These
had varied objectives, but increasingly SSD II became a focus. Sud-
denly these manifestations spilled over into North America and Japan
and their leaders increasingly realized the utility of relating these efforts to SSD II.

National Lobbying
In this period immediately preceeding SSD II, NGOs in some
world capitals tried to make an impact on evolving governmental policy
for SSD II. In London, a range of NGOs met regularly and discussed
SSD II with the Arms Control and Disarmament Research Unit of the
Foreign and Commonwealth Office. In Washington, the U.S. Arms
Control and Disarmament Agency held a day's meeting with selected
NGOs on SSD II. In Japan, the U.N. Information Center was the
venue of a number of meetings of NGOs preparing for SSD II, with the
Japanese Government also involved.

NGO Preparations
The number of meetings, seminars, conferences, teach-ins, and
rallies focusing on SSD II are too extensive to catalogue here—or
anywhere. A small sample, perhaps not even representative, follows:

○ World Assembly for Religious Workers for Nuclear Disarmament discussed preparations for SSD II in Tokyo in April 1981.

○ Stanley Foundation's 12th U.N. Procedures Conference for diplomats was devoted to SSD II at Lake Mohonk in May 1981.[22]

○ Special NGO Committee on Disarmament held an Urgent Action Conference at Geneva in August 1981.

○ Independent Commission on Disarmament and Security Issues (Palme Commission) held meetings during 1981 and 1982 at various world capitals to make a report to SSD II.[23]

○ Seminars for diplomats on SSD II were sponsored by Quaker offices at U.N. Headquarters and Geneva.

○ NGO Committee on Disarmament held one-day consultation on preparing NGOs for SSD II at U.N. Headquarters in October 1981.

○ World Council of Churches conducted hearings on nuclear issues at Amsterdam in November 1981 for transmission to SSD II.[24]

○ Second Swedish People's Parliament for Disarmament convened in January 1982 to make proposals for Swedish positions on SSD II.

○ World Peace Council sponsored an international conference on preparations for SSD II at Athens in February 1982.

○ NGO Committee on Disarmament conducted a short course on disarmament for NGOs at U.N. Headquarters in the spring of 1982.

○ Special NGO Committee on Disarmament convened a conference on World Public Opinion and SSD II at Geneva in April 1982.[25]

○ Russian Orthodox Church sponsored a Conference of Religious Workers on Nuclear Catastrophe in May 1982.[26]

○ Parliamentarians for World Order sent missions to Moscow and Washington to discuss SSD II.

○ World Conference on Religion and Peace sent a multi-religious mission to Beijing in May 1982 to talk with political and religious officials about SSD II.[27]

Early June Events

By early June 1982, parallel activities were beginning in the U.N. community in New York. These included the following:

○ Concert for Disarmament by U.N. Symphony at St. Patrick's Cathedral.

○ Fast for Peace. A month-long inter-religious fast began in 12 countries on May 30.

○ Tree of Life Exhibit of drawings about peace by children from 80 countries, sponsored by Radda Barnen of Sweden and UNICEF at U.N. Headquarters.

○ Nuclear Threat to our World Exhibit, using photographs of Hiroshima and Nagasaki. Sponsored by Soka Gakkai and U.N. Department of Public Information at U.N. Headquarters.

○ Forum of Parliamentarians. Fifty members of parliament attended. Sponsored by Parliamentarians for World Order at U.N. Headquarters.[28]

○ International Symposium on Morality and Legality of Nuclear Weapons. Lawyers Committee on Nuclear Policy.

○ The Social Scientists and Nuclear War. Sponsored by Rutgers University and Graduate Center of the City College of New York, with 400 persons attending.

○ International Feminist Disarmament Conference. Women's International League for Peace and Freedom.

○ Children's Rally for a Nuclear Freeze.

Disarmament Information Bureau

At SSD I and SSD II this storefront information service was useful to hundreds of persons who wanted to know more about the happenings at the U.N. event. Sponsored by the NGO Committee on Disarmament (at U.N. Headquarters) and located in the UNITAR building opposite U.N. Headquarters, the Bureau distributed free and low-cost literature. It also was a source of answers for queries and a place where NGOs could apply for passes to U.N. Headquarters. The Bureau also became a popular meeting place for NGOs.[29]

Plowshare Coffeehouse

Sponsored by the Fellowship of Reconciliation and other groups, as at SSD I, this was located in the Church Center for the U.N. immediately opposite U.N. Headquarters. It was notable for sponsoring an array of speakers—some diplomats, other national and international NGOs—at least twice daily on topics related to SSD II. Also disarmament films were shown. The Coffeehouse distributed free and low-cost literature and light refreshments were available.[30]

NGO Media Center

The NGO Committee on Disarmament (at U.N. Headquarters) sponsored an independent press service nine months before SSD II began and a NGO Media Center during SSD II. The purpose was to provide a forum, outside U.N. Headquarters, where journalists could have in-depth interviews and press conferences with disarmament experts (both diplomats and NGOs). In addition, the Center provided several daily news spots of the progress of SSD II and these were available by telephone to radio stations. Directed by Ms. Caroline Krebs, the Center was located in the B'nai B'rith building opposite U.N. Headquarters.[31]

Mid-June Activities

While parallel activities occurred throughout the five-week session, many occurred during the first two weeks:

○ World Peace March, taking different routes through the U.S., arrived at U.N. Headquarters on June 7th as did the Olympic Torch carried from ceremonies originating in Greece.

○ Reverence for Life Conference, sponsored by the Temple of Understanding and other religious groups.[32]

○ International Action Conference, sponsored by the International Confederation for Disarmament and Peace.

○ Benefit concert for June 12th Rally, featuring Jackson Browne, Linda Rondstadt, and James Taylor.

○ International Religious Convocation at Cathedral of St. John the Divine. Ten thousand persons participated and marched to Central Park, with an all-night vigil at U.N. Headquarters. Sponsored by Religious Task Force of Mobilization for Survival.

○ Vigils at the U.S.A. and the U.S.S.R. Missions in support of a nuclear freeze. Sponsored by American Friends Service Committee.

○ Children's Walk for Life. Sponsored by five children's organizations.

○ Reception for NGOs and delegates at U.N. Headquarters with presentation of Pomerance Awards. Sponsored by International Association for Religious Freedom and World Conference on Religion and Peace.[33]

June 12th Demonstration

The march/demonstration on June 12th was the largest political and thus peace/disarmament rally in North American history. Over 750,00 persons participated, gathering in the U.N. community, marching past U.N. Headquarters, and then walking to Central Park for a giant five-hour rally featuring many speakers. The latter included major world and American peace activists and there was entertainment by such stars as Joan Baez, Jackson Browne, Linda Ronstadt, Bruce Springstein, and James Taylor.

Preparations were made for the rally a year in advance, first by the Mobilization for Survival and then by a large group of primarily peace, labor, and other organizations. Great organizational if not ideological differences developed. The public response to the rally was so overwhelming that the organizers had to bury their differences and then they produced an outstanding, memorable event.

The march was led by the Children's Walk for Life, followed by giant puppets of the Bread and Puppet Theater. Participants came from all over the world, but mostly from the Eastern U.S.A. and Canada. The crowd was gentle, not angry, and the police responded in kind. The two official rally slogans were "Freeze and Reduce all Nuclear Weapons" and "Transfer Military Budgets to Human Needs." Some of the individual, often home-made placards were notable. Informal signs included the following: "You can't hug your children with nuclear arms;" "Blow up balloons, not kids;" "Bear babies, not arms;" "Don't nuke our spuds—Idaho;" "The bomb is an equal opportunity destroyer;" "Take the toys from the boys;" "The next war will start by computers;" "Raygun-Breznife Disarmament Now;" "Reagan Activity means Radioactivity;" "We're not asking please, we demand a nuclear freeze;" "Freeze now or fry later;" "Civil defense is a pretense;" "Brahmns not bombs;" and "I made history today."[34]

Civil Disobedience

On June 14th civil disobedience (CD) was directed to the Permanent Mission to the U.N. of the five nuclear-weapon States. (In 1978 the CD was directed only to the U.S.A.) Almost 1,600 persons were arrested, but most were released without immediately offering bail or paying fines. At court, almost nobody was sentenced and most were released without a fine. The participants tried to block the entrance to these missions in a Gandhian way to show their anguish at the slowness of negotiations to eliminate nuclear weapons.[35]

Petitions

A spontaneous spate of petitions on nuclear disarmament emerged for circulation and signature in the months before SSD II in various parts of the world. So many were scheduled to be presented to the U.N. that it was decided to provide one public presentation on June 10th. A thousand persons were outside the public entrance to U.N. Headquarters when U.N. Secretary-General Javier Perez de Cuellar was presented with a total of 90 million signatures. These came from 20 international and national organizations. Kinjiro Niwano of Rissho Kosei-kai, a lay Buddhist group with headquarters in Japan, presented the largest number of signatures—36.7 million—with the second largest coming from the National Liaison Committee on Nuclear and General Disarmament, also of Japan. Hundreds of separate petitions arrived at Headquarters, especially from the Soviet Union. The Secretariat issued a list of petitions.[36]

Religious Activity[37]

Of all the special groupings preparing for SSD II, and participating as NGOs in SSD II, the religious organizations may have been most active. A great number of conferences, seminars, and other meetings were held before SSD II. Outstanding were perhaps three: A Public Hearing on Nuclear War, sponsored by the World Council of Churches in Amsterdam in November 1981; a Multi-Religious Mission on Disarmament to Beijing in May 1982; and a World Conference of Religious Workers in Moscow also in May 1982. At SSD II, religious organizations were among the lobbyists—especially a five-person team from the Friends World Committee for Consultation. Sixteen religious organizations made oral presentations to the Ad Hoc Committee. A great number of written communications to SSD II originated from religious organizations. During SSD II, three parallel activities by religious groups were outstanding: the Rissho Kosei-kai Mission of Buddhists from Japan to SSD II for ten days; the Plowshares Coffeehouse run by an interreligious group; and the International Religious Convocation. The latter held on June 11th at the Cathedral of St. John the Divine, attracted 10,000 persons, the largest interreligious gathering ever held in New York. It ended in an all-night prayer vigil opposite U.N. Headquarters.[38] Also a Reverence for Life Conference was held for three days with several hundred persons present.

5. Initial Follow-Up

During the final days of SSD II, the NGOs present resolved to continue at least the NGO momentum surrounding SSD II and convene an early conference, especially related to the evolving World Disarmament Campaign. The Ad Hoc NGO Liaison Group, meeting in September at New York, voted to sponsor a NGO Consultation for the World Disarmament Campaign at U.N. Headquarters on November 8–10, 1982. In the meantime, the annual NGO conference of the U.N.'s Department of Public Information in September featured disarmament and included much discussion of SSD II.

Representatives from 61 NGOs and research institutions, from 22 countries, attended the NGO Consultation in November. However, once again there were visa problems and representatives of four international NGOs with headquarters in Finland, the Soviet Union, the German Democratic Republic, and Hungary were denied U.S. visas. Affronted, the Conference participants at its first meeting voted to cancel the Conference itself and become instead an Informal NGO Seminar on Disarmament. It discussed at length the World Disarmament Campaign and its relation to NGOs. It recommended that "NGO participation in the decision-making processes of the World Disarmament Campaign should be recognized officially by the U.N." Also the Seminar discussed the permanent NGO role in disarmament at the U.N. and made a recommendation that a comprehensive resolution on the subject be drafted by the General Assembly. Finally, the Seminar discussed substantive disarmament issues and found remarkable agreement on a short list of disarmament measures: 1) a nuclear weapons freeze, 2) a Comprehensive Test-Ban Treaty, 3) commitment by nuclear powers to either no use or no first use of nuclear weapons, 4) reverse the conventional arms race, and 5) strengthen mechanisms for the peaceful settlement of international disputes.[39]

The Seminar, and the Ad Hoc Group meeting afterwards, voted to attempt to convene another meeting sometime in 1983, hopefully with the close cooperation of the U.N. Centre for Disarmament.

Another dimension of follow-up was the publication by many of the organizations and institutions of their oral addresses to SSD II. Many were reproduced unabridged in organizational periodicals, often with supplementary materials on SSD II itself. One of the best examples is a 70-page pamphlet, "Ecumenical Presence at the United Nations," issued by the Commission of the Churches on International Affairs of the World Council of Churches.[40]

Influence?

The peace marches were not unnoticed inside U.N. Headquarters. A number of Heads of State or Government, and other speakers in the general debate of SSD II, heard and commented upon the drums and demonstrations through the thick walls of the "glass house on the East River." Despite this recognition of the mass demonstrations, there was no reflection of these demands in the substantive work of SSD II, except perhaps in the memorandum adopted on the World Disarmament Campaign. Perhaps U.N. Secretary-General Javier Perez de Cuellar best reflected opinion about the demonstrations when he wrote in his first annual report on the work of the U.N.: "Our peoples, especially the young, take to the streets in the hundreds of thousands in many parts of the world to proclaim their peaceful protest against the existing situation and their deep fear of the consequences of the arms race and nuclear catastrophe. Who can say that these gentle protesters are wrong or misguided? . . . The States Members of this Organization should not ignore the significance of what they are trying to say."[41]

6. Rationalization of the NGO Role

Article 71 of the U.N. Charter gives a role to NGOs in the economic and social field. Some NGOs in consultative relationship with the U.N. Economic and Social Council (ECOSOC) carried their work into the disarmament field, without any explicit permission. Others, registered with the Department of Public Information (DPI) or with U.N. specialized agencies, also worked on disarmament issues. However, it soon became apparent that some rationalization (formalization? legitimization?) of the role of NGOs in the field of disarmament in the whole U.N. system would be helpful.

One early effort, by NGOs to codify and expand their role, was at an annual conference of the International Peace Bureau at Bradford, England, in 1974.[42] In the hope that a World Disarmament Conference might be convened, the IPB proposed a greatly expanded NGO role, including the full rights of 30 NGOs and their funding.

The establishment of the Ad Hoc Committee on the Review of the Role of the U.N. in the Field of Disarmament appeared to be an occasion in 1976 for a breakthrough in the recognition of a NGO role. Despite the interest of the Chairman, Mrs. Inga Thorsson of Sweden, no progress was made. However a group of 13 NGOs submitted an important statement in June 1976 on "Strengthening the Role of International NGOs in the Field of Disarmament."[43]

In May 1977, the Eighth Conference of the Stanley Foundation on U.N. Procedures was devoted to the forthcoming SSD I and a whole chapter of this report was devoted to a role for NGOs.[44]

In early 1979 the NGO Committee on Disarmament (at U.N. Headquarters) completed a memorandum on "Proposals for the Development of the Role of the NGO at the U.N. in the Field of Disarmament."[45] After discussing five functions in disarmament performed by NGOs at the U.N., the memorandum made a number of specific suggestions covering disarmament bodies in the greater U.N. system, including the Committee on Disarmament (CD) and plenipotentiary conferences.

Efforts were made during SSD II for a resolution to be submitted on rationalizing the role of NGOs. None was submitted. However, the 15th General Assembly of the Conference of NGOs in Consultative Status with ECOSOC—known as CONGO—in September 1982 adopted a resolution urging an explicit role for NGOs in disarmament. NGOs began working toward this end during the 37th regular session of the General Assembly during September/December 1982. The obvious prerogatives for NGOs in disarmament include at least the following: access to meetings, including working groups; written statements and their reproduction, distribution, and indexing; hearings and oral statements and the process of screening applicants; access to documentation; and the process of accreditation. Also the definition of a NGO is pertinent here, although the tradition in the field of disarmament has increasingly been to include any local, national, regional, or international non-governmental organization which expressed an interest in disarmament, whether or not it had a previous connection with the U.N. system. This has now included peace and disarmament research institutions and other academic institutions, including colleges and universities.[46]

7. Conclusions and the Future

NGOs have gradually increased or broadened their role is disarmament in most parts of the U.N. system. This has occurred over several decades, but has not yet equalled the prerogatives given NGOs in the economic and social field.

The increase in the NGO role has been almost wholly due to united, persistent pressures by NGOs. Member States and members of the U.N. Secretariat have not been eager to help NGOs attain new prerogatives, being bound by precedent and some by the fear that somehow "NGOs will take over the U.N."

A rationalization of the role of NGOs in disarmament is overdue. An explicit role might be given to NGOs by the U.N. General Assembly in the next few years. The fear that the U.N. will be inundated by NGOs if the door were slightly widened appears groundless. So far, with rare exceptions, more seats have been made available to NGOs than they have been able to fill. This reflects the inability of NGOs to seize the opportunities given to them. This situation might change, but not unless there will be a sudden increase in the professionalization of NGOs in the field of disarmament. Also NGOs must be shown that their presence at the U.N. will someday make a difference in U.N. and thus national policy formulation.

Local, national, and regional NGOs have as much status in disarmament as international NGOs, unlike the ECOSOC system where international NGOs tend to receive priority. Also peace and disarmament research institutions and academic institutions generally are increasingly being considered as NGOs and being given the same opportunities in the U.N. as traditional NGOs.

Despite a kind of praise given to the actions of NGOs by Member States and members of the U.N. Secretariat, the fact is that NGOs have made little impact on the disarmament policies of States as reflected in the U.N., either at the two Special Sessions or in other U.N. bodies. This lack of results must surely make NGOs want to re-evaluate their strategies and tactics. How have they done wrong in their programs of education, mass education, demonstrations, lobbying, electoral politics, or civil disobedience? NGOs in the U.N. system have recognized that their pressure counts more in national capitals than in the U.N. itself.[47]

REFERENCES

1. For an account of the NGO role before and during SSD I, see "NGOs and Disarmament." In *SIPRI Yearbook 1979.* London: Taylor and Francis. 1979. 698 pp. pp. 666–80.

2. U.N. document A/S-10/4. *Final Document of the Tenth Session of the General Assembly.*

3. 33/71 G.

4. One of the most recent is Fact Sheet No. 25 on *International Satellite Monitoring Agency: A Proposal.* Twenty-five thousand copies of this 12-page pamphlet were published by the Centre and the Department of Public Information in August 1982.

5. In 1982, these lists were A/C-N.10/INF. 3, 5, and 7.

6. In 1982, these lists were CD/NGO. 5 and 6.

7. 35/46.

8. A/AC.206/SR.1, p. 6.

9. A/AC.206/INF/1, and Add.1 and Add.2. These contained a total of nine items.

10. A/AC.206/SR.17, p. 5.

11. A/AC.206/SR.25, pp. 1–17.

12. Some of these inventories are found in the following publications: *The Work of the First Substantive Session of the Preparatory Committee for the Second Special Session on Disarmament,* by Homer A. Jack. New York: WCRP. 1981. 21 pp. pp. 18–20. "NGOs and the Second Special Session on Disarmament: An Inventory." October 1981. 6 pp. "Global Round-up of NGO Activities." *Disarmament Times.* September/October 1981.

13. A/S-12/1, paragraph 28, p. 9.

14. "Statement of Recommendations to the President, Officers, and Members of the Preparatory Committee of SSD II." New York: NGO Committee on Disarmament. April 1981.

15. A/AC.206/SR.5, p. 3 and SR.7, pp. 7–8.

16. "NGOs and the Second Special Session on Disarmament," by Homer A. Jack. May 1981. 4 pp. Also, "A Note on Inviting World Religious Leaders to the Second Special Session," by Homer A. Jack. New York: WCRP. May 1981. 3 pp.

17. For a major paper on this subject, see *Jack v. Haig: How 318 NGOs Were Denied U.S. Visas To Attend The Second U.N. Special Session on Disarmament,* by

Homer A. Jack. New York: WCRP. 1982. 20 pp.

18. June 11, 1982.

19. A/INF/S-12/2. 21 pp.

20. *Freeze or Burn: The Nuclear Freeze at the Second U.N. Special Session on Disarmament*, by Homer A. Jack. New York: WCRP. 1982. p. 18.

21. Text in *Fellowship*. July–August 1982. pp. 19–20.

22. United Nations Second Special Session on Disarmament. Muscatine, Iowa: The Stanley Foundation. May 1981. 48pp.

23. *Common Security: A Programme for Disarmament*. Independent Commission on Disarmament and Security Issues. London: Pan Books. 202 pp. 1982.

24. *Before It's Too Late*. (Report of Public Hearings.) Geneva: World Council of Churches. 1982. 24 pp. "In Amsterdam, Thinking About the Bomb." *Christianity and Crisis*. Jan. 18, 1982. pp. 369–400.

25. *World Public Opinion and the Second Special Session of the U.N. General Assembly*. Geneva: Special NGO Committee on Disarmament. 1982. 43 pp.

26. *World Conference of Religious Workers for Saving the Sacred Gift of Life from Nuclear Catastrophe: Final Documents*. Moscow: Russian Orthodox Church. 1982. 22 pp.

27. *WCRP Multi-Religious Mission on Disarmament to China*. New York: WCRP. 1982. 15 pp.

28. *Politicians for Peace*. New York: Parliamentarians for World Order. 1982. 20 pp.

29. *Disarmament Times*, July 8, 1982, p. 1.

30. *Fellowship*. July–August 1982, pp. 17–18.

31. *Disarmament Times*, June 17, 1982, p. 3.

3. *Reverence for Life*. Edited Version of Transcripts. New York: Temple of Understanding. 1982. 58 pp.

33. Picture book of Rissho Kosei-kai Mission to SSD II. (In Japanese). Tokyo: Rissho Kosei-kai. 1982. 32 pp.

34. For one description, *Disarmament Times*, June 14, 1982 pp. 1–4. For a list of slogans, *Disarmament Times*, July 9, 1982, p. 4. For photographs, see *You Can't Hug With Nuclear Arms*, edited by Jennifer Warburg and Doug Lowe. Dobbs Ferry. 1982. 128 pp.

35. *Disarmament Times*, June 16, 1982, pp. 1–4. "Bread and Peonies," by Ursula Scott. *Fellowship*. July–August 1982. pp. 16–17.

36. For a list of originators of petitions, and numbers of signatures, see A/INF/S-12/2 and Add.1.

37. For a fuller description, see "Religion, Peace, and the Second U.N. Special Session on Disarmament," by Homer A. Jack. *Echoes of Peace*. Tokyo: Niwano Peace Foundation. February 1983.

38. "A Gathering of Many Faiths," by Richard Newell Myers. *Fellowship*. July–August. 1982. p. 13.

39. *Informal NGO Seminar on Disarmament: Report of Findings*. New York: NGO Committee on Disarmament. 1982. pp. 1–15.

40. "Ecumenical Presence at the United Nations: Second Special Session on Disarmament." *CCIA Background Information*. 1982/4. 70 pp.

41. A/37/1, p. 3.

42. International Peace Bureau, 41 rue de Zurich, 1201 Geneva, Switzerland.

43. See *Rationalizing the Role of NGOs in Disarmament in the U.N. System*, by Homer A. Jack. New York: WCRP. 1982. 15pp. pp. 9–10.

44. U.N. Special Session on Disarmament. Muscatine, Iowa: Stanley Foundation. 1977. 52 pp. pp. 33–37.

45. Jack, *Rationalizing the Role*. *Op. Cit.*, pp. 13–14.

46. A detailed discussion of the issues in this section is found in Jack, *Ibid*.

47. Parts of this essay will appear in a chapter by the author in the *SIPRI Yearbook 1983*. Also a briefer version appeared as "Non-Governmental Organizations and Public Opinion at SSOD II." *Disarmament*. Nov. 1982. Vol. V, No. 2. pp. 73–83.

11.

NGO Days

A total of 77 representatives of non-governmental organizations—NGOs—and peace and disarmament research organizations delivered oral statements to SSD II. These were given in the Ad Hoc Committee on June 24th and 25th—the so-called "NGO Days."

These interventions were the result, in the first instance, of the precedent set by SSD I to hear speakers from the NGO community. Also the precedent was repeated only after negotiations with the Prep Comm and among NGOs themselves.

This chapter discusses the selection of NGOs and research institutions. Also brief excerpts are given from the texts of a minority of the organizations making statements. Finally, there is a summary of a few of the common themes enunciated by the speakers.

1. Negotiating the NGO Role

The Final Document of SSD I in its penultimate paragraph acknowledged that "spokesmen [sic] of 25 non-governmental organizations and six research institutes also made valuable contributions to the proceedings of the session." The participation of NGOs as speakers then was no accident, since there are serious obstacles to allowing non-States to address plenary meetings of the General Assembly because the precedent opens the door to various quasi-governmental groups. However, careful negotiations made it possible for 31 non-governmental speakers to address the Ad Hoc Committee of SSD I. In retrospect, most credit goes to some NGOs in the U.K. and the U.K. Government itself for initiating this process.[1]

It was assumed by NGOs that they would be able at SSD II to obtain at least the same privileges they acquired at SSD I, including the right to address the Ad Hoc Committee. This turned out to be a correct assumption, but again serious, long negotiations were involved. For these negotiations, NGOs had a new instrument: the Ad Hoc NGO Liaison Group. This was formed shortly after SSD I was held in an effort to bring more cooperation between the Special NGO Committee on Disarmament at Geneva and the NGO Committee on Disarmament at New York. The Swedish Government donated some travel funds to make this possible, and the Group in the end was composed of officers of both NGO committees. While it operated several years before SSD II was convened, the Groups' greatest usefulness was as a conduit between the Prep Comm for SSD II and the NGO and disarmament institute community. The principal negotiators for the Ad Hoc Group were its co-chairmen, Mr. Serge Wourgaft of the World Veterans Federation and the author of this volume representing the World Conference on Religion and Peace.

After some preliminary discussions the Prep Comm at its second substantive session in 1981 made the following statement about procedures for oral statements: "With regard to oral statements, the Ad Hoc NGO Liaison Group of the two NGO disarmament committees at Geneva and U.N. Headquarters would make an appropriate speakers' list of representatives of non-governmental organizations and peace and disarmament research institutions. This would be transmitted to the Preparatory Committee, through its Chairman, at its final session for appropriate recommendation to the Special Session."[2] This was approximately the same procedure used for SSD I, except that the Ad Hoc Group had not existed in 1977–78 and relations among the NGOs were then more fragile and competitive. However, the Ad Hoc Group did not ask for the task of screening NGOs and its members approached it with the greatest reluctance and only because both the Prep Comm and the U.N. Secretariat refused—probably rightfully—to assume the task.

The Ad Hoc Group did insist that the U.N. Centre for Disarmament circularize a large cross-section of NGOs and research institutions with an interest in disarmament, whether or not they were related previously to the U.N. More than 500 were thus asked whether they would want an opportunity to deliver an oral statement to SSD II. Some 120 applied to speak, including 56 international or regional organizations, 47 national organizations, and 17 institutions. The screening process which fell into the lap of the Ad Hoc Group was compounded because the Group had initially to judge how much time, and thus how many speakers, the Prep Comm would recommend to be devoted to oral statements in the Ad Hoc Committee. At SSD I, 31 speakers were scheduled over three meetings.

The Ad Hoc NGO Group finally assumed that it might be possible to schedule four meetings of the Ad Hoc Committee. It suggested interventions of not more than ten minutes each, or an estimated total of 73 statements or speakers. In the end, the Group—meeting in New York late in April 1982 during the final session of the Prep Comm— selected 56 international and national NGOs, balanced carefully as to geography, ideology, and other factors, both tangible and intangible. However, the Ad Hoc Group found it impossible to screen the 17 research institutions which applied. It recommended in effect that all research institutions applying should speak unless the Prep Comm could find some criteria for screening. The final session of the Prep Comm recommended that all 56 NGOs be invited to speak. Pressures were exerted on the Prep Comm by Member States to add another six research institutions, and a total of 23 were invited to speak.[3]

2. Excerpts from Statements

The "NGO Days" were on June 24–25, 1982. The 77 speakers took a total of 14 hours and 19 minutes, spread over four extended meetings of the Ad Hoc Committee. In the end, three NGOs and one institution did not appear. On the other hand, two speakers spoke for each of two organizations. Thus the total was 77 speakers or just over 11 minutes for each speaker. For the full list of organizations and institutions, and the individuals who represented them, see Appendix E. There was some criticism that not too many diplomats—or NGOs—were present in the General Assembly Hall during the NGO Days. However, many diplomats were involved in SSD II negotiations in other parts of U.N. Headquarters. Also some of the final days of the general debate, featuring addresses by foreign ministers and ambassadors, were not better attended.

This volume cannot include the unabridged texts of all statements; indeed, below are given brief excerpts from only a random sample of some of the statements.

Bishop Kurt Scharf, Action Reconciliation/Service for Peace, Federal Republic of Germany: "I come to you from the country which in two world wars in this century has borne a great burden of guilt of war; the guilt of holocaust and genocide weighs on the nation as a whole. And how terribly that guilt has come home, down to the third and fourth generation . . . Our organization was founded after the Second

World War by Christians who wanted to counteract bitterness, hatred, and self-justification with the power of peace through reconciliation. We strive to achieve this aim through the devoted endeavors of thousands of young Germans who go out into those very countries and to those very peoples that have suffered most and are still suffering as a result of the National Socialist persecution and occupation. By working for reconciliation and peace we want to learn from the history of our own nation and of the Protestant Christian community in Germany and help shape a future in which man will no longer be man's worst enemy . . . In obedience to God and listening to His word, I venture to say that nuclear weapons are not a political means; even to threaten to use them is to blaspheme God . . ."[4]

Mrs. Joan Ruddock, Campaign for Nuclear Disarmament, United Kingdom: "We now have a mobilized, aware, and expectant public opinion, informed of the risks and costs of the arms race and impatient for action. Various opinion polls taken over the past 12 months show that a majority of British people are opposed to buying Trident submarines, opposed to the siting of American cruise missiles and indeed opposed to the continued presence of American nuclear bases in our country . . . Every country can and should decide what steps it can take without waiting for some bilateral or multilateral agreement . . . A favorite saying in the CND is 'a unilateralist is a multilateralist who means it.' "[5]

Dr. Philip Potter, General Secretary, World Council of Churches: "It has been argued at this session that deterrence provides the basis for international security. Deterrence is based on the intention and readiness to use nuclear weapons. It thus negates the very security it seeks to achieve. New weapons and new strategies have introduced new elements to deterrence. Deterrence offers no reliable basis for peace. It does not provide international security. It can in no way be a step towards disarmament. On the contrary, it has fueled and continues to fuel the arms race at various levels. The concept of deterrence is thus politically unacceptable and morally indefensible . . . The churches do not come to this arena with any self-righteousness. We are conscious of our failures. But I take this opportunity to assure members of the renewed commitment among churches around the world to disarmament and peace-making . . ."[6]

Mr. David R. Brower, President, Friends of the Earth: "Thirty years of futile attempts at disarmament have proved that fresh ideas are called for, and they are now being conceived with refreshing speed. I hope members hear them . . . We are looking at new definitions.

Conservation in the old sense meant strengthening the resources budget. It needs now to encompass the preservation of the world's life-support systems. Security sounds nice but is ambiguous. One can be secure in the army, in jail, and in the grave. We need something better; not a higher standard of living fed by a lower standard of environment, but a better life in a society that is sustainable because it is determined that it will not steal from the unborn and wishes, in the words of George Dyson, 'to find freedom without taking it from someone else.' Somehow the earth's peoples must determine that conservation and equity can mitigate the causes of war and drain on the resources that are needed to sustain human progress on the only livable planet we know of."[7]

Mr. Stephen Thiermann, Friends World Committee for Consultation: "As Friends we have a vision of a world free from war. We see that day coming when nation-States are prepared to hand over regulation of their arms to a world authority. We foresee a radical evolution of the U.N. We believe that modern technology makes world monitoring and verification of disarmament not a matter of wild idealism but a necessity for survival and for the right sharing of the precious and limited resources of the globe. We are encouraged by the confluence of the rising tides at work in the world that are more or less independent of the goodwill of Governments, the peace movements, and pressures for economic reform . . . Technological advance, especially nuclear weapons research, has rendered any conception of the 'just war' obsolete. It fills us with hope that in ever-increasing numbers the churches are speaking out against nuclear weapons: no use at all—neither for devastation nor death, nor stockpiling as a deterrent."[8]

Mayor Takeshi Araki of Hiroshima, Hiroshima Peace Culture Foundation: "The citizens of Hiroshima are firmly determined that nuclear weapons shall not be used again, no matter what the reasons . . . 'Let all the souls here rest in peace, for we shall not repeat the evil.' The words on the epitaph of the A-bomb Memorial Cenotaph in Hiroshima compose the pledge that each and all standing before the Cenotaph share the desire for peace, and are the 'Heart of Hiroshima' itself. The 'Heart of Hiroshima' is based on humanism in a true sense, by which the hatred and sorrow of the past are transcended, and the coexistence and prosperity of all humankind are genuinely sought. On behalf of the citizens of Hiroshima, I wish to call in particular for the immediate and complete banning of nuclear tests and the freezing of all nuclear weapons stocks, which should ultimately be eliminated . . . Furthermore, Hiroshima calls for the solidarity of cities throughout the

world which share a common cause with Hiroshima. This inter-city
solidarity which will be formed, regardless of national boundaries and
racial differences, to share efforts in paving the way to nuclear abolition
will give great momentum to the building of a new order of peace in
the nuclear age . . ."[9]

*Mr. Hitoshi Motoshima, Mayor of Nagasaki, Nagasaki Atomic
Bomb Casualty Council:* "I pray for the repose of the souls of war
victims all over the world, in particular of those who were killed by
atomic bombs. I am here to bear witness to the truth about the horrify-
ing effect of nuclear weapons. None of you have ever in reality seen the
destruction of the world or the annihilation of mankind. We from
Nagasaki have seen it with our own eyes . . . During the last 37 years
we have striven to reconstruct our city and at the same time to overcome any feeling of hatred. With the ideal of mankind's living in
mutual coexistence, we have been appealing for the total banning of
nuclear weapons. Our present town has been rebuilt from the ashes of
innumerable victims, for there still live in our city many who are
suffering from the effects of radiation—sometimes totally disabled,
sometimes leading an unbearable solitary life of pain. We are talking
about our own experience, knowing what kind of menace for humanity
nuclear weapons are. There must never be a third nuclear attack. The
city of Nagasaki has to be the last city on our planet ever destroyed by
nuclear weapons."[10]

Mr. Wim Bartels, Interchurch Peace Council, the Netherlands: "In
1977 the Interchurch Peace Council based its campaign to rid the
world of nuclear weapons on the very specific demand that the effort
should start with the denuclearization of the Netherlands. This should
not be seen as an element of an approach towards complete unilateral
disarmament, but as a first step, which is unilateral and independent
yet designed to promote a bilateral and multilateral process towards
disarmament and also to function as a confidence-building measure, a
step that should be drastic enough to reflect an alternative approach,
but at the same time small enough to enable allies and others to respond to it on the military and political level . . . In general the
approach that predominates in such (bilateral) arms talks is the numbers game, that is, an attempt to compare various weapons systems,
both in numbers and in properties. But that is meaningless, since there
are already far more warheads than conceivable targets. It is not sur-
prising that arms-control talks fail to bring positive results because they
fail to address the major cause of the arms race, the pursuit of power
politics expressed in military alliances and spheres of interest . . . The

Top Left: Archbishop Dom Helder Camara of Pax Christi International

Top Right: Ms. Randall Forsberg of the National Nuclear Weapons Freeze Campaign, U.S.A.

Bottom Left: Dr. Viqar A. Hamdani of the World Muslim Congress

Bottom Right: Dr. Homer A. Jack of the World Conference on Religion and Peace

Top Left: Rear-Admiral (Ret.) Gene La Rocque of the Center for Defense Information, U.S.A.
Top Right: Hon. Sean MacBride of the International Peace Bureau
Bottom Left: President Nikkyo Niwano of the International Association for Religious Freedom
Bottom Right: Patriarch Pimen of the Russian Orthodox Church

Top Left: Dr. Philip Potter of the World Council of Churches
Top Right: Shri Radhakrishna of the Gandhi Peace Foundation
Bottom Left: Mr. Douglas Roche, M.P., of the Parliamentarians for
    World Order
Bottom Right: Ms. Joan Ruddock of the Campaign for Nuclear Dis-
    armament, U.K.

Top Left: Mr. C. Maxwell Stanley of the Stanley Foundation, U.S.A.
Top Right: Mayor Hotoshi Motoshima of Nagasaki
Bottom Left: Demonstrators at United Nations Plaza on June 12th
Bottom Right: United Nations Headquarters at Night

link with the rapidly growing American peace movement is getting stronger and stronger and we are working out the complementary functions of the European peace campaigns and the freeze campaign in the U.S., which we firmly support . . . We beg every man and woman who hears these words to join us in the massive demonstrations and actions we are going to organize in 1983 for the cause of nuclear disarmament in the Netherlands and in Europe as a whole."[11]

President Nikkyo Niwano, President, International Association for Religious Freedom: "As a Buddhist from Japan, the only nation ever to suffer atomic attack, I feel it is my duty to call to the attention of all peoples everywhere the drastic alteration the existence of nuclear weapons makes in the meaning of war. In the past, belligerents have usually been able to find some kind of justification for bellicose action. But, in the face of the horrendous destruction and slaughter caused by nuclear war, all justifications become less than meaningless. There can be no victor in a war without survivors, a war in which it is impossible to remain an onlooker. Such a war is impiety against the sacredness of life itself . . . As a Buddhist, I cannot but fully understand the Buddha's law of cause and effect, as well as feel deep repentance, whenever I recall the tragic atomic bombings suffered by Japan in return for its sudden attack on Pearl Harbor some 40 years ago."[12]

Lord Philip Noel-Baker, International Association for the Work of Dr. Albert Schweitzer: " 'The armaments,' said the great Pope John XXIII, 'kill their millions while they lie unused in their silos and their stores.' They kill their millions because they absorb vast resources that should be used to feed the hungry and give shelter to the cold. This misuse of human wealth has been the cause of mortal peril and of a scandal that should shame us all . . . All history has proved that if you prepare for war, war is what you get. If you want peace, you must prepare for peace; make the law and the institutions and the cooperative practices that are required . . . Can the magic change proposed in the Final Document of the First Special Session, the change from armaments and war to a world in which mankind's wealth is used for welfare, be brought about? Only by a change in the thinking of the peoples of the world. Can that change of thinking be achieved? Yes, said the great Albert Schweitzer, yes, it can be and it must be if mankind is to survive."[13]

Mr. John Vanderveken, Assistant General Secretary, International Confederation of Free Trade Unions: "One of the problems that concerns trade unions is reconversion. For the ICFTU there is no question of getting out of an economic recession by increasing military expenditures. On the contrary, alternative socially useful products for peaceful purposes must be found, products that would create more jobs, rather than military machines that devour capital . . . The military producers' lobby must be monitored and measures of reconversion and recycling planned to make it possible to take full advantage of the potential to create more jobs and satisfy essential needs. Reconversion cannot be left to chance . . . As for nuclear strategy, it is an illusion. Nuclear weapons are by their very nature weapons of mass destruction. A limited nuclear war is unthinkable; it would incontrovertibly bring about a response—a nuclear world war—which mankind would have little chance of surviving."[14]

Ms. Hildegard Goss-Mayr, International Fellowship of Reconciliation: "Through our firm refusal to enter into the spiral of violence, through techniques of solidarity, through non-cooperation with injustice, and through moral pressure, through creative initiatives for peaceful solutions and through confidence-building and, above all, through the willingness, ourselves, to accept the consequence of our commitment, we in the non-violent movement struggle to bring violence to a halt and to create a climate for disarmament and the peaceful resolution of conflict . . . We appeal to you in your responsibility for billions of lives to open your eyes and conscience to the non-violent conflict solutions of social, political, and defense issues; welcome the growing numbers of conscientious objectors to military service who seek to offer unarmed peace service, and help build a vast and comprehensive program of education in non-violence and peacemaking."[15]

Mr. Sean MacBride, President, International Peace Bureau: "The great world leaders who founded this world body, the U.N., had lived through the holocaust of the last world war; they were fully conscious of the threat that faced humanity. After years of anxious and earnest discussion, they unanimously came to the conclusion that the only way of avoiding a third world war, which in turn would inevitably be a nuclear war, was by the achievement of general and complete disarmament under international supervision and control . . . Ever since the adoption of the Hague and Geneva Humanitarian Conventions, two types of weapons have been prohibited by international humanitarian law. Those are weapons which are unnecessarily cruel and weapons which are indiscriminate in their effect on combatants and civilians. Their use has been prohibited both by the Hague and Geneva Conventions and by international law. What weapon could be more cruel and more indiscriminate than a nuclear warhead or bomb? Why outlaw dum-dum bullets and not outlaw atomic weapons? Yet, for some unexplained reason, there has been a refusal on the part of the super-Powers to include nuclear weapons among the weapons to be specifically outlawed in the revised text of the Geneva Convention. If any meaningful credibility is to be given to the rule of law and to humanitarian law, it is essential as a first step to adopt, without any further delay, a short convention outlawing the use of nuclear weapons and making the use of such weapons an offense under international law . . . The ordinary people of the world are losing patience with Governments for their failure to take meaningful measures for disarmament. We in the peace movement, throughout the world, are in close, direct contact with the ordinary people of the world, and we know that they will no longer tolerate the dangerous complacency which is rapidly leading us to World War III."[16]

Dr. Herbert Abrams, International Physicians for the Prevention of Nuclear War: "Doctors have never before been involved in an anti-war movement because they have always observed that war, as an extension of national policy, has characterized the behavior of man over centuries and yet society has been able to emerge intact. But physicians have never before been faced with such a life- and health-threatening possibility, nor with a sense that the planet could be so changed . . . We hear talk that nuclear war is winnable; but we know that there is nothing but mutual suicide in a massive nuclear war. We hear talk that nuclear war is survivable; yet we know that the living may envy the dead . . . We are simply doctors who are concerned about the greatest threat to life and health in this century. We feel a professional and ethical and humane obligation to become involved and to warn you and the whole world that much as we would like to help you in your time of sickness and disease and injury and radiation exposure, we simply will not be here. We will be dead, like the nurses and other health workers; our hospitals will be destroyed, just like your homes and buildings and this great U.N. General Assembly Hall."[17]

Patriarch Pimen, Russian Orthodox Church: "It is the duty of churches and religious organizations to educate believers in peace, to humanize international relations, and to seek out and strive to follow the roads to peace . . . The threat of nuclear war now hangs over the whole of mankind. Will people be able to find in themselves sufficient moral force to overcome what would appear to be a hopeless situation? Will we be able to understand that today the security of one can be guaranteed only by the security of all? We are convinced that an alternative answer to those questions depends to a large extent on the

position of the States you represent at this Special Session on disarmament . . . I believe that I am expressing the view of all the world's
religious leaders in asserting that we shall support all resolutions of this
session and shall exercise all of our moral authority so that, by the
prayers of believers and through their active involvement, those resolutions may be implemented."[18]

*Ms. Randall Forsberg, U.S. National Campaign for a Bilateral
Nuclear Weapons Freeze:* "The Campaign is a coalition representing
nearly 80 national organizations and hundreds of local organizations in
all 50 States. The goal of the Campaign is to stop U.S. and Soviet
testing, production, and deployment of nuclear warheads and of missiles and aircraft designed to deliver nuclear warheads, as a first step
towards a global halt in nuclear weapons production and towards the
reduction and eventual elimination of nuclear weapons . . . Stopping
the production of nuclear weapons is a reasonable step, which clearly
deserves priority in the process of controlling and reversing the steady
global increase in armaments . . . What has mobilized an unprecedented mass movement in the U.S. is the notion of working for a
meaningful yet realistic first step, which can make subsequent, more
ambitious steps in arms control and disarmament possible."[19]

Mr. Roman Bedor, Pacific Concerns Resource Center: "The Pacific
region covers nearly one third of the earth. It includes many thousands
of islands, a huge ocean and hundreds of diverse cultures. It is an
exploited region and remains a region where the heavy hand of foreign
domination continues to be felt. To France the Pacific is a nuclear-
bomb testing ground; to Japan it is a low-level nuclear-waste dump; to
China the Pacific is a missile-testing site; to the Soviet Union it is a
military toe-hold. And to the U.S., the Pacific is a market for nuclear
power plants, a testing site for nuclear weapon delivery systems, a
high-level waste dump, a deployment theatre for the mighty nuclear
submarine fleet, and the lodging for an expanding string of military
bases . . . The peoples of the South Pacific face two direct nuclear
threats to their survival; the testing of nuclear weapons by the Government of France in its Polynesian colonies, and the mining of uranium
in Aboriginal Australia."[20]

*Mr. Douglas Roche, Chairman, Parliamentarians for World Or-
der:* "We call for negotiations on a world treaty for simultaneous, balanced, verifiable, and enforceable disarmament, which must
eventually include: disarmament by all nations to the level of arms
required for internal security; an international inspection organization
able to monitor disarmament, using both satellites and on-site inspec-

tion; a world peace force able to enforce disarmament and prevent
international aggression, the members of which should be individually
recruited; an effective system of world courts and arbitration tribunals;
a world development fund through which a fixed proportion of the
resources made available through disarmament will be devoted to development of the poorest nations. We commit ourselves to this task.
We recognize that the chief obstacle to disarmament and development
is not technical difficulty but a lack of political will. On behalf of the
millions we represent, we affirm that political will. We make this
appeal on behalf of our constituencies who, whatever their culture,
whatever their ideology, whatever their nationality, share one desire:
the desire for life. I emphasize that, in making such an appeal, I am not
standing here alone. The call for global survival that I have just transmitted has been signed by 610 parliamentarians around the world, who
represent more than 50 million people."

Archbishop Dom Helder Camara, Pax Christi International:
"There are moments so grave in human history that, rather than accus-
ing one another, we all, not only as individuals, but as peoples and
institutions, have need of prophets—who, in the name of the Lord,
would call us to true conversion, to true change in our lives, to true
rebirth. How great our woe: we have no prophets and we smile at
prophecy . . . The North frequently manipulates the Governments of
the South, encouraging dictatorships, particularly the military type,
which seem stabler than the few weak constitutional Governments.
Through advertising, the North imposes its life style, its patterns, and
even its dietary habits on the South. The North has forced the South to
participate in the arms race. Dear United Nations, teach us the lesson
of rebirth and renaissance. Discover the speediest and surest way to
liberate yourself from the anti-democratic privilege of the right of veto,
which was usurped from the time of your creation by some super-
Powers, the victors of the Second World War . . . Encourage women
the world over to help dispel the fear of unilateral disarmament. This
should occur throughout the entire world, so that there will no longer
be a first world, second world, or third world, but one world."[22]

Ms. Myrtle Solomon, War Resisters' International: "The basis of
non-violence is no irresponsible dream, as is the nightmare of war. It
involves a dedicated commitment which is no longer a prerequisite of
those who are called or forced to wage war. Because non-violent resist-
ance rejects war itself, it cannot truly be called an alternative to war.
But it is a way of breaking through the shackles of armed force and
diverting our skills to a better purpose and to the benefit of all people,

especially to those who live and die all too soon in the poorer countries. The war resister is a troublesome person who frequently challenges accepted traditions by unusual methods which range from mass civil disobedience to extensive educational programs among the young, but most of us are quite sane and have learnt to fight for values without killing for those values. The conscientious objector understands the meaning of unilateral disarmament—an example to be followed by the States . . . The U.N. Organization awarded first prize this year to the symbol of the broken rifle. This symbol has been that of the War Resisters' International since its inception 60 years ago. But we have truly broken our rifles and refused to support their further use or manufacture. Will you, too, friends, turn that symbol into fact and come along with us and scrap the lot?"[23]

Mr. Willard McGuire, World Confederation of Organizations of the Teaching Profession: "As a teacher, I have a very strong feeling that my students will not accept the concept of the 'age of deterrence' as a substitute for the 'age of peace' that we have promised them and that we have promised ourselves. So what do we tell the children? We must tell them the truth . . . The children, our students, and the students of teachers who march to different political drummers around the world, must be told the truth. The nuclear arms race is really not a race at all, for in a race there is always a victor and losers. But in the nuclear arms race there can only be losers . . . In the past teachers remained silent while national leaders systematically, and most effectively, misused the instrument of education to shape policies which have led tragically and inevitably to international ill will, aggression, and war . . . We must educate the world's children to believe that real peace is possible, a peace free of nuclear threats and counter-threats, a peace where human life is something more than a list of numbers on some benighted general's chart. Such a peace can only be possible through world disarmament. The world's teachers must work toward this goal."[24]

Mr. Edgar Bronfman, World Jewish Congress: "The World Jewish Congress has a unique reason for raising its voice at this U.N. session on disarmament. In the history of the world, nations have been destroyed by war, religious groups have been persecuted, whole societies have been plundered and ravaged. But we Jews have been the first and main victims of a twentieth-century technology organized for the purpose of ethnocide, of group murder . . . We Jews, who experienced technological holocaust, insist that nuclear holocaust, whether it be launched by super-Powers or by smaller nations who have nuclear capacity, can, should, and must be curtailed . . . There is an old Jewish saying from the second century: If I am not for myself, who will be for me? But if I am only for myself, what am I? The nations of the world would do well to heed that wisdom."[25]

Dr. Viqar A. Hamdani, World Muslim Congress: "For the Muslim world there can be no perceived benefits from disarmament without, first and foremost, a complete repudiation of the relationship between armament and aggression, without an immediate end to bloodshed, without the condemnation of all acts of hostility and hegemony by Member States and without the institution of a genuine process to rectify past injustices and to undo the cumulative territorial, political, economic, and social usurpations of colonialism . . . The concept of a defensive war in the cause of the highest ethical principles ordained by God plays an important role in the socio-political scheme of Islam. Only self-defense in the widest sense of the term enjoins Muslims to resort to arms."[26]

Mr. Romesh Chandra, President, World Peace Council: "The World Peace Council condemns the major upsurge of the arms build-up that has characterized recent years and led to the rise of the spectre of nuclear annihilation. This upsurge can be seen vividly in the production of the neutron bomb; the doctrine of the first strike; the U.S. refusal to ratify SALT II; the further development of nuclear armaments; the projected development of medium-range nuclear arms in Europe; the deployment of new armaments systems and rapid deployment forces; the new doctrines on the use of nuclear arms; the use or threat of use of control of food supplies as a weapon; and the plans to manufacture new chemical weapons . . . I believe that this session will be remembered in history because of the great mass interest it evoked among the peoples of the world. A wave of enthusiasm swept across the world when the peoples learned that the Soviet Union had at this session made a clear unilateral declaration that it had renounced the first use of nuclear weapons. Peace and disarmament movements have for many years urged that all nuclear Powers should make such a declaration. We appeal to all other nuclear Powers to follow the lead given in this regard by the Soviet Union. One can only regret that certain Washington spokesmen should have thought fit to declare that the U.S. would never make such a declaration and that its entire strategy was based on the concept of a first strike."[27]

Mr. W. Ch. J. M. Lanschot, World Veterans Federation: "I have the honor of addressing you on behalf of tens of millions of veterans and war victims, of the West and of the East, of the South and of the North, who have known the sufferings and tragedies of war, who have fought side by side or one against the other and who for many years have worked together over and above their differences to save humanity from another, still more terrible, more destructive tragedy . . . At a time when the enormous advances in the space sciences make possible a better understanding of the relative fragility of life on earth, it is inconceivable that living beings themselves should destroy it. We support the decisions of the U.N., in particular regarding attempts to avoid a nuclear confrontation, and we ask that its work in that field be accelerated. In memory of the tens of millions of combattants who have sacrificed their lives, and speaking on behalf of those who bear forever on their bodies and in their minds the visible and invisible scars of the tragedies they have lived through, we therefore solemnly recall to the representatives of Governments at the Second Special Session on disarmament that the immediate future of mankind is at stake."[28]

Prof. Bernard Feld, Pugwash Conference on Science and World Affairs: "There are no simple mechanistic solutions to the problem of nuclear weapons proliferation. There is no way, short of the political will and political decision, to keep the nuclear genie in the bottle, to keep nuclear weapons proliferation under control. And increasingly, as we advance towards and into the twenty-first century, the fate of the human species will depend on its political wisdom and on its ability to organize that wisdom into an effective mechanism for controlling not only the production and the dissemination of nuclear weapons but, ultimately war itself. At the end of the twentieth century and as we advance into the twenty-first century, war is no longer a possible means of settling anything, and the sooner this is universally recognized and universally brought into our international system, the less danger there will be that, in fact, we will destroy ourselves . . . We now appeal to our colleagues of the world's scientific community: accept responsibility and become directly involved in actions to avert nuclear war; to the Governments of the world: seek a comprehensive international agreement aimed at eliminating the risk of nuclear war, and the danger to civilization involved in any use of nuclear weapons; to all peoples: support measures to remove the nuclear menace that threatens the survival of mankind."[29]

Rear-Admiral Gene La Rocque (Retd.), Center for Defense Information, Washington, D.C.: "Does anyone believe civilization will survive a nuclear war? Does anyone, any sane rational person, believe our different philosophies and economic and political competition warrant a nuclear war? We, the representatives of non-governmental organizations, have come here in the hope that we would witness world leaders in serious, constructive discussion of measures to slow, stop, and reverse the arms race. So far we have heard far too much fear, distrust, and animosity expressed here. Has the U.N. become merely a forum to castigate our adversaries, build competing blocks, and rattle sabres? Do those national leaders who pollute this platform with the diatribes against other peoples, other nations, other systems, serve their own nations, or do they condemn them and all of us to the calamity of a nuclear war? . . . Put very simple, will the Soviet Union and the U.S. destroy civilization to ensure that their economic system and their political philosophy dominate the world? The answer is clear: both the U.S. and the Soviet Union are planning, training, arming, and practicing to destroy each other and all civilization. Neither side expects to win. Neither can avoid losing. As we proceed at ever-increasing speed down the converging courses which lead toward a nuclear war, little time remains to alter course to avoid the catastrophe ahead of us. It is no longer a question of whether we will have a nuclear war, only one of 'how soon will it start?' "[30]

Sri Radhakrishna, Gandhi Peace Foundation, India: "Disarmament can never be achieved if it is left to the ruling elites; it has to be made a people's movement; and it has to be pursued as a goal along with other goals like human rights and the international distribution of justice. We believe that the time has come when we should adopt a holistic approach to disarmament. We believe also that the U.N. can make a significant contribution to disarmament with the help of this holistic approach. Let us realize that peace keeping and conflict resolution are not enough by themselves, unless accompanied by a simultaneous effort at building a world community. Thus, an entirely new approach to disarmament has to be developed incorporating elements of development, conflict resolution, and community-building . . . The U.N. has to convince itself that disarmament can be achieved if it can develop a total approach in its own building and not a casual compartmental approach. The problems of development, peace-keeping, environment, human rights, and justice are all so interrelated that, unless we shed the usual sectorial approach and evolve the methodology of a holistic approach to problems, the problem will continue to dodge us because, if we put it off at one end, it will reappear at the other end and we will be caught in the network of our own creation."[31]

Mr. Burton Yale Pines, The Heritage Foundation, Washington, D.C.: "What is questionable is just how serious is this Second Special Session on Disarmament. All that can be done here for five weeks is talk. And, while words can be very powerful weapons, they can be so only if they are spoken and taken seriously. The question is: are we engaging in serious discussion or merely playing a ritualistic parlor game? I wonder . . . Where is the outcry at this conference—from the official representatives and from my fellow representatives of non-governmental organizations—against weapons being used at this moment? Why do so many of you from third-world nations seem to be much more concerned with the distant and extremely unlikely threat of nuclear arms than with the present use and further imminent threat of chemical arms, which a highly industrialized nation, the Soviet Union, is using against third-world populations? Can it be that you and your nations are not really serious about disarmament? . . . In the 1970s, in fact, imports of arms by the third-world soared 150 per cent. Those with the most voracious, insatiable appetites for arms have been Libya, Iraq, Syria, Iran, Viet Nam, and India . . . Such a discussion must ask also why third-world countries such as Iraq, Libya, Syria, Tanzania, and South Yemen, as well as the Soviet Union and its East European allies, have been spending more of their gross national product on arms than have NATO members on average."[32]

Prof. Oleg Bykov, Institute of World Economics and International Relations of the U.S.S.R. Academy of Sciences: "As for the Soviet Union, its position is extremely clear: it has not sought, nor does it seek, military superiority; it has not intended, nor does it intend, to threaten any State or group of States. As Leonid Brezhnev declared in his message to the Second Special Session devoted to disarmament, the Soviet Union has undertaken not to be the first to use nuclear weapons. The ruling circles of the U.S.A., as is clear from their official statements and concrete actions, have taken a different position. A massive build-up of American military might is coupled with a strategy geared to a first use of nuclear weapons, either in a generalized confrontation or initially in a 'limited' conflict, which would inevitably become a prelude to world war . . . Logic dictates above all the urgency of freezing the strategic arms of the U.S.S.R. and the U.S.A. for the duration of the current talks. That important measure would facilitate progress towards radical nuclear arms limitation and reduction."[33]

Major-General Indar Jit Rikhye (Retd.), International Peace Academy, New York: "Disarmament and international security are not only linked—they are interlocked. No nation here will agree to lay down or reduce its arms, be they conventional or nuclear in nature, without assurances of viable alternative measures to provide for its security . . . Two concepts which would alter and modify the international relations of States in such a way as to enhance security deserve to be strongly promoted. One is the proposal for a U.N. treaty on military non-intervention which would clarify and limit the uses of Article 51 of the Charter. Another is the concept of nuclear-free zones. "[34]

Mr. Yoshikazu Sakamoto, International Peace Research Association: "This Special Session should officially endorse the establishment of a non-governmental organization consultative committee on disarmament that would act as a counterpart to the Committee on Disarmament in Geneva, and should request that government representatives to the Committee on Disarmament cooperate in the exchange of views with such a non-governmental organization committee. Furthermore, a non-governmental, independent expert committee on disarmament, designated by research institutes and non-governmental organizations, should be established and attached to the U.N. Centre for Disarmament . . . In brief, the U.N. should utilize the human and intellectual resources of the non-governmental organizations and movements by taking innovative steps in its Disarmament Campaign to strengthen ties with the people of the world . . . The citizens' movement has emerged, and is here to stay, to help Governments restore genuine political leadership committed to and capable of creating a new demilitarized international order. "[35]

Mr. C. Maxwell Stanley, President, The Stanley Foundation, U.S.A.: "Accelerated multilateral disarmament progress is not just important, it is critical, for five reasons. First, only the multilateral approach can effectively reduce conventional weapons and forces. Secondly, even nuclear weapons reduction measures must ultimately be multilateral. Thirdly, the multilateral approach, in contrast to the secrecy of bilateral negotiations, stimulates public interest. Fourthly, the visibility of the multilateral approach, in contrast to the secrecy of bilateral negotiations, stimulates public interest. And, fifthly, vigorous multilateral activities prod the two major nuclear Powers to get on with bilateral negotiations . . . The success of the Second Special Session on disarmament will depend on how well it responds to four immediate needs: first, to take prompt and definite steps to reduce the danger of nuclear war; secondly, to agree on a short list of specific arms control and reduction measures that can be negotiated in the near future; thirdly, to increase the number, intensity, and effectiveness of negotiations on specific arms control and disarmament agreements; and, fourthly, to build stronger support for disarmament and enlarge the active disarmament constituency. "[36]

Dr. Frank Blackaby, Stockholm International Peace Research Institute (SIPRI): "In making suggestions for what might be done in the field of disarmament there is always a dilemma. Ambitious proposals are open to the objection that they are politically unrealistic. Proposals which are judged to be in the range of the politically possible are open to the objection that their effects may well be very small . . . Regarding space, three quarters of all satellites launched since Sputnik, in 1957, have been launched for military purposes. Because of their increased dependence on such spacecraft, the military are now turning their attention to sophisticated weapons for disabling the satellites of the other side and so gaining military advantage. Here again is a development still in its early stages. Every year without some arms control constraints will make the possibility of control more difficult. As a first modest step towards reducing the military use of outer space, the two major Powers should at least agree to a treaty banning anti-satellite operations . . . There are two points we wish to make about the conduct of negotiations. The offer to negotiate about arms control or disarmament should not be treated as a favor done to another State or as a reward for good international behavior. Arms limitation and disarmament agreements serve the interests of all parties. If, every time there is a tension between major Powers, arms-control negotiations are suspended or postponed, there is little hope for progress. The second point on negotiations [is that] there is a case for negotiations about packages of measures rather than separate negotiations about small individual steps. Any individual proposal, however carefully constructed, may often be seen to benefit some participants in the negotiations more than others. Negotiations about a package of measures could make more trade-offs possible."[37]

3. Common Themes

The context of the NGO speeches varied widely. The U.N. Centre for Disarmament, in its index to the subject matter discussed in the Ad Hoc Committee, showed the wide variety of NGO themes—and their frequency. These are shown in Table 10.

TABLE 10
THEMES MOST ENDORSED BY NGOs AND INSTITUTIONS
DELIVERING ORAL STATEMENTS*

Nuclear arms limitation and disarmament	62
Disarmament and international security	60
Information on disarmament	55
Dissemination of information on disarmament	55
Role of non-governmental organizations	39
Second Special Session on disarmament	30
Nuclear freeze	30**
Confidence-building measures	29
General and complete disarmament	29
Reduction of military budgets	28
U.N. role in disarmament	27
Cessation of nuclear weapons tests	24
Regional approach to disarmament	22
Nuclear-free zones	21
Unilateralism	21***
World Disarmament Campaign	20***
No first use of nuclear weapons	19
Importance of U.S./U.S.S.R. negotiations	19

*—Based on Index compiled by the U.N. Centre for Disarmament of statements delivered by 75 NGOs and research institutions made to the Ad Hoc Committee[38]
**—Based on an independent analysis of speeches delivered
***—Based on survey by Leah Halper[39]

REFERENCES

1. For details about the selection process for SSD II, see the author's *Disarmament Workbook: The U.N. Special Session and Beyond* (1978) and his article, "NGOs and Disarmament," in the 1979 SIPRI Yearbook.
2. A/S-12/1, p. 9.
3. For more details about the selection process, see "The Final Meeting of the Preparatory Committee for the Second U.N. Special Session on Disarmament," by Homer A. Jack. WCRP Report. June 1982. 17 pp. pp. 11–13.
4. A/S-12/AC.1/PV.5, pp. 3–7.
5. *Ibid.*, pp. 21–26.
6. *Ibid.*, pp. 31–36.
7. *Ibid.*, pp. 37–41.
8. *Ibid.*, pp. 41–46.
9. *Ibid.*, pp. 46–48.
10. *Ibid.*, pp. 49–52.
11. *Ibid.*, pp. 52–58.
12. *Ibid.*, pp. 58–62.
13. *Ibid.*, pp. 63–71.
14. *Ibid.*, pp. 82–88.
15. *Ibid.*, pp. 92–95.
16. A/S-12/AC.1/PV.6, pp. 8–16.
17. *Ibid.*, pp. 16–22.
18. *Ibid.*, pp. 22–30.
19. *Ibid.*, pp. 41–45.
20. *Ibid.*, pp. 46–52.
21. *Ibid.*, pp. 52–56.
22. *Ibid.*, pp. 57–62.
23. *Ibid.*, pp. 96–101.
24. A/S-12/AC.1/PV.7, pp. 7–12.
25. *Ibid.*, pp. 36–41.
26. *Ibid.*, pp. 41–46.

27. *Ibid.*, pp. 46–52.
28. *Ibid.*, pp. 58–62.
29. *Ibid.*, pp. 68–78.
30. A/S-12/AC.1/PV.8, pp. 7–11.
31. *Ibid.*, pp. 31–38.
32. *Ibid.*, pp. 38–41.
33. *Ibid.*, pp. 63–68.
34. *Ibid.*, pp. 76–80.
35. *Ibid.*, pp. 81–86.
36. A/S-12/AC.1/PV.8/Add.1, pp. 22–27.
37. *Ibid.*, pp. 27–32.

38. "Index to Statements on Disarmament at the Meetings of the Ad Hoc Committee of the Twelfth Special Session." U.N. Centre for Disarmament. June/July 1982. 52 pp.

39. "Measures Advocated by NGOs and Peace Research Institutions at the Second Special Session," by Leah Halper. New York: NGO Consultation for the World Disarmament Campaign. November 1982. 6 pp.

12.

Why Did the Special Session Fail?

Why did SSD II fail? To some—diplomats, Secretariat members, NGOs—"failure" is a negative word and, in fact, SSD II was *not* a failure. To others, SSD II was a failure all right, but only because some starry-eyed NGOs and a few diplomats had invested too high expectations in the session.

In any case, an assessment of SSD II is essential, not only to look backwards, or to indict individuals and institutions, but to contribute to progress in the future. Thus this chapter will attempt to assess SSD II, especially from the viewpoint of diplomats on the last day of the session, and the Editorial Advisory Board of *Disarmament Times*.

1. The Diplomats' Assessment

If diplomats at SSD II could not agree on assessing the implementation of the Final Document of SSD I—and thus this disagreement itself constituted one of the chief failures of SSD II—they could also not agree on assessing SSD II itself. However, the final two plenary meetings of SSD II on July 10th, held a day after the scheduled adjournment of the session, consisted of a parade of diplomats taking the podium of the General Assembly Hall to assess their collective relative failure.[1]

A total of 42 States participated in this evaluation, not counting the President of the Special Session who began the assessment. (The Secretary-General was away from Headquarters.) The evaluation came immediately after the report of the Ad Hoc Committee was presented by its Rapporteur, Mr. Omer Ersun of Turkey. The President announced that, once the report was approved, those delegates "wishing to do so will be free to make statements of position or reservations."

The report was adopted by consensus and a total of 42 States made interventions. The list is found in Table 11. It is of some interest to discover that only three African States and four Latin American States participated in this evaluation. On the other hand, 17 Western States, ten Eastern European States, and eight Asian States did so.

It is difficult to know how best to reflect the flavor of these evaluations, but perhaps the classification below can be of most utility.

Disappointment

Most delegations had little trouble in designating the outcome of SSD II in one or two words, or a phrase. The most common word was "disappointment." The range of judgements about SSD II is as follows:

"Failed." (President Kittani) (Sri Lanka) (India) (Pakistan) (Egypt) (China) (Algeria) (Cyprus).

"Regret." "Deep" (Netherlands) (Japan) "Profound" (Pakistan) (Poland) (Tunisia) (Brazil).

"Disappointment." (Pres. Kittani) (Belgium) "Great" (Sweden) "Bitter" (Indonesia) "Grave" (India) (Canada) "Profound" (Italy) (Bulgaria) (New Zealand) "Deep" (Romania) (France) (Cuba) (Norway) (Finland).

"Infinitesmal result" (Sweden).

"Dismal outcome" (Sweden) "Unsuccessful outcome" (Indonesia).

"A little sad" (Netherlands).

"Serious setback" (Ireland).

"Sombre note" (Pakistan).

"Expectations betrayed" (Yugoslavia).

"Unable to fulfill its mandate" (Tunisia).

Some delegates were not that pessimistic and tried to make the best of admittedly a bad situation:

"Our hopes . . . remain far from fulfillment" (Pres. Kittani).

"Temporary setback" (Netherlands).

"Missed opportunity" (Sri Lanka).

"Successes and failures" (U.S.A.).

"Not an irreparable failure" (Turkey).

"Opportunity missed" (Ireland).

"So few results" (Australia).

"Ended inconclusively" (Bangladesh).

Other delegates wanted to make sure that the process of disarmament deliberations would continue and tried, with some desperation, to see light at the end of the tunnel:

"Can't despair" (Pres. Kittani) "not despair" (Netherlands) "despair must be avoided" (Egypt).

TABLE 11
STATES PARTICIPATING IN THE EVALUATION OF SSD II IN THE FINAL PLENARY MEETINGS

African: Algeria, Egypt, Tunisia

Asian: Bangladesh, China, Cyprus, India, Indonesia, Japan, Pakistan, Sri Lanka

Eastern European: Bulgaria, Byelorussian SSR, Czechoslovakia, German Democratic Republic, Hungary,* Poland, Romania, Ukrainian SSR, U.S.S.R., Yugoslavia

Latin American: Bahamas, Brazil, Cuba, Mexico

Western European and Others: Australia, Austria, Belgium,** Canada, Denmark, Finland, France, German Federal Republic, Ireland, Italy, Netherlands, New Zealand, Norway, Sweden, Turkey, U.K., U.S.A.

---

*Speaking for some socialist States
**Speaking for the ten members of the European Community

"Not be discouraged" (Sweden) "Not lead to despair" (Norway) (Denmark).

"Not lessen our resolve" (U.K.).

"Provide stimulus" (Turkey).

"Part of a process" (Ireland).

"Not weaken our resolve" (Pakistan).

"Warning signal" (Yugoslavia).

"Not lose heart" (Australia).

"Not duly despondent" (Australia).

"No evil without benefit" (Cyprus).

During the final two meetings of SSD II, many delegates tried to discover some of the reasons for the failure of the session. Four reasons were repeatedly given, although admittedly these did not cover the full basis for failure.

Western Culpability

1. The U.S.A. and NATO were the culprits:

○ "It is the fault of the U.S. and the NATO bloc that the demands of the peoples . . . are being blocked and remain unimplemented." (U.S.S.R.).

○ "These members timed their Summit meeting in Bonn to coincide with the Special Session." (U.S.S.R.).

○ "These States came to this disarmament forum virtually empty-handed . . . they failed to submit a single specific proposal." (U.S.S.R.).

o "Obstructionist position of the U.S. and some other NATO countries." (Hungary).

o "Certain delegations have obstinately defied the wish and determination of the majority and even the popular masses of their own countries and stubbornly blocked every effort aimed at reaching agreement." (Hungary).

o "Full responsibility for the unsatisfactory results falls on the shoulders of the leading circles in the U.S. and their closest allies in NATO." (Bulgaria).

o "They have attempted to revise the priorities agreed on" at SSD I. (Ukrainian SSR).

o "All this has been frustrated by the unchanging rhetoric and chauvinistic positions of those who have built their political careers on the basis of threat, blackmail, and disregard to the fundamental interests of peace." (Cuba).

o "The fault of the forces of imperialism and reaction." (Byelorussian SSR).

o "Responsibility for this outcome of the session lies wholly on the shoulders of the delegations of the countries which, as in the past, have avoided constructive businesslike negotiations and have striven to divert our negotiations." (Czechoslovakia).

Eastern Culpability

2. The U.S.S.R. and the Warsaw Bloc were responsible:

o "Attempts have been made to shift the center of gravity at this session towards matters whose unbalanced treatment was not likely to win consensus." (Belgium for the European Community).

o "Their tenacious efforts to achieve agreement did not meet with a corresponding response in some quarters." (The Netherlands).

o "Shortly after the First Special Session one major Power violated the most fundamental principles of the U.N. Charter and invaded its Non-Aligned neighbor." (U.S.A.).

Joint Culpability

3. Both Super-Powers and their allies were to blame:

o "The political challenge of our time, in which a handful of nations cling to the illusion of exclusive and absolute power in utter disregard of the vital interests of all nations." (Brazil).

o "Most of the leading Powers, and especially the super-Powers, have again not shown themselves to be prepared to make use of the U.N. as an instrument for genuine disarmament efforts." (Sweden).

o "An uncooperative attitude on the part of the super-Powers toward multilateral negotiations." (Sweden).

o "Political bickering among delegations." (Indonesia).

o "The interplay of the narrow approach adopted by the powerful nations among us." (India).

o "Primary responsibility falls upon nuclear-weapon and other heavily-armed States." (Romania).

o "The States possessing the largest arsenals have resorted to every possible means inside and outside the session to dodge their responsibility and have raised extraneous issues to obstruct the reaching of the necessary common agreement." (China).

o "Those who have prevented the achievement of the smallest concrete results by adopting rigid stands and deliberately uncompromising arguments." (Algeria).

International Climate
4. The other major reason given for the disappointment about SSD II was the miserable international climate and its effect on disarmament deliberations:

o "It lies in the sad state of the world in which we live." (Pres. Kittani).

o "It would be an illusion to expect the U.N. to insulate itself from the general climate and fabric of relations among Member States and produce miracles." (Pres. Kittani).

o "The international political climate is much more severe today than it was in 1978." (Sweden).

o "The cause of disarmament has again become an important casualty of the present climate of mistrust and suspicion." (Indonesia).

o "Politically, the world is in poor shape. Confidence has been eroded and little is left of the détente that marked the early 1970s." (The Netherlands).

o "The present political environment." (Sri Lanka).

o "Disarmament cannot be viewed in isolation; it is an integral part of international politics and as such is subject to the same forces and influences as international politics in general." (Finland).

o "A worsening international situation." (U.S.S.R.).

o "The background of an accelerating arms race and rising tensions and mistrust." (Austria).

o "The occurence in certain regions of the world of events greatly detrimental to whatever is left of peace and stability." (Turkey).

o "The reciprocal relations between the growth of international tension and the build-up of armaments." (Ireland).

o "An unpromising time in international relations." (Canada).

o "The grave and deteriorating international situation has eroded the prospects for progress." (Pakistan).

o "The strained international situation resulting from constant disregard of general international order." (Egypt).

o "Disarmament can hardly make progress in circumstances in which international security is constantly breached and the hegemonists and aggressors refuse to renounce their designs." (China).

o "Disarmament does not operate in a political vacuum . . . Four years ago something of a peak in international confidence existed. That confidence has since been severely shaken." (Australia).

o "The international climate was not propitious for working out a future disarmament program." (Denmark).

During the final two meetings, delegates also suggested some of the accomplishments of SSD II, against the backdrop of general failure. New Zealand, among other States, pointed out that, although SSD II was "disappointing and its achievements limited, it has nevertheless served a number of useful purposes." Two major by-products listed obviously and repeatedly were the approval by consensus of the World Disarmament Campaign and the Fellowship Program. These needed little explanation, but were repeatedly recalled. However, other by-products were also suggested:

General Debate

1. The General Debate:

o "Many prominent world leaders chose to address this forum." (Pres. Kittani).

o "Penetrating statements made in plenary meetings at the highest level." (The Netherlands).

o "The participation in the general debate of many world leaders." (Finland).

o "The participation of statesmen from all regions." (Austria).

o "An impressively large number of other Heads of State or Government and Foreign Ministers." (U.K).

o "Participation of so many world leaders." (Canada).

o "Many Heads of State and Government and a great many other dignitaries participated." (Japan).

○ "The general debate was of outstanding quality." (France).

○ "There is a role for rhetoric in general debate which can lift our eyes to the horizon." (Australia).

New Proposals

2. New disarmament proposals were presented:

○ "A great number of new ideas, suggestions, and proposals." (Finland).

○ "During the past weeks we have offered concrete proposals and initiatives on a wide range of issues." (U.S.A).

○ "Some valuable proposals at least were made." (Ireland).

○ "The socialist countries have proposed a number of important new elements." (Hungary)

○ "A large number of proposals have been submitted." (Romania).

○ "Socialist and developing countries . . . put forward a whole range of ideas and constructive proposals." (Ukrainian SSR).

Reaffirmation

3. The Final Document of SSD I was reaffirmed. This was widely hailed as an achievement, only because efforts might have succeeded, in effect, to scuttle it.

○ "The validity of the Final Document has been unanimously and categorically confirmed." (Sweden).

○ "Efforts were exerted by some States to turn upside-down the priority measures already agreed upon in the Final Document . . . tantamount to backtracking on the steps that were taken in 1978." (Indonesia).

○ "We are encouraged by the unanimous reaffirmation of the validity of the Final Document." (The Netherlands).

○ "At least we have all reaffirmed our commitment to the Final Document." (Sri Lanka).

○ "Confirmed the value of the Final Document." (Finland).

○ "All delegations have reaffirmed the validity of the Final Document and their commitment to it." (Austria).

○ "We have all reaffirmed the validity of the Final Document and pledged ourselves to renewed efforts toward disarmament." (U.S.A.).

○ "The Final Document has been upheld and confirmed . . . something of an achievement." (Ireland).

○ "Reaffirmed the Final Document . . . This in itself is an important act." (Canada).

o "The unanimous and categorical reaffirmation of the Final Document acquires special importance." (Italy).

o "The validity of the Final Document . . . has been reaffirmed." (Japan).

o "Welcomes the unanimous reaffirmation by all States of their commitment to the privileges and provisions of the Final Document." (Pakistan).

o "Special importance must be attached that the General Assembly has reaffirmed the validity of the Final Document as well as the commitment entered into by all countries to ensure its practical implementation." (Bulgaria).

o "In difficult circumstances, we have been able to maintain and to preserve the achievements inherited from SSD I." (France).

o "We have built upon and confirmed the Final Document." (German Fed. Republic).

o "Reaffirmed the significance and the lasting value of the Final Document." (Yugoslavia).

o "Above all . . . we have reaffirmed the validity of the Final Document and pledged to respect the priorities in its Program of Action." (Norway).

Role of NGOs

4. The active role of NGOs was repeatedly mentioned:

o "Extensive and welcome participation of thousands of representatives from NGOs all over the world." (Pres. Kittani).

o "This session has also benefitted from the presence and the activities of the representatives of a great number of NGOs." (Sweden).

o "The presence of a multitude of NGOs at this session shows the depth and the universality of that opinion. NGOs are in fact invaluable in channeling the weight of public opinion on disarmament questions." (Finland).

o "My delegation has very much welcomed the attendance at this session of large numbers of representatives of international NGOs, including a prominent and dedicated group from Britain." (U.K.).

o "Many Canadians marched in New York last month." (Canada).

o "A large number of members of parliament and representatives of NGOs and of peace and disarmament research institutions, as well as countless private citizens from all over the world, including Japan, have come to New York." (Japan).

o "The supportive role of NGOs and research institutes is considered by my delegation to be a positive service." (Bangladesh).

○ "We heard . . . the anxious voices of NGOs united in demanding general and complete disarmament." (Algeria).

○ "The appeals of NGOs, including the survivors of the Hiroshima and Nagasaki massacres, who, along with hundreds of thousands of others, marched a few days ago before U.N. Headquarters." (Cuba).

○ "The statements made by representatives of NGOs from this rostrum. The delegation of the Byelorussian SSR expresses its gratitude for their important contribution to the work of the Special Session." (Byelorussian SSR).

○ "The Special Session has provided us the opportunity of hearing the voice of peoples from all over the world who have been alerted to the dangers of an approaching nuclear conflagration and who have expressed themselves in emphatic terms against the continuation of the arms race." (Cyprus).

○ "[The Session] provided a forum in which NGOs could express the profound concern of people all over the world to be freed from the danger and burden of armaments." (New Zealand).

Public Opinion

5. The role of public opinion for disarmament was widely recognized:

○ "Increasing concern manifest in world public opinion about the need to relieve humanity of the fear and danger of universal annihilation." (Pres. Kittani).

○ "A catalyst for one of the most impressive manifestations of free popular movements ever witnessed, not only in this city but wherever free opinion can be expressed." (Sweden).

○ "Pay its tribute to the thousands of women, men, and children across the globe who individually and through their organizations gave a new dimension to our endeavors." (Sri Lanka).

○ "The Special Session generated an unprecedented degree of public attention and interest." (Finland).

○ "A widespread anti-war movement which swept across all continents." (U.S.S.R.).

○ "The great interest and involvement shown by the public all over the world." (Austria).

○ "The way in which [SSD II] has acted as a focus for world public opinion." (U.K.).

○ "The wide public interest in Canada in this Special Session." (Canada).

○ "We note with satisfaction the role that well-informed public opinion . . . if it enjoys freedom of expression . . . can play." (Italy).

○ "The widespread interest among the peoples of the world to establish and preserve peace through disarmament." (Japan).

○ "The socialist countries express their full solidarity with the anti-war movement of the popular masses, which acquired unprecedented dimensions on the eve and during the course of the Special Session." (Hungary, in behalf of Socialist States).

○ "The demands of the world-wide peace movement have made an imprint on the session's discussions." (German Democratic Republic).

○ "The session has served as the focal point for the widespread expression of public concern about the arms race. We hope that the massive public support for disarmament demonstrated all over the world in recent months will have an impact on policy makers." (Pakistan).

○ "The large demonstrations that have taken place throughout the world before and during the Special Session, the participation of representatives of world public opinion in the discussions of this session, and the numerous messages and appeals addressed to the session have all demonstrated what the people of the world expect from their leaders and Governments." (Romania).

○ "A remarkable popular movement which has given abundant proof that disarmament can no longer be considered a matter for the Powers but, on the contrary, as a concern of all the peoples." (Algeria).

○ "This Assembly has encouraged and strengthened to an extraordinary degree the active interest of all the peoples of the world in promoting peace and disarmament. This interest which was unquestionably shown in this very city when nearly one million human beings gathered in Central Park, New York, to demonstrate it." (Mexico).

○ "[The Session] has helped stimulate public consiousness of the world for genuine and substantial measures of disarmament." (New Zealand).

2. Other Evaluations

While the diplomats at SSD II had the last word in the final plenary meetings, the diplomatic assessment continued a few weeks after adjournment when the Committee on Disarmament resumed in Geneva in August 1982 and when the 37th regular session of the General Assembly resumed in New York in September. Some of the same diplomats who played a role in SSD II participated in these other bodies, and both included a further post-mortem of SSD II. However, few additional insights were produced beyond those articulated on July tenth.

Another kind of evaluation was given by NGOs and the press, both immediately after SSD II concluded and for weeks and months afterward. Because of the failure of SSD II, perhaps not as many articles appeared as had been anticipated. These contain valuable insights, but it is beyond the competence of this volume to examine their contents. A short, incomplete bibliography of these articles is found in Chapter 9 above.

Another level of evaluation was given by the Editorial Advisory Board of *Disarmament Times,* the NGO newspaper published four times a week during SSD II. Some members of the Board followed the proceedings of SSD II in great detail even though they were attached neither to governments nor to the U.N. This Board, including some of its same members, made a similar evaluation of SSD I four years earlier.[2] The 1982 assessment is reprinted below from *Disarmament Times* unabridged.[3]

Members of the Editorial Advisory Board of *Disarmament Times,* and its editor, met two hours after the adjournment of the final meeting of the Ad Hoc Committee on July 9th to assess their reactions to SSD II. Edited excerpts from their taped conversations follow:

DISARMAMENT TIMES: What to you was the main achievement of SSD II?

PETER WHITTLE, Co-Director, Quaker U.N. Office, Geneva: Public involvement in disarmament affairs. This is a continuous process, of which the June 12th demonstration in New York was one manifestation.

ALAN GEYER, Executive Director of the Churches' Center for Theology and Public Policy, Washington: SSD II made blatantly clear the onus of political responsibility for the arms race—primarily the U.S.A., U.K., and the U.S.S.R.—while bringing the potential of the new multinational public disarmament movement to a timely focus.

WILLIAM EPSTEIN, former Director of U.N. Disarmament Affairs: The June 12th rally and what resulted directly from it—the World Disarmament Campaign. The demonstration would not have happened without SSD II which provided its raison d'étre. The approval of the Campaign was aided by worldwide demonstrations.

KAY CAMP, Former President, Women's International League for Peace and Freedom, Philadelphia: The no-first-use announcement by the Soviet Union. Another achievement, if indirect, is the clarification of the situation: the inability of governments to deal with the major crisis in the world—the nuclear arms race—and the necessity for the public to do it ourselves.

JOZEF GOLDBLAT, senior researcher of the Stockholm International Peace Research Institute (SIPRI): The impressive reaffirmation of the Final Document of SSD I, especially after very clear attacks upon it.

RICHARD HUDSON: Editor, *Disarmament Times:* NGOs achieved a higher level of activity and sophistication.

HOMER A. JACK, Secretary-General of the World Conference on Religion and Peace: The injection of the U.S. nuclear freeze movement massively into the U.N. system.

DISARMAMENT TIMES: What was the chief disappointment of SSD II?

WHITTLE: Discovering what we already knew: the intransigence of the super-Powers and their failure of imagination.

EPSTEIN: The Non-Aligned States were fractured and no longer played an independent stimulative role, as each of the super-Powers succeeded in drawing some of the Non-Aligned to their side on disarmament issues.

HUDSON: The final confirmation of the bankruptcy of the existing international system as exemplified in the U.N. The system is hopeless as it now stands. To work on international security is more important for nations, and individuals, than to work on disarmament.

GOLDBLAT: The paucity of imaginative disarmament initiatives, especially compared to SSD I. Also, the total inability to come to terms with the new situation of the nuclear threat.

CAMP: The actors on the world stage who are chiefly responsible for this situation have so little perception of their responsibility to do something about it. The failure to adopt a reasonable Comprehensive Program of Disarmament is very serious.

JACK: Some of us expected that growing out of SSD II there would be new impetus to the Geneva disarmament negotiations on a whole range of next steps to nuclear disarmament. But never mind the new measures, there has been no new thrust on hoary measures such as the comprehensive test ban treaty. Unfortunately, the Committee on Disarmament will meet perfunctorily for one month or so and then adjourn routinely until February, as if SSD II had never occurred.

GEYER: SSD II achieved absolutely nothing with regard to the highest priority: nuclear disarmament. There was no agreed short list of substantive measures, not even with regard to the single, long-standing commitment to a comprehensive test ban.

DISARMAMENT TIMES: Why did SSD II fail?

CAMP: A deteriorated political and military situation, the determination of the major powers to carry on the arms race, and their unwillingness to consider alternatives.

GOLDBLAT: The cold war, and also unrealistic goals of SSD II itself. One cannot negotiate in five weeks a change in the strategic doctrine of the U.S.A. or the opening up of Soviet society. Also, SSD II coincided with the U.S.A. openly saying that it would build up its armaments. The Soviets may have been doing the same thing, but they do not express it so openly or clearly. Also, the U.S.S.R. converted the initiative of preventing nuclear war into a propaganda exercise; when it didn't work out that way, they simply gave up.

GEYER: Regression to cold war diplomacy and confrontation. The rigidity of NATO and the Warsaw Pact bloc behavior frustrated all efforts of other States to achieve a significant consensus. The address of President Reagan and the policies of the U.S.A. did more to obstruct the prospects for a successful session than any other factor.

EPSTEIN: There is really no political will amongst the major powers to achieve disarmament. Also, the involvement of the public was too late to affect the policies of governments.

HUDSON: The political force for disarmament that is emerging in Europe and the U.S.A. did not get through the glass walls of the U.N.

JACK: While I have no illusions about the Soviet Union, I think SSD II failed because of the policies of the Reagan Administration. Two-thirds of the failure is due to the American people voting for the wrong presidential candidate.

DISARMAMENT TIMES: What lessons can be learned from SSD II?

HUDSON: There is a new threat to human survival: Special Sessions on Disarmament! SSD I did accomplish something, but it had a disastrous second act. A next Special Session, if any, should be devoted to international security.

AN OBSERVER to the dialogue: A Special Session is a fairly bad system because it mixes up too many different things at once. If we had concentrated on a single disarmament measure, such as a test ban treaty, we might have gotten somewhere. The main lesson is never to schedule a Special Session on Disarmament again unless it is a public relations exercise to help the World Disarmament Campaign.

GEYER: NGOs and research institutes must bring political influence to bear upon their governments well in advance of any Special Session. It is too late to change policies when the session is under way. The June 12th rally should have been held weeks, if not months, earlier—and in Washington.

GOLDBLAT: No disarmament measure should have been brought to SSD II unless most of its contentious issues had been solved.

JACK: SSD II should have dealt with only a short list of measures to prevent nuclear war. If the 38th floor of the U.N. Secretariat does not want to exert political leadership then an executive secretary of top stature should have been appointed to make SSD II less of a political failure. Also, a small group of non-governmental disarmament experts should have met during SSD II to issue daily substantive conclusions and act as a "shadow cabinet."

EPSTEIN: Unless the public gets more involved, as the mothers of the U.S.A. did in ending nuclear testing in the atmosphere in the early 1960s, then no disarmament progress can occur.

DISARMAMENT TIMES: What is your final judgment—in a sentence—of SSD II?

GOLDBLAT: A sad non-event, which hopefully will not be decisive for the future of disarmament efforts.

GEYER: A deeply distressing political fiasco which failed in any way to reverse the trends toward nuclear war, yet which highlighted the political obstacles to disarmament as perhaps no other event in modern history.

CAMP: Since the governments are not going to bring disarmament, we the people are going to have to do it ourselves.

OBSERVER: Disarmament is too important a topic to be left to the super-Powers.

EPSTEIN: Unless the public is involved in exercising pressure, there will never be disarmament. No government of any nuclear power really wants disarmament—only the public and some smaller States. Public pressure is the only way.

JACK: An unmitigated failure; unless public pressure escalates faster than the arms race, the disarmament conference of 1982 will be remembered as the disarmament conference of 1932: a harbinger of world war.

HUDSON: To get 157 sovereign nation-states together trying to make decisions on the basis of consensus virtually guarantees failure—and we really got a mammoth failure this time.

Disarmament Times asked a similar last question in 1978. Here are the anwers of four members of the above panel:

EPSTEIN: The new ideas and proposals made could become increasingly important in the next few years.

GEYER: Progress on many secondary concerns, and yet a dismaying failure on the primary issues.

GOLDBLAT: Perhaps a modest beginning in a process of mobilizing public opinion for disarmament.

JACK: Hopes deferred within the U.N. system while the arms race outside accelerates to an estimated $600 billion when the Second Special Session is held in 1981.

3. A Short Inventory

The author made, during the last week of SSD II, a simple, perhaps simplistic, evaluation of SSD II in a terse format. This may be of some interest, going slightly beyond some of the assessments made by both the diplomats and the journalists.[4]

Positive Results of SSD II

1. The media (TV, radio, newspapers, magazines) gave the initial weeks of SSD II good coverage, worldwide, and some to its close.

2. A World Disarmament Campaign was launched.

3. Many Heads of State or Government participated in the general debate, giving SSD II prestige and publicity.

4. The occasion of SSD II was used by NGOs throughout the world for intensive disarmament activities.

5. A large number of speakers (77) representing NGOs and research institutions gave oral statements.

6. The nuclear freeze concept was injected into the session through several different proposals.

7. The Soviet Union made a unilateral announcement that it would not be the first to use nuclear weapons. (China, however, made this announcement 18 years ago.)

8. Observers now know that currently the reason for the continuation and escalation of the arms race lies primarily on the shoulders of the U.S.A. and the U.S.S.R.

Some Disappointments About SSD II

1. The chances of a nuclear detonation were not lessened by SSD II; indeed, the quantitative and qualitative arms race (nuclear and conventional) continues unabated, despite SSD II.

2. The Member States, and thus the U.N., were unable to react

positively to large-scale demands of world public opinion for the beginnings of nuclear disarmament.

3. Preparations for SSD II did not stimulate the completion of any disarmament treaty and SSD II itself was not the occasion for the announcement of any treaty.

4. SSD II was unable to complete what had been hoped would be its "centerpiece"—A Comprehensive Program of Disarmament.

5. The continued tension between the U.S.A. and the U.S.S.R. made any new thrust for negotiating substantive issues impossible, including a Comprehensive Test-Ban Treaty, a no use or no first use treaty, and nuclear freeze treaty.

6. The visas of 318 persons were denied and perhaps 500 delayed—a serious indictment of the U.S.A. as an "open society."

7. The addresses of U.S. President Ronald Reagan and Prime Minister Thatcher were unbelievably disappointing.

8. Very few Heads of State or Government of Non-Aligned States, and none of Eastern Europe, participated in the general debate.

9. Contributions to the new voluntary fund for the World Disarmament Campaign were disappointingly low. A total of $271,615 was raised—less than the cost of receptions for one year at U.N. Headquarters.

10. NATO showed contempt for SSD II by scheduling a Summit of its Heads of State or Government during the first week of SSD II.

11. The U.N. Secretariat gave little political leadership to SSD II.

12. The leadership of the Non-Aligned States was less effective than at SSD I partly because of its internal political divisions.

13. Attempts were made in effect to weaken the Final Document of SSD I.

14. No consultative role for NGOs was given in the World Disarmament Campaign and no continuing role for NGOs in disarmament in the U.N. system was formulated.

Lessons Learned From SSD II

1. While the arms race contributes to world tension, the latter often makes it difficult to engender the degree of trust necessary to engage in compromise and therefore successful disarmament deliberations.

2. Disarmament deliberations must be prepared more carefully, and their agendas must be more modest.

3. The U.N. Secretariat must give more political leadership for a Special Session to have a chance of success. Perhaps an Executive Secretary for a Special Session should be appointed.

4. Preparations by NGOs to change governmental policies must begin months if not years before a Special Session. Perhaps a group of non-governmental experts should be appointed by the NGO community to work alongside a Special Session.

5. The people cannot wait for statesmen to prevent nuclear war.

6. Future Special Sessions as deliberative (and not negotiating) forums need not function by consensus.

Memories of SSD II

1. Hundreds of thousands of persons marched past U.N. Headquarters at the beginning of the June 12th demonstration.

2. Sixteen hundred persons offered civil disobedience in front of the Missions of the five nuclear weapon States on June 14th.

3. Tight security at U.N. Headquarters was evident, especially for the visits of President Reagan and Prime Minister Begin.

4. The General Assembly Hall was relatively empty when Prime Minister Begin spoke, due to a boycott by 100 Member States because of the Israeli invasion of Lebanon.

5. One ambassador tried to turn a meeting of the Ad Hoc Committee into a seminar of the conservative Heritage Foundation.

6. A military aide carried President Reagan's "black box" (to "command" nuclear war) while the President was visiting the U.N. to speak to a disarmament conference.

7. The Mayors of Hiroshima and Nagasaki visited New York twice during SSD II and gave oral statements to the Ad Hoc Committee.

8. The July 7th meeting of the Ad Hoc Committee saw the hopes for SSD II completely dissolve with the announcement of no progress possible on either a Comprehensive Program of Disarmament or a document assessing the implementation of SSD I.

Honor Roll of Individuals

A. Ambassador Alfonso Garcia Robles of Mexico for constantly submitting excellent initiatives.

2. Mrs. Inga Thorsson of Sweden for piloting the useful Swedish delegation.

3. Ambassador Olu Adeniji of Nigeria for assuming the impossible task of Chairman of the Ad Hoc Committee.

4. Ambassador A. P. Venkateswaran of India for giving leadership to the Non-Aligned caucus.

5. Ambassador Constantin Ene of Romania for convening the drafting group which produced a consensus paper on the World Disarmament Campaign.

REFERENCES

1. A/S-12/PV.28 and PV.29.
2. *Disarmament Times,* June 29, 1978.
3. *Disarmament Times,* July 13, 1982.
4. This is adapted from the author's assessment published in *Gandhi Marg,* August 1982. pp. 566–68.

Appendix A.
Final Document of the
First Special Session*

The General Assembly,

Alarmed by the threat to the very survival of mankind posed by the existence of nuclear weapons and the continuing arms race, and recalling the devastation inflicted by all wars,

Convinced that disarmament and arms limitation, particularly in the nuclear field, are essential for the prevention of the danger of nuclear war and the strengthening of international peace and security and for the economic and social advancement of all peoples, thus facilitating the achievement of the new international economic order,

Having resolved to lay the foundations of an international disarmament strategy which, through co-ordinated and persevering efforts in which the United Nations should play a more effective role, aims at general and complete disarmament under effective international control,

Adopts the following Final Document of this special session of the General Assembly devoted to disarmament:

I. Introduction

1. The attainment of the objective of security, which is an inseparable element of peace, has always been one of the most profound

---

*Adopted by consensus on July 1, 1978. While the spelling and punctuation of this volume is according to the country of publication (the U.S.A.), the spelling and punctuation of the Final Document is according to U.N. style (English).

aspirations of humanity. States have for a long time sought to maintain their security through the possession of arms. Admittedly, their survival has, in certain cases, effectively depended on whether they could count on appropriate means of defence. Yet the accumulation of weapons, particularly nuclear weapons, today constitutes much more a threat than a protection for the future of mankind. The time has therefore come to put an end to this situation, to abandon the use of force in international relations and to seek security in disarmament, that is to say, through a gradual but effective process beginning with a reduction in the present level of armaments. The ending of the arms race and the achievement of real disarmament are tasks of primary importance and urgency. To meet this historic challenge is in the political and economic interests of all the nations and peoples of the world as well as in the interests of ensuring their genuine security and peaceful future.

2. Unless its avenues are closed, the continued arms race means a growing threat to international peace and security and even to the very survival of mankind. The nuclear and conventional arms build-up threatens to stall the efforts aimed at reaching the goals of development, to become an obstacle on the road of achieving the new international economic order and to hinder the solution of other vital problems facing mankind.

3. The dynamic development of détente, encompassing all spheres of international relations in all regions of the world, with the participation of all countries, would create conditions conducive to the efforts of States to end the arms race, which has engulfed the world, thus reducing the danger of war. Progress on détente and progress on disarmament mutually complement and strengthen each other.

4. The Disarmament Decade solemnly declared in 1969 by the United Nations is coming to an end. Unfortunately, the objectives established on that occasion by the General Assembly appear to be as far away today as they were then, or even further because the arms race is not diminishing but increasing and outstrips by far the efforts to curb it. While it is true that some limited agreements have been reached, "effective measures relating to the cessation of the nuclear arms race at an early date and to nuclear disarmament" continue to elude man's grasp. Yet the implementation of such measures is urgently required. There has not been any real progress either that might lead to the conclusion of a treaty on general and complete disarmament under effective international control. Furthermore, it has not been possible to free any amount, however modest, of the enormous resources, both material and human, which are wasted on the unpro-

ductive and spiralling arms race and which should be made available for the purpose of economic and social development, especially since such a race "places a great burden on both the developing and developed countries."

5. The Members of the United Nations are fully aware of the conviction of their peoples that the question of general and complete disarmament is of utmost importance and that peace, security and economic and social development are indivisible, and they have therefore recognized that the corresponding obligations and responsibilities are universal.

6. Thus a powerful current of opinion had gradually formed, leading to the convening of what will go down in the annals of the United Nations as the first special session of the General Assembly devoted entirely to disarmament.

7. The outcome of this special session, whose deliberations have to a large extent been facilitated by the five sessions of the Preparatory Committee which preceded it, is the present Final Document. This introduction serves as a preface to the document which comprises also the following three sections: a Declaration, a Programme of Action and recommendations concerning the international machinery for disarmament negotiations.

8. While the final objective of the efforts of all States should continue to be general and complete disarmament under effective international control, the immediate goal is that of the elimination of the danger of a nuclear war and the implementation of measures to halt and reverse the arms race and clear the path towards lasting peace. Negotiations on the entire range of those issues should be based on the strict observance of the purposes and principles enshrined in the Charter of the United Nations, with full recognition of the role of the United Nations in the field of disarmament and reflecting the vital interest of all peoples of the world in this sphere. The aim of the Declaration is to review and assess the existing situation, outline the objectives and the priority tasks and set forth fundamental principles for disarmament negotiations.

9. For disarmament—the aims and purposes of which the Declaration proclaims—to become a reality, it was essential to agree on a series of specific disarmament measures, selected by common accord as those on which there is a consensus to the effect that their subsequent realization in the short term appears to be feasible. There is also a need to prepare through agreed procedures a comprehensive disarmament programme. That programme, passing through all the neces-

sary stages, should lead to general and complete disarmament under effective international control. Procedures for watching over the fulfilment of the obligations thus assumed had also to be agreed upon. That is the purpose of the Programme of Action.

10. Although the decisive factor for achieving real measures of disarmament is the "political will" of States, especially of those possessing nuclear weapons, a significant role can also be played by the effective functioning of an appropriate international machinery designed to deal with the problems of disarmament in its various aspects. Consequently, it would be necessary that the two kinds of organs required to that end, the deliberative and the negotiating organs, have the appropriate organization and procedures that would be most conducive to obtaining constructive results. The last section of the Final Document, section IV, has been prepared with that end in view.

II. Declaration

11. Mankind today is confronted with an unprecedented threat of self-extinction arising from the massive and competitive accumulation of the most destructive weapons ever produced. Existing arsenals of nuclear weapons alone are more than sufficient to destroy all life on earth. Failure of efforts to halt and reverse the arms race, in particular the nuclear arms race, increases the danger of the proliferation of nuclear weapons. Yet the arms race continues. Military budgets are constantly growing, with enormous consumption of human and material resources. The increase in weapons, especially nuclear weapons, far from helping to strengthen international security, on the contrary weakens it. The vast stockpiles and tremendous build-up of arms and armed forces and the competition for qualitive refinement of weapons of all kinds, to which scientific resources and technological advances are diverted, pose incalculable threats to peace. This situation both reflects and aggravates international tensions, sharpens conflicts in various regions of the world, hinders the process of détente, exacerbates the differences between opposing military alliances, jeopardizes the security of all States, heightens the sense of insecurity among all States, including the non-nuclear-weapon States, and increases the threat of nuclear war.

12. The arms race, particularly in its nuclear aspect, runs counter to efforts to achieve further relaxation of international tension, to establish international relations based on peaceful coexistence and trust between all States, and to develop broad international co-operation

and understanding. The arms race impedes the realization of the purposes, and is incompatible with the principles, of the Charter of the United Nations, especially respect for sovereignty, refraining from the threat or use of force against the territorial integrity or political independence of any State, the peaceful settlement of disputes and non-intervention and non-interference in the internal affairs of States. It also adversely affects the right of peoples freely to determine their systems of social and economic development, and hinders the struggle for self-determination and the elimination of colonial rule, racial or foreign domination or occupation. Indeed, the massive accumulation of armaments and the acquisition of armaments technology by racist régimes, as well as their possible acquisition of nuclear weapons, present a challenging and increasingly dangerous obstacle to a world community faced with the urgent need to disarm. It is, therefore, essential for purposes of disarmament to prevent any further acquisition of arms or arms technology by such régimes, especially through strict adherence by all States to relevant decisions of the Security Council.

13. Enduring international peace and security cannot be built on the accumulation of weaponry by military alliances nor be sustained by a precarious balance of deterrence or doctrines of strategic superiority. Genuine and lasting peace can only be created through the effective implementation of the security system provided for in the Charter of the United Nations and the speedy and substantial reduction of arms and armed forces, by international agreement and mutual example, leading ultimately to general and complete disarmament under effective international control. At the same time, the causes of the arms race and threats to peace must be reduced and to this end effective action should be taken to eliminate tensions and settle disputes by peaceful means.

14. Since the process of disarmament affects the vital security interests of all States, they must all be actively concerned with and contribute to the measures of disarmament and arms limitation, which have an essential part to play in maintaining and strengthening international security. Therefore the role and responsibility of the United Nations in the sphere of disarmament, in accordance with its Charter, must be strengthened.

15. It is essential that not only Governments but also the peoples of the world recognize and understand the dangers in the present situation. In order that an international conscience may develop and that world public opinion may exercise a positive influence, the United Nations should increase the dissemination of information on the arma-

ments race and disarmament with the full co-operation of Member States.

16. In a world of finite resources there is a close relationship between expenditure on armaments and economic and social development. Military expenditures are reaching ever higher levels, the highest percentage of which can be attributed to the nuclear-weapon States and most of their allies, with prospects of further expansion and the danger of further increases in the expenditures of other countries. The hundreds of billions of dollars spent annually on the manufacture or improvement of weapons are in sombre and dramatic contrast to the want and poverty in which two thirds of the world's population live. This colossal waste of resources is even more serious in that it diverts to military purposes not only material but also technical and human resources which are urgently needed for development in all countries, particularly in the developing countries. Thus, the economic and social consequences of the arms race are so detrimental that its continuation is obviously incompatible with the implementation of the new international economic order based on justice, equity and co-operation. Consequently, resources released as a result of the implementation of disarmament measures should be used in a manner which will help to promote the well-being of all peoples and to improve the economic conditions of the developing countries.

17. Disarmament has thus become an imperative and most urgent task facing the international community. No real progress has been made so far in the crucial field of reduction of armaments. However, certain positive changes in international relations in some areas of the world provide some encouragement. Agreements have been reached that have been important in limiting certain weapons or eliminating them altogether, as in the case of the Convention on the Prohibition of the Development, Production and Stockpiling of Bacteriological (Biological) and Toxin Weapons and on Their Destruction[1] and excluding particular areas from the arms race. The fact remains that these agreements relate only to measures of limited restraint while the arms race continues. These partial measures have done little to bring the world closer to the goal of general and complete disarmament. For more than a decade there have been no negotiations leading to a treaty on general and complete disarmament. The pressing need now is to translate into practical terms the provisions of this Final Document and to proceed along the road of binding and effective international agreements in the field of disarmament.

18. Removing the threat of a world war—a nuclear war—is the

most acute and urgent task of the present day. Mankind is confronted with a choice: we must halt the arms race and proceed to disarmament or face annihilation.

19. The ultimate objective of the efforts of States in the disarmament process is general and complete disarmament under effective international control. The principal goals of disarmament are to ensure the survival of mankind and to eliminate the danger of war, in particular nuclear war, to ensure that war is no longer an instrument for settling international disputes and that the use and the threat of force are eliminated from international life, as provided for in the Charter of the United Nations. Progress towards this objective requires the conclusion and implementation of agreements on the cessation of the arms race and on genuine measures of disarmament, taking into account the need of States to protect their security.

20. Among such measures, effective measures of nuclear disarmament and the prevention of nuclear war have the highest priority. To this end, it is imperative to remove the threat of nuclear weapons, to halt and reverse the nuclear arms race until the total elimination of nuclear weapons and their delivery systems has been achieved, and to prevent the proliferation of nuclear weapons. At the same time, other measures designed to prevent the outbreak of nuclear war and to lessen the danger of the threat or use of nuclear weapons should be taken.

21. Along with these measures, agreements or other effective measures should be adopted to prohibit or prevent the development, production or use of other weapons of mass destruction. In this context, an agreement on elimination of all chemical weapons should be concluded as a matter of high priority.

22. Together with negotiations on nuclear disarmament measures, negotiations should be carried out on the balanced reduction of armed forces and of conventional armaments, based on the principle of undiminished security of the parties with a view to promoting or enhancing stability at a lower military level, taking into account the need of all States to protect their security. These negotiations should be conducted with particular emphasis on armed forces and conventional weapons of nuclear-weapon States and other militarily significant countries. There should also be negotiations on the limitation of international transfer of conventional weapons, based in particular on the same principle, and taking into account the inalienable right to self-determination and independence of peoples under colonial or foreign domination and the obligations of States to respect that right, in ac-

cordance with the Charter of the United Nations and the Declaration
on Principles of International Law concerning Friendly Relations and
Co-operation among States,[2] as well as the need of recipient States to
protect their security.

23. Further international action should be taken to prohibit or
restrict for humanitarian reasons the use of specific conventional
weapons, including those which may be excessively injurious, cause
unnecessary suffering or have indiscriminate effects.

24. Collateral measures in both the nuclear and conventional
fields, together with other measures specifically designed to build
confidence, should be undertaken in order to contribute to the creation of favourable conditions for the adoption of additional disarmament measures and to further the relaxation of international tension.

25. Negotiations and measures in the field of disarmament shall be
guided by the fundamental principles set forth below.

26. All States Members of the United Nations reaffirm their full
commitment to the purposes of the Charter of the United Nations and
their obligation strictly to observe its principles as well as other relevant and generally accepted principles of international law relating to
the maintenance of international peace and security. They stress the
special importance of refraining from the threat or use of force against
the sovereignty, territorial integrity or political independence of any
State, or against peoples under colonial or foreign domination seeking
to exercise their right to self-determination and to achieve independence; non-intervention and non-interference in the internal affairs of
other States; the inviolability of international frontiers; and the peaceful settlement of disputes, having regard to the inherent right of States
to individual and collective self-defence in accordance with the Charter.

27. In accordance with the Charter, the United Nations has a central role and primary responsibility in the sphere of disarmament. In
order effectively to discharge this role and facilitate and encourage all
measures in this field, the United Nations should be kept appropriately
informed of all steps in this field, whether unilateral, bilateral, regional
or multilateral, without prejudice to the progress of negotiations.

28. All the peoples of the world have a vital interest in the success
of disarmament negotiations. Consequently, all States have the duty to
contribute to efforts in the field of disarmament. All States have the
right to participate in disarmament negotiations. They have the right to
participate on an equal footing in those multilateral disarmament
negotiations which have a direct bearing on their national security.

While disarmament is the responsibility of all States, the nuclear-weapon States have the primary responsibility for nuclear disarmament and, together with other militarily significant States, for halting and reversing the arms race. It is therefore important to secure their active participation.

29. The adoption of disarmament measures should take place in such an equitable and balanced manner as to ensure the right of each State to security and to ensure that no individual State or group of States may obtain advantages over others at any stage. At each stage the objective should be undiminished security at the lowest possible level of armaments and military forces.

30. An acceptable balance of mutual responsibilities and obligations for nuclear and non-nuclear-weapon States should be strictly observed.

31. Disarmament and arms limitation agreements should provide for adequate measures of verification satisfactory to all parties concerned in order to create the necessary confidence and ensure that they are being observed by all parties. The form and modalities of the verification to be provided for in any specific agreement depend upon and should be determined by the purposes, scope and nature of the agreement. Agreements should provide for the participation of parties directly or through the United Nations system in the verification process. Where appropriate, a combination of several methods of verification as well as other compliance procedures should be employed.

32. All States, in particular nuclear-weapon States, should consider various proposals designed to secure the avoidance of the use of nuclear weapons, and the prevention of nuclear war. In this context, while noting the declarations made by nuclear-weapon States, effective arrangements, as appropriate, to assure non-nuclear-weapon States against the use or the threat of use of nuclear weapons could strengthen the security of those States and international peace and security.

33. The establishment of nuclear-weapon-free zones on the basis of agreements or arrangements freely arrived at among the States of the zone concerned and the full compliance with those agreements or arrangements, thus ensuring that the zones are genuinely free from nuclear weapons, and respect for such zones by nuclear-weapon States constitute an important disarmament measure.

34. Disarmament, relaxation of international tension, respect for the right to self-determination and national independence, the peace-

ful settlement of disputes in accordance with the Charter of the United Nations and the strengthening of international peace and security are directly related to each other. Progress in any of these spheres has a beneficial effect on all of them; in turn, failure in one sphere has negative effects on others.

35. There is also a close relationship between disarmament and development. Progress in the former would help greatly in the realization of the latter. Therefore resources released as a result of the implementation of disarmament measures should be devoted to the economic and social development of all nations and contribute to the bridging of the economic gap between developed and developing countries.

36. Non-proliferation of nuclear weapons is a matter of universal concern. Measures of disarmament must be consistent with the inalienable right of all States, without discrimination, to develop, acquire and use nuclear technology, equipment and materials for the peaceful use of nuclear energy and to determine their peaceful nuclear programmes in accordance with their national priorities, needs and interests, bearing in mind the need to prevent the proliferation of nuclear weapons. International co-operation in the peaceful uses of nuclear energy should be conducted under agreed and appropriate international safeguards applied on a non-discriminatory basis.

37. Significant progress in disarmament, including nuclear disarmament, would be facilitated by parallel measures to strengthen the security of States and to improve the international situation in general.

38. Negotiations on partial measures of disarmament should be conducted concurrently with negotiations on more comprehensive measures and should be followed by negotiations leading to a treaty on general and complete disarmament under effective international control.

39 Qualitative and quantitative disarmament measures are both important for halting the arms race. Efforts to that end must include negotiations on the limitation and cessation of the qualitative improvement of armaments, especially weapons of mass destruction and the development of new means of warfare so that ultimately scientific and technological achievements may be used solely for peaceful purposes.

40. Universality of disarmament agreements helps create confidence among States. When multilateral agreements in the field of disarmament are negotiated, every effort should be made to ensure that they are universally acceptable. The full compliance of all parties

with the provisions contained in such agreements would also contribute to the attainment of that goal.

41. In order to create favourable conditions for success in the disarmament process, all States should strictly abide by the provisions of the Charter of the United Nations, refrain from actions which might adversely affect efforts in the field of disarmament, and display a constructive approach to negotiations and the political will to reach agreements. There are certain negotiations on disarmament under way at different levels, the early and successful completion of which could contribute to limiting the arms race. Unilateral measures of arms limitation or reduction could also contribute to the attainment of that goal.

42. Since prompt measures should be taken in order to halt and reverse the arms race, Member States hereby declare that they will respect the objectives and principles stated above and make every effort faithfully to carry out the Programme of Action set forth in section III below.

III. Program of Action

43. Progress towards the goal of general and complete disarmament can be achieved through the implementation of a programme of action on disarmament, in accordance with the goals and principles established in the Declaration on disarmament. The present Programme of Action contains priorities and measures in the field of disarmament that States should undertake as a matter of urgency with a view to halting and reversing the arms race and to giving the necessary impetus to efforts designed to achieve genuine disarmament leading to general and complete disarmament under effective international control.

44. The present Programme of Action enumerates the specific measures of disarmament which should be implemented over the next few years, as well as other measures and studies to prepare the way for future negotiations and for progress towards general and complete disarmament.

45. Priorities in disarmament negotiations shall be: nuclear weapons; other weapons of mass destruction, including chemical weapons; conventional weapons, including any which may be deemed to be excessively injurious or to have indiscriminate effects; and reduction of armed forces.

46. Nothing should preclude States from conducting negotiations on all priority items concurrently.

47. Nuclear weapons pose the greatest danger to mankind and to the survival of civilization. It is essential to halt and reverse the nuclear arms race in all its aspects in order to avert the danger of war involving nuclear weapons. The ultimate goal in this context is the complete elimination of nuclear weapons.

48. In the task of achieving the goals of nuclear disarmament, all the nuclear-weapon States, in particular those among them which possess the most important nuclear arsenals, bear a special responsibility.

49. The process of nuclear disarmament should be carried out in such a way, and requires measures to ensure, that the security of all States is guaranteed at progressively lower levels of nuclear armaments, taking into account the relative qualitative and quantitative importance of the existing arsenals of the nuclear-weapon States and other States concerned.

50. The achievement of nuclear disarmament will require urgent negotiation of agreements at appropriate stages and with adequate measures of verification satisfactory to the States concerned for:

(a) Cessation of the qualitative improvement and development of nuclear-weapon systems;

(b) Cessation of the production of all types of nuclear weapons and their means of delivery, and of the production of fissionable material for weapons purposes;

(c) A comprehensive, phased programme with agreed time-frames, whenever feasible, for progressive and balanced reduction of stockpiles of nuclear weapons and their means of delivery, leading to their ultimate and complete elimination at the earliest possible time. Consideration can be given in the course of the negotiations to mutual and agreed limitation or prohibition, without prejudice to the security of any State, of any types of nuclear armaments.

51. The cessation of nuclear-weapon testing by all States within the framework of an effective nuclear disarmament process would be in the interest of mankind. It would make a significant contribution to the above aim of ending the qualitative improvement of nuclear weapons and the development of new types of such weapons and of preventing the proliferation of nuclear weapons. In this context the negotiations now in progress on "a treaty prohibiting nuclear-weapon tests, and a protocol covering nuclear explosions for peaceful purposes, which would be an integral part of the treaty," should be concluded urgently and the result submitted for full consideration by the multilateral negotiating body with a view to the submission of a draft treaty to the General Assembly at the earliest possible date. All efforts should be

made by the negotiating parties to achieve an agreement which, following endorsement by the General Assembly, could attract the widest possible adherence. In this context, various views were expressed by non-nuclear-weapon States that, pending the conclusion of this treaty, the world community would be encouraged if all the nuclear-weapon States refrained from testing nuclear weapons. In this connexion, some nuclear-weapon States expressed different views.

52. The Union of Soviet Socialist Republics and the United States of America should conclude at the earliest possible date the agreement they have been pursuing for several years in the second series of the strategic arms limitation talks. They are invited to transmit in good time the text of the agreement to the General Assembly. It should be followed promptly by further strategic arms limitation negotiations between the two parties, leading to agreed significant reductions of, and qualitative limitations on, strategic arms. It should constitute an important step in the direction of nuclear disarmament and, ultimately, of establishment of a world free of such weapons.

53. The process of nuclear disarmament described in the paragraph on this subject should be expedited by the urgent and vigorous pursuit to a successful conclusion of ongoing negotiations and the urgent initiation of further negotiations among the nuclear-weapon States.

54. Significant progress in nuclear disarmament would be facilitated both by parallel political or international legal measures to strengthen the security of States and by progress in the limitation and reduction of armed forces and conventional armaments of the nuclear-weapon States and other States in the regions concerned.

55. Real progress in the field of nuclear disarmament could create an atmosphere conducive to progress in conventional disarmament on a world-wide basis.

56. The most effective guarantee against the danger of nuclear war and the use of nuclear weapons is nuclear disarmament and the complete elimination of nuclear weapons.

57. Pending the achievement of this goal, for which negotiations should be vigorously pursued, and bearing in mind the devastating results which nuclear war would have on belligerents and non-belligerents alike, the nuclear-weapon States have special responsibilities to undertake measures aimed at preventing the outbreak of nuclear war, and of the use of force in international relations, subject to the provisions of the Charter of the United Nations, including the use of nuclear weapons.

58. In this context all States, in particular nuclear-weapon States, should consider as soon as possible various proposals designed to secure the avoidance of the use of nuclear weapons, the prevention of nuclear war and related objectives, where possible through international agreement, and thereby ensure that the survival of mankind is not endangered. All States should actively participate in efforts to bring about conditions in international relations among States in which a code of peaceful conduct of nations in international affairs could be agreed and which would preclude the use or threat of use of nuclear weapons.

59. In the same context, the nuclear-weapon States are called upon to take steps to assure the non-nuclear-weapon States against the use or threat of use of nuclear-weapons. The General Assembly notes the declarations made by the nuclear-weapon States and urges them to pursue efforts to conclude, as appropriate, effective arrangements to assure non-nuclear-weapon States against the use or threat of use of nuclear weapons.

60. The establishment of nuclear-weapon-free zones on the basis of arrangements freely arrived at among the States of the region concerned constitutes an important disarmament measure.

61. The process of establishing such zones in different parts of the world should be encouraged with the ultimate objective of achieving a world entirely free of nuclear weapons. In the process of establishing such zones, the characteristics of each region should be taken into account. The States participating in such zones should undertake to comply fully with all the objectives, purposes and principles of the agreements or arrangements establishing the zones, thus ensuring that they are genuinely free from nuclear weapons.

62. With respect to such zones, the nuclear-weapon States in turn are called upon to give undertakings, the modalities of which are to be negotiated with the competent authority of each zone, in particular:

(a) To respect strictly the status of the nuclear-weapon-free zone;

(b) To refrain from the use or threat of use of nuclear weapons against the States of the zone.

63. In the light of existing conditions, and without prejudice to other measures which may be considered in other regions, the following measures are especially desirable:

(a) Adoption by the States concerned of all relevant measures to ensure the full application of the Treaty for the Prohibition of Nuclear Weapons in Latin America (Treaty of Tlatelolco),[3] taking into account the views expressed at the tenth special session on the adherence to it;

(*b*) Signature and ratification of the Additional Protocols of the Treaty for the Prohibition of Nuclear Weapons in Latin America (Treaty of Tlatelolco) by the States entitled to become parties to those instruments which have not yet done so;

(*c*) In Africa, where the Organization of African Unity has affirmed a decision for the denuclearization of the region, the Security Council of the United Nations shall take appropriate effective steps whenever necessary to prevent the frustration of this objective;

(*d*) The serious consideration of the practical and urgent steps, as described in paragraphs above, required for the implementation of the proposal to establish a nuclear-weapon-free zone in the Middle East, in accordance with the relevant General Assembly resolutions, where all parties directly concerned have expressed their support for the concept and where the danger of nuclear-weapon proliferation exists. The establishment of a nuclear-weapon-free zone in the Middle East would greatly enhance international peace and security. Pending the establishment of such a zone in the region, States of the region should solemnly declare that they will refrain on a reciprocal basis from producing, acquiring or in any other way possessing nuclear weapons and nuclear explosive devices and from permitting the stationing of nuclear weapons on their territory by any third party, and agree to place all their nuclear activities under International Atomic Energy Agency safeguards. Consideration should be given to a Security Council role in advancing the establishment of a nuclear-weapon-free zone in Middle East;

(*e*) All States in the region of South Asia have expressed their determination to keep their countries free of nuclear weapons. No action should be taken by them which might deviate from that objective. In this context, the question of establishing a nuclear-weapon-free zone in South Asia has been dealt with in several resolutions of the General Assembly, which is keeping the subject under consideration.

64. The establishment of zones of peace in various regions of the world under appropriate conditions, to be clearly defined and determined freely by the States concerned in the zone, taking into account the characteristics of the zone and the principles of the Charter of the United Nations, and in conformity with international law, can contribute to strengthening the security of States within such zones and to international peace and security as a whole. In this regard, the General Assembly notes the proposals for the establishment of zones of peace, *inter alia*, in:

(*a*) South-East Asia where States in the region have expressed interest in the establishment of such a zone, in conformity with their views;

(b) The Indian Ocean, taking into account the deliberations of the General Assembly and its relevant resolutions and the need to ensure the maintenance of peace and security in the region.

65. It is imperative, as an integral part of the effort to halt and reverse the arms race, to prevent the proliferation of nuclear weapons. The goal of nuclear non-proliferation is on the one hand to prevent the emergence of any additional nuclear-weapon States besides the existing five nuclear-weapon States, and on the other progressively to reduce and eventually eliminate nuclear weapons altogether. This involves obligations and responsibilities on the part of both nuclear-weapon States and non-nuclear-weapon States, the former undertaking to stop the nuclear arms race and to achieve nuclear disarmament by urgent application of the measures outlined in the relevant paragraphs of this Final Document, and all States undertaking to prevent the spread of nuclear weapons.

66. Effective measures can and should be taken at the national level and through international agreements to minimize the danger of the proliferation of nuclear weapons without jeopardizing energy supplies or the development of nuclear energy for peaceful purposes. Therefore, the nuclear-weapon States and the non-nuclear-weapon States should jointly take further steps to develop an international consensus of ways and means, on a universal and non-discriminatory basis, to prevent the proliferation of nuclear weapons.

67. Full implementation of all the provisions of existing instruments on non-proliferation, such as the Treaty on the Non-Proliferation of Nuclear Weapons[4] and/or the Treaty for the Prohibition of Nuclear Weapons in Latin America (Treaty of Tlatelolco) by States parties to those instruments will be an important contribution to this end. Adherence to such instruments has increased in recent years and the hope has been expressed by the parties that this trend might continue.

68. Non-proliferation measures should not jeopardize the full exercise of the inalienable rights of all States to apply and develop their programmes for the peaceful uses of nuclear energy for economic and social development in conformity with their priorities, interests and needs. All States should also have access to and be free to acquire technology, equipment and materials for peaceful uses of nuclear energy, taking into account the particular needs of the developing countries. International co-operation in this field should be under agreed

and appropriate international safeguards applied through the International Atomic Energy Agency on a non-discriminatory basis in order to prevent effectively the proliferation of nuclear weapons.

69. Each country's choices and decisions in the field of the peaceful uses of nuclear energy should be respected without jeopardizing their respective fuel cycle policies or international co-operation, agreements and contracts for the peaceful uses of nuclear energy, provided that the agreed safeguard measures mentioned above are applied.

70. In accordance with the principles and provisions of General Assembly resolution 32/50 of 8 December 1977, international co-operation for the promotion of the transfer and utilization of nuclear technology for economic and social development, especially in the developing countries, should be strengthened.

71. Efforts should be made to conclude the work of the International Nuclear Fuel Cycle Evaluation strictly in accordance with the objectives set out in the final communiqué of its Organizing Conference.[5]

72. All States should adhere to the Protocol for the Prohibition of the Use in War of Asphyxiating, Poisonous or Other Gases, and of Bacteriological Method of Warfare, signed at Geneva on 17 June 1925.[6]

73. All States which have not yet done so should consider adhering to the Convention on the Prohibition of the Development, Production and Stockpiling of Bacteriological (Biological) and Toxin Weapons and on Their Destruction.

74. States should also consider the possibility of adhering to multilateral agreements concluded so far in the disarmament field which are mentioned below in this section.

75. The complete and effective prohibition of the development, production and stockpiling of all chemical weapons and their destruction represent one of the most urgent measures of disarmament. Consequently, the conclusion of a convention to this end, on which negotiations have been going on for several years, is one of the most urgent tasks of multilateral negotiations. After its conclusion, all States should contribute to ensuring the broadest possible application of the convention through its early signature and ratification.

76. A convention should be concluded prohibiting the development, production, stockpiling and use of radiological weapons.

77. In order to help prevent a qualitative arms race and so that scientific and technological achievements may ultimately be used solely for peaceful purposes, effective measures should be taken to

avoid the danger and prevent the emergence of new types of weapons of mass destruction based on new scientific principles and achievements. Efforts should be appropriately pursued aiming at the prohibition of such new types and new systems of weapons of mass destruction. Specific agreements could be concluded on particular types of new weapons of mass destruction which may be identified. This question should be kept under continuing review.

78. The Committee on Disarmament should keep under review the need for a further prohibition of military or any other hostile use of environmental modification techniques in order to eliminate the dangers to mankind from such use.

79. In order to promote the peaceful use of and to avoid an arms race on the sea-bed and the ocean floor and the subsoil thereof, the Committee on Disarmament is requested—in consultation with the States parties to the Treaty on the Prohibition of the Emplacement of Nuclear Weapons and Other Weapons of Mass Destruction on the Sea-Bed and the Ocean Floor and in the Subsoil Thereof,[7] and taking into account the proposals made during the 1977 Review Conference of the parties to that Treaty and any relevant technological developments—to proceed promptly with the consideration of further measures in the field of disarmament for the prevention of an arms race in that environment.

80. In order to prevent an arms race in outer space, further measures should be taken and appropriate international negotiations held in accordance with the spirit of the Treaty on Principles Governing the Activities of States in the Exploration and Use of Outer Space, including the Moon and Other Celestial Bodies.[8]

81. Together with negotiations on nuclear disarmament measures, the limitation and gradual reduction of armed forces and conventional weapons should be resolutely pursued within the framework of progress towards general and complete disarmament. States with the largest military arsenals have a special responsibility in pursuing the process of conventional armaments reductions.

82. In particular the achievement of a more stable situation in Europe at a lower level of military potential on the basis of approximate equality and parity, as well as on the basis of undiminished security of all States with full respect for security interests and independence of States outside military alliances, by agreement on appropriate mutual reductions and limitations would contribute to the strengthening of security in Europe and constitute a significant step towards enhancing international peace and security. Current efforts to this end should be continued most energetically.

83. Agreements or other measures should be resolutely pursued on a bilateral, regional and multilateral basis with the aim of strengthening peace and security at a lower level of forces, by the limitation and reduction of armed forces and of conventional weapons, taking into account the need of States to protect their security, bearing in mind the inherent right of self-defence embodied in the Charter of the United Nations and without prejudice to the principle of equal rights and self-determination of peoples in accordance with the Charter, and the need to ensure balance at each stage and undiminished security of all States. Such measures might include those in the following two paragraphs.

84. Bilateral, regional and multilateral consultations and conferences should be held where appropriate conditions exist with the participation of all the countries concerned for the consideration of different aspects of conventional disarmament, such as the initiative envisaged in the Declaration of Ayacucho subscribed to by eight Latin American countries on 9 December 1974.[9]

85. Consultations should be carried out among major arms supplier and recipient countries on the limitation of all types of international transfer of conventional weapons, based in particular on the principle of undiminished security of the parties with a view to promoting or enhancing stability at a lower military level, taking into account the need of all States to protect their security as well as the inalienable right to self-determination and independence of peoples under colonial or foreign domination and the obligations of States to respect that right, in accordance with the Charter of the United Nations and the Declaration on Principles of International Law concerning Friendly Relations and Co-operation among States.

86. The United Nations Conference on Prohibitions or Restrictions of Use of Certain Conventional Weapons Which May Be Deemed to Be Excessively Injurious or to Have Indiscriminate Effects, to be held in 1979, should seek agreement, in the light of humanitarian and military considerations, on the prohibition or restriction of use of certain conventional weapons including those which may cause unnecessary suffering or have indiscriminate effects. The Conference should consider specific categories of such weapons, including those which were the subject-matter of previously conducted discussions.

87. All States are called upon to contribute towards carrying out this task.

88. The result of the Conference should be considered by all States, especially producer States, in regard to the question of the transfer of such weapons to other States.

89. Gradual reduction of military budgets on a mutually agreed basis, for example, in absolute figures or in terms of percentage points, particularly by nuclear-weapon States and other militarily significant States, would be a measure that would contribute to the curbing of the arms race and would increase the possibilities of reallocation of resources now being used for military purposes to economic and social development, particularly for the benefit of the developing countries. The basis for implementing this measure will have to be agreed by all participating States and will require ways and means of its implementation acceptable to all of them, taking account of the problems involved in assessing the relative significance of reductions as among different States and with due regard to the proposals of States on all the aspects of reduction of military budgets.

90. The General Assembly should continue to consider what concrete steps should be taken to facilitate the reduction of military budgets, bearing in mind the relevant proposals and documents of the United Nations on this question.

91. In order to facilitate the conclusion and effective implementation of disarmament agreements and to create confidence, States should accept appropriate provisions for verification in such agreements.

92. In the context of international disarmament negotiations, the problem of verification should be further examined and adequate methods and procedures in this field be considered. Every effort should be made to develop appropriate methods and procedures which are non-discriminatory and which do not unduly interfere with the internal affairs of other States or jeopardize their economic and social development.

93. In order to facilitate the process of disarmament, it is necessary to take measures and pursue policies to strengthen international peace and security and to build confidence among States. Commitment to confidence-building measures could significantly contribute to preparing for further progress in disarmament. For this purpose, measures such as the following, and other measures yet to be agreed upon, should be undertaken:

(a) The prevention of attacks which take place by accident, miscalculation or communications failure by taking steps to improve communications between Governments, particularly in areas of tension, by the establishment of "hot lines" and other methods of reducing the risk of conflict;

(b) States should assess the possible implications of their military research and development for existing agreements as well as for further efforts in the field of disarmament;

(c) The Secretary-General shall periodically submit reports to the General Assembly on the economic and social consequences of the armaments race and its extremely harmful effects on world peace and security.

94. In view of the relationship between expenditure on armaments and economic and social development and the necessity to release real resources now being used for military purposes to economic and social development in the world, particularly for the benefit of the developing countries, the Secretary-General should, with the assistance of a group of qualified governmental experts appointed by him, initiate an expert study on the relationship between disarmament and development. The Secretary-General should submit an interim report on the subject to the General Assembly at its thirty-fourth session and submit the final results to the Assembly at its thirty-sixth session for subsequent action.

95. The expert study should have the terms of reference contained in the report of the *Ad Hoc* Group on the Relationship between Disarmament and Development[10] appointed by the Secretary-General in accordance with General Assembly resolution 32/88 A of 12 December 1977. It should investigate the three main areas listed in the report, bearing in mind the United Nations studies previously carried out. The study should be made in the context of how disarmament can contribute to the establishment of the new international economic order. The study should be forward-looking and policy-oriented and place special emphasis on both the desirability of a reallocation, following disarmament measures, of resources now being used for military purposes to economic and social development, particularly for the benefit of the developing countries, and the substantive feasibility of such a reallocation. A principal aim should be to produce results that could effectively guide the formulation of practical measures to reallocate those resources at the local, national, regional and international levels.

96. Taking further steps in the field of disarmament and other measures aimed at promoting international peace and security would be facilitated by carrying out studies by the Secretary-General in this field with appropriate assistance from governmental or consultant experts.

97. The Secretary-General shall, with the assistance of consultant experts appointed by him, continue the study of the interrelationship between disarmament and international security requested in Assem-

bly resolution 32/87 C of 12 December 1977 and submit it to the thirty-fourth session of the General Assembly.

98. At its thirty-third and subsequent sessions the General Assembly should determine the specific guidelines for carrying out studies, taking into account the proposals already submitted including those made by individual countries at the special session, as well as other proposals which can be introduced later in this field. In doing so, the Assembly would take into consideration a report on these matters prepared by the Secretary-General.

99. In order to mobilize world public opinion on behalf of disarmament, the specific measures set forth below, designed to increase the dissemination of information about the armaments race and the efforts to halt and reverse it, should be adopted.

100. Governmental and non-governmental information organs and those of the United Nations and its specialized agencies should give priority to the preparation and distribution of printed and audio-visual material relating to the danger represented by the armaments race as well as to the disarmament efforts and negotiations on specific disarmament measures.

101. In particular, publicity should be given to the Final Document of the tenth special session.

102. The General Assembly proclaims the week starting 24 October, the day of the foundation of the United Nations, as a week devoted to fostering the objectives of disarmament.

103. To encourage study and research on disarmament, the United Nations Centre for Disarmament should intensify its activities in the presentation of information concerning the armaments race and disarmament. Also, the United Nations Educational, Scientific and Cultural Organization is urged to intensify its activities aimed at facilitating research and publications on disarmament, related to its fields of competence, especially in developing countries, and should disseminate the results of such research.

104. Throughout this process of disseminating information about developments in the disarmament field of all countries, there should be increased participation by non-governmental organizations concerned with the matter, through closer liaison between them and the United Nations.

105. Member States should be encouraged to ensure a better flow of information with regard to the various aspects of disarmament to avoid dissemination of false and tendentious information concerning armaments, and to concentrate on the danger of escalation of the arma-

ments race and on the need for general and complete disarmament under effective international control.

106. With a view to contributing to a greater understanding and awareness of the problems created by the armaments race and of the need for disarmament, Governments and governmental and non-governmental international organizations are urged to take steps to develop programmes of education for disarmament and peace studies at all levels.

107. The General Assembly welcomes the initiative of the United Nations Educational, Scientific and Cultural Organization in planning to hold a world congress on disarmament education and, in this connexion, urges that organization to step up its programme aimed at the development of disarmament education as a distinct field of study through the preparation, *inter alia*, of teachers' guides, textbooks, readers and audio-visual materials. Member States should take all possible measures to encourage the incorporation of such materials in the curricula of their educational institutes.

108. In order to promote expertise in disarmament in more Member States, particularly in the developing countries, the General Assembly decides to establish a programme of fellowships on disarmament. The Secretary-General, taking into account the proposal submitted to the special session, should prepare guidelines for the programme. He should also submit the financial requirements of twenty fellowships to the General Assembly at its thirty-third session for inclusion in the regular budget of the United Nations, bearing in mind the savings that can be made within the existing budgetary appropriations.

109. Implementation of these priorities should lead to general and complete disarmament under effective international control, which remains the ultimate goal of all efforts exerted in the field of disarmament. Negotiations on general and complete disarmament shall be conducted concurrently with negotiations on partial measures of disarmament. With this purpose in mind, the Committee on Disarmament will undertake the elaboration of a comprehensive programme of disarmament encompassing all measures thought to be advisable in order to ensure that the goal of general and complete disarmament under effective international control becomes a reality in a world in which international peace and security prevail and in which the new international economic order is strengthened and consolidated. The comprehensive programme should contain appropriate procedures for ensuring that the General Assembly is kept fully informed of the progress of the

negotiations including an appraisal of the situation when appropriate and, in particular, a continuing review of the implementation of the programme.

110. Progress in disarmament should be accompanied by measures to strengthen institutions for maintaining peace and the settlement of international disputes by peaceful means. During and after the implementation of the programme of general and complete disarmament, there should be taken, in accordance with the principles of the Charter of the United Nations, the necessary measures to maintain international peace and security, including the obligation of States to place at the disposal of the United Nations agreed manpower necessary for an international peace force to be equipped with agreed types of armaments. Arrangements for the use of this force should ensure that the United Nations can effectively deter or suppress any threat or use of arms in violation of the purposes and principles of the United Nations.

111. General and complete disarmament under strict and effective international control shall permit States to have at their disposal only those nonnuclear forces, armaments, facilities and establishments as are agreed to be necessary to maintain internal order and protect the personal security of citizens and in order that States shall support and provide agreed manpower for a United Nations peace force.

112. In addition to the several questions dealt with in this Programme of Action, there are a few others of fundamental importance, on which, because of the complexity of the issues involved and the short time at the disposal of the special session, it has proved impossible to reach satisfactory agreed conclusions. For those reasons they are treated only in very general terms and, in a few instances, not even treated at all in the Programme. It should be stressed, however, that a number of concrete approaches to deal with such questions emerged from the exchange of views carried out in the General Assembly which will undoubtedly facilitate the continuation of the study and negotiation of the problems involved in the competent disarmament organs.

IV. Machinery

113. While disarmament, particularly in the nuclear field, has become a necessity for the survival of mankind and for the elimination of the danger of nuclear war, little progress has been made since the end of the Second World War. In addition to the need to exercise political will, the international machinery should be utilized more effectively and also improved to enable implementation of the Programme of

Action and help the United Nations to fulfil its role in the field of disarmament. In spite of the best efforts of the international community, adequate results have not been produced with the existing machinery. There is, therefore, an urgent need that existing disarmament machinery be revitalized and forums appropriately constituted for disarmament deliberations and negotiations with a better representative character. For maximum effectiveness, two kinds of bodies are required in the field of disarmament—deliberative and negotiating. All Member States should be represented on the former, whereas the latter, for the sake of convenience, should have a relatively small membership.

114. The United Nations, in accordance with the Charter, has a central role and primary responsibility in the sphere of disarmament. Accordingly, it should play a more active role in this field and, in order to discharge its functions effectively, the United Nations should facilitate and encourage all disarmament measures—unilateral, bilateral, regional or multilateral—and be kept duly informed through the General Assembly, or any other appropriate United Nations channel reaching all Members of the Organization, of all disarmament efforts outside its aegis without prejudice to the progress of negotiations.

115. The General Assembly has been and should remain the main deliberative organ of the United Nations in the field of disarmament and should make every effort to facilitate the implementation of disarmament measures. An item entitled "Review of the implementation of the recommendations and decisions adopted by the General Assembly at its tenth special session" shall be included in the provisional agenda of the thirty-third and subsequent sessions of the General Assembly.

116. Draft multilateral disarmament conventions should be subjected to the normal procedures applicable in the law of treaties. Those submitted to the General Assembly for its commendation should be subject to full review by the Assembly.

117. The First Committee of the General Assembly should deal in the future only with questions of disarmament and related international security questions.

118. The General Assembly establishes, as successor to the Commission originally established by resolution 502(VI) of 11 January 1952, a Disarmament Commission, composed of all States Members of the United Nations, and decides that:

(*a*) The Disarmament Commission shall be a deliberative body, a subsidiary organ of the General Assembly, the function of which shall be to consider and make recommendations on various problems in the field of disarmament and to follow up the relevant decisions and recommendations of the special session devoted to disarmament. The Disarmament Commission should, *inter alia*, consider the elements of a comprehensive programme for disarmament to be submitted as recommendations to the General Assembly and, through it, to the negotiating body, the Committee on Disarmament;

(b) The Disarmament Commission shall function under the rules of procedure relating to the committees of the General Assembly with such modifications as the Commission may deem necessary and shall make every effort to ensure that, in so far as possible, decisions on substantive issues be adopted by consensus;

(c) The Disarmament Commission shall report annually to the General Assembly and will submit for consideration by the Assembly at its thirty-third session a report on organizational matters; in 1979, the Disarmament Commission will meet for a period not exceeding four weeks, the dates to be decided at the thirty-third session of the Assembly;

(d) The Secretary-General shall furnish such experts, staff and services as are necessary for the effective accomplishment of the Commission's functions.

119. A second special session of the General Assembly devoted to disarmament should be held on a date to be decided by the Assembly at its thirty-third session.

120. The General Assembly is conscious of the work that has been done by the international negotiating body that has been meeting since 14 March 1962 as well as the considerable and urgent work that remains to be accomplished in the field of disarmament. The Assembly is deeply aware of the continuing requirement for a single multilateral disarmament negotiating forum of limited size taking decisions on the basis of consensus. It attaches great importance to the participation of all the nuclear-weapon States in an appropriately constituted negotiating body, the Committee on Disarmament. The Assembly welcomes the agreement reached following appropriate consultations among the Member States during the special session of the General Assembly devoted to disarmament that the Committee on Disarmament will be open to the nuclear-weapon States, and thirty-two to thirty-five other States to be chosen in consultation with the President of the thirty-second session of the Assembly; that the membership of the Committee on Disarmament will be reviewed at regular intervals; that the Committee on Disarmament will be convened in Geneva not later than January 1979 by the country whose name appears first in the alphabetical list of membership; and that the Committee on Disarmament will:

(a) Conduct its work by consensus;

(b) Adopt its own rules of procedure;

(c) Request the Secretary-General of the United Nations, following consultations with the Committee on Disarmament, to appoint the Secretary of the Committee, who shall also act as his personal representative, to assist the Committee and its Chairman in organizing the business and time-tables of the Committee;

(d) Rotate the chairmanship of the Committee among all its members on a monthly basis;

(e) Adopt its own agenda taking into account the recommendations made to it by the General Assembly and the proposals presented by the members of the Committee;

(f) Submit a report to the General Assembly annually, or more frequently as appropriate, and provide its formal and other relevant documents to the States Members of the United Nations on a regular basis;

(g) Make arrangements for interested States, not members of the Committee, to submit to the Committee written proposals or working documents on measures of disarmament that are the subject of negotiation in the Committee and to participate in the discussion of the subject-matter of such proposals or working documents;

(h) Invite States not members of the Committee, upon their request, to express views in the Committee when the particular concerns of those States are under discussion;

(i) Open its plenary meetings to the public unless otherwise decided.

121. Bilateral and regional disarmament negotiations may also play an important role and could facilitate negotiations of multilateral agreements in the field of disarmament.

122. At the earliest appropriate time, a world disarmament conference should be convened with universal participation and with adequate preparation.

123. In order to enable the United Nations to continue to fulfil its role in the field of disarmament and to carry out the additional tasks assigned to it by this special session, the United Nations Centre for Disarmament should be adequately strengthened and its research and information functions accordingly extended. The Centre should also take account fully of the possibilities offered by specialized agencies and other institutions and programmes within the United Nations system with regard to studies and information on disarmament. The Centre should also increase contacts with non-governmental organizations and research institutions in view of the valuable role they play in

the field of disarmament. This role could be encouraged also in other ways that may be considered as appropriate.

124. The Secretary-General is requested to set up an advisory board of eminent persons, selected on the basis of their personal expertise and taking into account the principle of equitable geographical representation, to advise him on various aspects of studies to be made under the auspices of the United Nations in the field of disarmament and arms limitation, including a programme of such studies.

125. The General Assembly notes with satisfaction that the active participation of the Member States in the consideration of the agenda items of the special session and the proposals and suggestions submitted by them and reflected to a considerable extent in the Final Document have made a valuable contribution to the work of the special session and to its positive conclusion. Since a number of those proposals and suggestions,[11] which have become an integral part of the work of the special session of the General Assembly, deserve to be studied further and more thoroughly, taking into consideration the many relevant comments and observations made in both the general debate in plenary meeting and the deliberations of the *Ad Hoc* Committee of the Tenth Special Session, the Secretary-General is requested to transmit, together with this Final Document, to the appropriate deliberative and negotiating organs dealing with the questions of disarmament all the official records of the special session devoted to disarmament, in accordance with the recommendations which the Assembly may adopt at its thirty-third session. Some of the proposals put forth for the consideration of the special session are listed below:

(*a*) Text of the decision of the Central Committee of the Romanian Communist Party concerning Romania's position on disarmament and, in particular, on nuclear disarmament, adopted on 9 May 1978;[12]

(*b*) Views of the Swiss Government on problems to be discussed at the tenth special session of the General Assembly;[13]

(*c*) Proposals of the Union of Soviet Socialist Republics on practical measures for ending the arms race;[14]

(*d*) Memorandum from France concerning the establishment of an International Satellite Monitoring Agency;[15]

(*e*) Memorandum from France concerning the establishment of an International Institute for Research on Disarmament;[16]

(*f*) Proposal by Sri Lanka for the establishment of a World Disarmament Authority;[17]

(*g*) Working paper submitted by the Federal Republic of Germany entitled "Contribution to the seismological verification of a comprehensive test ban";[18]

(*h*) Working paper submitted by the Federal Republic of Germany entitled "Invitation to attend an international chemical-weapon verification workshop in the Federal Republic of Germany";[19]

(*i*) Working paper submitted by China on disarmament;[20]

(*j*) Working paper submitted by the Federal Republic of Germany concerning zones of confidence-building measures as a first step towards the preparation of a world-wide convention on confidence-building measures;[21]

(*k*) Proposal by Ireland for a study of the possibility of establishing a system of incentives to promote arms control and disarmament;[22]

(*l*) Working paper submitted by Romania concerning a synthesis of the proposals in the field of disarmament;[23]

(*m*) Proposal by the United States of America on the establishment of a United Nations Peace-keeping Reserve and on confidence-building measures and stabilizing measures in various regions, including notification of manoeuvres, invitation of observers to manoeuvres, and United Nations machinery to study and promote such measures;[24]

(*n*) Proposal by Uruguay on the possibility of establishing a polemological agency;[25]

(*o*) Proposal by Belgium, Canada, Denmark, Germany, Federal Republic of, Ireland, Italy, Japan, Luxembourg, the Netherlands, New Zealand, Norway, Sweden, the United Kingdom of Great Britain and Northern Ireland and the United States of America on the strengthening of the security role of the United Nations in the peaceful settlement of disputes and peace-keeping;[26]

(*p*) Memorandum from France concerning the establishment of an International Disarmament Fund for Development;[27]

(*q*) Proposal by Norway entitled "Evaluation of the impact of new weapons on arms control and disarmament efforts";[28]

(*r*) Note verbale transmitting the text, signed in Washington on 22 June 1978 by the Ministers for Foreign Affairs of Argentina, Bolivia, Chile, Colombia, Ecuador, Panama, Peru and Venezuela, reaffirming the principles of the Declaration of Ayacucho with respect to the limitation of conventional weapons;[29]

(*s*) Memorandum from Liberia entitled "Declaration of a new philosophy on disarmament";[30]

(*t*) Statements made by the representatives of China, on 22 June 1978, on the draft Final Document of the tenth special session;[31]

(*u*) Proposal by the President of Cyprus for the total demilitarization and disarmament of the Republic of Cyprus and the implementation of the resolutions of the United Nations;[32]

(v) Proposal by Costa Rica on economic and social incentives to halt the arms race;[33]

(w) Amendments submitted by China to the draft Final Document of the tenth special session;[34]

(x) Proposals by Canada for the implementation of a strategy of suffocation of the nuclear arms race;[35]

(y) Draft resolution submitted by Cyprus, Ethiopia and India on the urgent need for cessation of further testing of nuclear weapons;[36]

(z) Draft resolution submitted by Ethiopia and India on the non-use of nuclear weapons and prevention of nuclear war;[37]

(aa) Proposal by the non-aligned countries on the establishment of a zone of peace in the Mediterranean;[38]

(bb) Proposal by the Government of Senegal for a tax on military budgets;[39]

(cc) Proposal by Austria for the transmission to Member States of working paper A/AC.187/109 and the ascertainment of their views on the subject of verification;[40]

(dd) Proposal by the non-aligned countries for the dismantling of foreign military bases in foreign territories and withdrawal of foreign troops from foreign territories;[41]

(ee) Proposal by Mexico for the opening, on a provisional basis, of an ad hoc account in the United Nations Development Programme to use for development the funds which may be released as a result of disarmament measures;[42]

(ff) Proposal by Italy on the role of the Security Council in the field of disarmament in accordance with Article 26 of the Charter of the United Nations;[43]

(gg) Proposal by the Netherlands for a study on the establishment of an international disarmament organization.[44]

126. In adopting this Final Document, the States Members of the United Nations solemnly reaffirm their determination to work for general and complete disarmament and to make further collective efforts aimed at strengthening peace and international security; eliminating the threat of war, particularly nuclear war; implementing practical measures aimed at halting and reversing the arms race; strengthening the procedures for the peaceful settlement of disputes; and reducing military expenditures and utilizing the resources thus released in a manner which will help to promote the well-being of all peoples and to improve the economic conditions of the developing countries.

127. The General Assembly expresses its satisfaction that the proposals submitted to its special session devoted to disarmament and the deliberations thereon have made it possible to reaffirm and define in this Final Document fundamental principles, goals, priorities and procedures for the implementation of the above purposes, either in the Declaration or the Programme of Action or in both. The Assembly also welcomes the important decisions agreed upon regarding the deliberative and negotiating machinery and is confident that these organs will discharge their functions in an effective manner.

128. Finally, it should be borne in mind that the number of States that participated in the general debate, as well as the high level of representation and the depth and scope of that debate, are unprecedented in the history of disarmament efforts. Several Heads of State or Government addressed the General Assembly. In addition, other Heads of State or Government sent messages and expressed their good wishes for the success of the special session of the Assembly. Several high officials of specialized agencies and other institutions and programmes within the United Nations system and spokesmen of twenty-five non-governmental organizations and six research institutes also made valuable contributions to the proceedings of the session. It must be emphasized, moreover, that the special session marks not the end but rather the beginning of a new phase of the efforts of the United Nations in the field of disarmament.

129. The General Assembly is convinced that the discussions of the disarmament problems at the special session and its Final Document will attract the attention of all peoples, further mobilize world public opinion and provide a powerful impetus for the cause of disarmament.

REFERENCES

1. Resolution 2826(XXVI), annex.
2. Resolution 2625(XXV), annex.
3. United Nations, *Treaty Series*, vol. 634, No. 9068.
4. Resolution 2373(XXII), annex.
5. See A/C.1/32/7.
6. League of Nations, *Treaty Series*, vol. XCIV(1929), No. 2138.
7. Resolution 2660(XXV), annex.
8. Resolution 2222(XXI), annex.
9. See A/10044, annex.
10. A/S-10/9, annex.
11. See *Official Records of the General Assembly, Tenth Special Session, Plenary Meetings*, 1st to 25th meetings; *ibid.*,

Tenth Special Session, Supplement No. 1 (A/S-10/1), *Supplement No. 2* (A/S-10/2 and Corr.1), *Supplement No. 2A* (A/S-10/2/Add.1/Rev.1) and *Supplement No. 3* (A/S-10/3 and Corr.1); *ibid., Tenth Special Session, Annexes*, agenda item 7, document A/S-10/10; and *ibid., Tenth Special Session*, Ad Hoc *Committee of the Tenth Special Session*, 1st to 16th meetings, and *ibid.*, Ad Hoc *Committee of the Tenth Special Session, Sessional Fascicle*, corrigendum; A/S-10/5, A/S-10/6 and Corr.1 and Add.1, A/S-10/7 and Corr.1, A/S-10/8 and Add.1 and 2, A/S-10/9, A/S-10/11–14 and A/S-10/17; A/S-

10/AC.1/1–8, A/S-10/AC.1/9 and Add.1,
A/S-10/AC.1/10 and 11, A/S-10/AC.1/
12 and Corr.1, A/S-10/AC.1/13–25, A/S-
10/AC.1/26 and Corr.1 and 2, A/S-10/
AC.1/27–36, A/S-10/AC.1/37 and Rev.1
and Corr.1 and Rev.1/Add.1, and A/S-10/
AC.1/38–40; A/S-10/AC.1/L.1 and Rev.1
and A/S-10/AC.1/L.2–17.

12. A/S-10/14.
13. A/S-10/AC.1/2.
14. A/S-10/AC.1/4.
15. A/S-10/AC.1/7.
16. A/S-10/AC.1/8.
17. A/S-10/AC.1/9 and Add.1.
18. A/S-10/AC.1/12 and Corr.1.
19. A/S-10/AC.1/13.
20. A/S-10/AC.1/17.
21. A/S-10/AC.1/20.
22. A/S-10/AC.1/21.
23. A/S-10/AC.1/23.
24. A/S-10/AC.1/24.

25. A/S-10/AC.1/25.
26. A/S-10/AC.1/26 and Corr.1 and 2.
27. A/S-10/AC.1/28.
28. A/S-10/AC.1/31.
29. A/S-10/AC.1/34.
30. A/S-10/AC.1/35.
31. A/S-10/AC.1/36.
32. A/S-10/AC.1/39.
33. A/S-10/AC.1/40.
34. A/S-10/AC.1/L.2–4, A/S-10/AC.1/L.7 and 8.
35. A/S-10/AC.1/L.6.
36. A/S-10/AC.1/L.10.
37. A/S-10/AC.1/L.11.
38. A/S-10/AC.1/37, para. 72.
39. *Ibid.*, para. 101.
40. *Ibid.*, para. 113.
41. *Ibid.*, para. 126.
42. *Ibid.*, para. 141.
43. *Ibid.*, para. 179.
44. *Ibid.*, para. 186.

Appendix B.
Conclusions of the Second
Special Session

57. The Tenth Special Session of the General Assembly, the First Special Session devoted to disarmament, held in 1978, was an event of historic significance. The Special Session was convened in response to a growing concern among the peoples of the world that the arms race, especially the nuclear-arms race, represented ever-increasing threats to human well-being and even to the survival of mankind. At that session the international community of nations achieved, for the first time in the history of disarmament negotiations, a consensus on an international disarmament strategy, the immediate goal of which was the elimination of the danger of nuclear war and implementation of measures to halt and reverse the arms race. The final objective of the strategy was to achieve general and complete disarmament under effective international control. The conviction that all peoples had a legitimate right to expect early and significant progress in disarmament and a vital interest in its success led to the United Nations being given a central role and primary responsibility in the field of disarmament.

58. The historic consensus embodied in the Final Document of the Tenth Special Session of the General Assembly (resolution S-10/2) was rooted in a common awareness that the accumulation of weapons, particularly nuclear weapons, constituted much more a threat to than a protection of mankind. It was also based on recognition that the time had come to put an end to that situation, to abandon the use of force in international relations and to seek security in disarmament, that is to say, through a gradual but effective process beginning with a reduction

in the current level of armaments. The Final Document recognized that in the contemporary world, the security of States could be greatly enhanced by effective action aimed at preventing nuclear war, ending the arms race and achieving real disarmament. Progress in disarmament would significantly contribute to pursuing the goals of economic and social development, particularly of developing countries. The consensus embodied in the Final Document sought to place disarmament negotiations in a unified perspective and became a most significant and integral part of the context within which negotiations on disarmament have been pursued.

59. In the course of the Twelfth Special Session, the Second Special Session devoted to disarmament, the General Assembly has noted that developments since 1978 have not lived up to the hopes engendered by the Tenth Special Session. Despite the efforts that have been made by the international community to implement the decisions and recommendations of that session on a multilateral, bilateral, and regional level, including action in the General Assembly and the Committee on Disarmament, and steps that have been taken on some specific measures contained in the Final Document, the objectives, priorities, and principles there laid down have not been generally observed. The Program of Action contained in the Final Document remains largely unimplemented. A number of important negotiations either have not begun or have been suspended, and efforts in the Committee on Disarmament and other forums have produced little tangible result. There has been some progress in certain negotiations and bilateral negotiations in the nuclear field have been initiated. The arms race, however, in particular the nuclear-arms race, has assumed more dangerous proportions and global military expenditures have increased sharply. In short, since the adoption of the Final Document in 1978, there has been no significant progress in the field of arms limitation and disarmament and the seriousness of the situation has increased.

60. The Final Document stated that disarmament, relaxation of international tension, respect for the right to self-determination and national independence, the peaceful settlement of disputes in accordance with the Charter of the United Nations, and the strengthening of international peace and security are directly related to each other. Progress in any of these spheres has a beneficial effect on all of them; in turn, failure in one sphere has negative effects on others. The past four years have witnessed increasing recourse to the use or threat of use of force against the sovereignty and territorial integrity of States, military

intervention, occupation, annexation and interference in the internal affairs of States, and denial of the inalienable right to self-determination and independence of peoples under colonial or foreign domination. The period has also witnessed other actions by States contrary to the Final Document. The consequent tensions and confrontations have retarded progress in disarmament and have in turn been aggravated by the failure to make significant progress towards disarmament.

61. It was stressed that in a world of finite resources there is an organic relationship between expenditures on armaments and economic and social development. The vastly increased military budgets since 1978 and the development, production, and deployment, especially by the States possessing the largest military arsenals, of new types of weapon systems represent a huge and growing diversion of human and material resources. Apart from the significant capital costs that these military expenditures represent, they have also contributed to current economic problems in certain States. Existing and planned military programs constitute a colossal waste of precious resources which might otherwise be used to elevate living standards of all peoples; furthermore, such waste greatly compounds the problems confronting developing countries in achieving economic and social development.

62. The General Assembly regrets that at its Twelfth Special Session it has not been able to adopt a document on the Comprehensive Program of Disarmament and on a number of other items on its agenda. However, on two agenda items, relating to the United Nations program of fellowships on disarmament and the World Disarmament Campaign, there are agreed texts for consideration and appropriate action by the General Assembly. The General Assembly was encouraged by the unanimous and categorical reaffirmation by all Member States of the validity of the Final Document of the Tenth Special Session as well as their solemn commitment to it and their pledge to respect the priorities in disarmament negotiations as agreed to in its Program of Action. Taking into account the aggravation of the international situation and being gravely concerned about the continuing arms race, particularly in its nuclear aspect, the General Assembly expresses its profound preoccupation over the danger of war, in particular nuclear war, the prevention of which remains the most acute and urgent task of the present day. The General Assembly urges all Member States to consider as soon as possible relevant proposals designed to

secure the avoidance of war, in particular nuclear war, thus ensuring that the survival of mankind is not endangered. The General Assembly also stresses the need for strengthening the central role of the United Nations in the field of disarmament and the implementation of the security system provided for in the Charter of the United Nations in accordance with the Final Document and to enhance the effectiveness of the Committee on Disarmament as the single multilateral negotiating body. In this regard the Committee on Disarmament is requested to report to the General Assembly at its thirty-seventh session on its consideration of an expansion of its membership, consistent with the need to enhance its effectiveness.

63. Member States have affirmed their determination to continue to work for the urgent conclusion of negotiations on and the adoption of the Comprehensive Program of Disarmament, which shall encompass all measures thought to be advisable in order to ensure that the goal of general and complete disarmament under effective international control becomes a reality in a world in which international peace and security prevail, and in which a new international economic order is strengthened and consolidated. To this end, the draft Comprehensive Program of Disarmament is hereby referred back to the Committee on Disarmament, together with the views expressed and the progress achieved on the subject at the Special Session. The Committee on Disarmament is requested to submit a revised draft Comprehensive Program of Disarmament to the General Assembly at its thirty-eighth session.

64. The other items on the agenda on which the Special Session has not reached decisions should be taken up at the thirty-seventh session of the General Assembly for further consideration.

65. The General Assembly is convinced that the discussion of disarmament problems, which it has undertaken at the Special Session and in which representatives of Member States—among them some heads of State or Government and many Foreign Ministers—have participated, and the active interest shown by peoples all over the world will provide a powerful impetus to Member States to redouble their efforts in the cause of disarmament. The General Assembly hopes that the World Disarmament Campaign, which it solemnly launched at the opening meeting of the Special Session, will further contribute to the mobilization of public opinion to the cause of disarmament and the strengthening of international peace and security. In this regard the campaign should provide an opportunity for discussion and debate in

all countries on all points of view relating to disarmament issues, objectives, and conditions.

66. The Third Special Session of the General Assembly devoted to disarmament should be held at a date to be decided by the General Assembly at its thirty-eighth session.

Appendix C.
World Disarmament
Campaign

1: Introduction

1. On 7 June 1982, the General Assembly at its Twelfth Special Session, the Second Special Session devoted to disarmament, launched a World Disarmament Campaign under United Nations auspices in conformity with the principles laid down in paragraphs 15 and 99 of the Final Document of the Tenth Special Session of the General Assembly (resolution S-10/2), the First Special Session devoted to disarmament, held in 1978 and bearing in mind the measures contemplated in paragraphs 100 to 107 of that document. The World Disarmament Campaign is intended to promote public interest in and support for the goals set out in the paragraphs referred to above and in particular for the reaching of agreements on measures of arms limitation and disarmament with a view to achieving the goal of general and complete disarmament under effective international control. Recognizing that world public opinion may exercise a positive influence on the attainment of meaningful measures of arms limitation and disarmament and the need for it to be well informed to discuss and debate all points of view relating to disarmament issues, its objectives and conditions, the General Assembly is aware of the public concern at the dangers of the arms race, particularly the nuclear arms race, and its negative social and economic consequences, as expressed in the oral and written presentations addressed to the Second Special Session devoted to disarmament by non-governmental organizations and research institutes. Taking into account the operational guidelines and modalities defined

in the reports of the Secretary-General contained in documents A/36/458 and A/S-12/27, the World Disarmament Campaign should be conducted on the following basis.

2. Objectives

2. The Campaign has three primary purposes: to inform, to educate, and to generate public understanding and support for the objectives of the United Nations in the field of arms limitation and disarmament as stated in the Final Document adopted at the First Special Session, with particular reference to the priorities and measures set out by its Program of Action, the decisions taken at the Second Special Session, the views expressed by Member States, and the recommendations in the Declaration of the 1980s as the Second Disarmament Decade.

3. The Campaign should be carried out in all regions of the world in a balanced, factual, and objective manner.

4. The universality of the Campaign should be guaranteed by the co-operation and participation of all States and by the widest possible dissemination of information and unimpeded access for all sectors of the public to a broad range of information and opinions on questions of arms limitation and disarmament, and the dangers relating to all aspects of the arms race and war, in particular nuclear war.

5. The United Nations system, Member States with respect for their sovereign rights, and other bodies, in particular non-governmental organizations, all have their roles to play in achieving the objectives of the Campaign.

3. Contents

6. The United Nations information and education activities conducted in accordance with the principles and purposes the Charter of the United Nations must be global in scope and content, and use those means of communication which are most appropriate in reaching the largest number of people. Although the means of informing and educating may vary from region to region, the basic thrust of the activities for the Campaign should be equally effective in all regions of the world. The elements of the Campaign should be of such a nature that they could be implemented at the global, regional, and national levels.

7. The Secretary-General is requested to make every effort to

make available to the public in all States, and on as wide a scale as possible, through the United Nations information centres, United Nations Development Program offices or other appropriate United Nations offices, the substance of the statements in the general debate at the Second Special Session as soon as possible in the official languages of the United Nations. Similarly, the texts adopted at the First and Second Special Sessions devoted to disarmament should be brought to the attention of the public in all countries.

8. Member States should be encouraged to cooperate with the United Nations in the implementation of paragraph 4 above to ensure a better flow of information with regard to the various aspects of disarmament and to avoid dissemination of false and tendentious information. In carrying out the Campaign, emphasis should be placed on the relationship between disarmament and international security and between disarmament and development, given the benefits that could be derived from the reduction of military outlays and the reallocation of released resources for socio-economic development.

9. In this regard, the Campaign should provide an opportunity for discussion and debate in all countries on all points of view relating to disarmament issues, objectives, and conditions.

10. The Campaign should encourage bilateral and multilateral exchanges on the basis of reciprocity and mutual agreement and give the widest possible dissemination to such exchanges, for example, among government officials, experts, academicians, and journalists of differing countries.

11. The Campaign should give full consideration to the role of mass media as the most effective way to achieve wide access to the public with a view to promoting a climate of understanding, confidence, and cooperation conducive to peace and disarmament.

12. In view of the fact that Disarmament Week has played a useful role in fostering the objectives of disarmament, the week starting 24 October should continue to be widely observed as Disarmament Week.

4. Modalities

13. In the light of the guidance given at the Second Special Session, the United Nations should provide the substance of information for and generally co-ordinate the implementation of the World Disarmament Campaign which should be carried out at the global, regional, and national levels under the United Nations auspices. The Secretary-

General is urged to take the necessary steps to ensure that all appropriate resources available, human, financial, and material, within the United Nations system are adequately coordinated in order to further the objectives of the Campaign as set out above.

14. Taking into account the existing mechanisms of coordination and in view for the need of reinforcing coordination, the Centre for Disarmament should provide the central guidance in coordinating the Campaign activities within the United Nations system and in maintaining liaison with the governmental and non-governmental organizations and research institutes. The Centre should also provide the substance of the information material to be disseminated in the implementation of the Campaign. Within the Campaign, the Department of Public Information should play its role as assigned by the General Assembly in utilizing its expertise and resources in public information to ensure its maximum effectiveness.

15. The Campaign should facilitate and complement existing programs of information, research, education, and training in the areas of disarmament. The promotion of such programs should be encouraged, particularly in the developing countries, and the United Nations and its agencies should be instrumental in this process.

16. Considering the ongoing activities of the United Nations Educational, Scientific, and Cultural Organization (UNESCO) in promoting disarmament education as a distinct field of study and the materials produced thereby, the program of action to be implemented by the Campaign should set out appropriate tasks for UNESCO in its fields of competence and in coordination with the Centre for Disarmament. The United Nations information centres should be drawn into the process of giving the widest possible dissemination to the materials for distribution, particularly among those countries where the existing facilities are not adequately utilized or equipped, bearing in mind the special needs of the developing countries in this respect.

17. Every effort should be made to ensure an equitable and timely distribution of materials in accordance with the principle of conducting the Campaign on a universal basis.

18. The General Assembly commends the Secretary-General for outlining a program of a World Disarmament Campaign as contained in document A/S-12/27 and requests him to submit to the Assembly at its thirty-seventh regular session the specifics of such a program, taking into account the views expressed by Member States during the Second Special Session.

19. Specific proposals for inclusion in the Campaign were made by

delegations pertaining to: the holding of a world conference on the role of mass media; instituting a council of consciences representing eminent personalities in the spiritual, scientific, cultural, and philosophical field; world-wide action for collecting signatures in favor of measures to prevent a nuclear war, curb the arms race, and for disarmament; installing in the United Nations the documentation and materials concerning Japan's atomic experiences; banning of war movies and war toys; televising or disseminating in other effective ways addresses and discussions by world statesmen of various regions and philosophies; and disseminating in an unhindered way a range of relevant materials provided by Governments and recognized international studies institutes.

20. The Secretary-General is further requested to submit at each subsequent regular session of the General Assembly for its review, a report on the implementation of the World Disarmament Campaign during the preceding year, and to convey to the Assembly the relevant views of the Advisory Board on Disarmament Studies, taking into account the tasks the Assembly may further entrust to it.

5. Financial Implications

21. Bearing in mind the need for additional human, financial, and material resources which may be necessary to implement an effective World Disarmament Campaign, the Secretary-General is urged to explore the possibilities of redeploying existing resources and to submit to the General Assembly at its thirty-seventh regular session a report in this respect. Member States are invited to supplement available United Nations resources with voluntary contributions to carry out the objectives of the Campaign on a world-wide basis. Voluntary contributions made by non-governmental organizations, foundations and trusts, and other private sources would also be welcome.

22. Member States should cooperate with the United Nations in the implementation of all the recommendations mentioned in this document.

Appendix D.
U.N. Program of
Fellowships on Disarmament

1. The United Nations program of fellowships on disarmament was established by the General Assembly at the initiative of Nigeria during its First Special Session devoted to disarmament in 1978 in order to promote expertise in disarmament in more Member States, particularly in the developing countries. The specialized training of government officials undertaken within the framework of the program since its inception in 1979 has become one of the more concrete results of the Special Session.

2. The result of the implementation of the program thus far, including the continuing contribution to disarmament negotiations by former fellows, confirms the view that the program has justified the hopes which inspired its establishment. In view of the growing interest which continues to be manifested in the program by an ever-increasing number of States, an expansion of the program in terms of its content and number of awards has become desirable. To this end, the Working Group recommends that the General Assembly should decide:

3.(a) To commend the Secretary-General for the diligence with which the program of fellowships on disarmament has been conducted so far;

(b) To endorse the report of the Secretary-General on the program as contained in document A/S-12/8 and Corr. 1;

(c) To continue the program;

(d) To increase the number of fellowships from 20 to 25 from 1983 onwards;

(e) To request the Secretary-General to continue to apply the same criteria of objectivity and balance in drawing up the future program for fellowships as he has done so far, in accordance with the guidelines established by the General Assembly at its thirty-third session (resolution 33/71 E of 14 December 1978);

(f) To express its appreciation to the Governments of the German Democratic Republic, the Federal Republic of Germany, Hungary, and Sweden for inviting fellows to their countries to study selected activities in the field of disarmament, thereby contributing to the fulfillment of the over-all objectives of the program, as well as providing additional information sources and practical knowledge for the fellows; in this connection, to welcome the offer of the Government of Japan to enable participants in the United Nations program of fellowships on disarmament to visit Hiroshima and Nagasaki and encourage other Member States to extend similar support for the program;

(g) To request the Secretary-General to submit to the General Assembly at its thirty-seventh session the financial implications of awarding 25 fellowships for inclusion in the regular budget of the United Nations, taking into account the necessary staffing requirements to meet the level of activities and structure of the program and bearing in mind the savings that can be made within the existing budgetary appropriations.

Appendix E.
NGOs and Institutions
Submitting Oral Statements

1. Non-Governmental Organizations*

1. Action Reconciliation/Service for Peace. (Federal Republic of Germany). Jebensstr. 1, 1 Berlin 12, Federal Republic of Germany. (Bishop Kurt Scharf)

2. Afro-Asian Peoples' Solidarity Organization.** # 89 Abdel Aziz al Saoud, St. Manial, Cairo, Egypt. (Mr. Mouri Abdel-Razzak)

3. Asian Buddhists Conference for Peace.** Gangdantekchenling Monastery, Ulan-Bator, Mongolian People's Republic. (Mr. Ch. Jogder)

4. Baha'i International Community. 866 U.N. Plaza, New York, N.Y. 10017, U.S.A. (Mr. Victor de Araujo)

5. Campaign for Nuclear Disarmament. (U.K.) 11 Goodwin Street, London M4 3HQ, U.K. (Ms. Joan Ruddock)

6. Christian Peace Conference. Jungmannova 9, P.O. Box 192, 111 21 Praha 1, Czechoslovakia. (Bishop Karoly Toth)

---

*Three student organizations invited to give oral presentations did not participate: All Africa Student Union, Continental Organization of Latin American Students, and the General Union of Arab Students.

**Organization gave oral statement at SSD I, but not necessarily the same speaker.

#Also submitted oral statement to Preparatory Committee for SSD II. In addition to the ten listed above, the Institute for Defense and Disarmament Studies (U.S.A.) was represented.

7. Commission of the Churches on International Affairs of the World Council of Churches.** P.O. Box 66, 150 route de Ferney, 1211 Geneva 20, Switzerland. (Dr. Philip Potter)

8. Friends of the Earth. 530 7th Street, S.E., Washington, D.C. 20003, U.S.A. (Mr. David R. Brower)

9. Friends World Committee for Consultation.** Religious Society of Friends, Drayton House, 30 Gordon Street, London WC1 HOAX, England. (Mr. Steve Thiermann)

10. Hiroshima Peace Culture Foundation/Nagasaki Atomic Bomb Casualty Council. (Japan). Hiroshima Peace Memorial Hall, 1–2 Nakajimacho, Hiroshima City 733, Japan. c/o Nagasaki International Cultural Hall, 7–8 Hirano-machi, Nagasaki, Japan. (Mayor Takeshi Araki/Mayor Hitoshi Motoshima)

11. Interchurch Peace Council. (Netherlands). Postbus 18747, 2502 ES's Gravenhage, The Netherlands. (Mr. Wim Bartels)

12. International Association for Religious Freedom.** Auf dem Muelberg 6, 6000 Frankfurt 70, Federal Republic of Germany. (President Nikkyo Niwano)

13. International Association for the Work of Dr. Albert Schweitzer of Lambaréné, 866 U.N. Plaza, Rm. 4054, New York, N.Y. 10017, U.S.A. (Lord Philip Noel-Baker)

14. International Association of Democratic Lawyers. Suite 202, 209 West 125th Street, New York, N.Y. 10027, U.S.A. (Mr. J. Nordmann)

15. International Committee for European Security and Cooperation. Rue Dautzenberg 42, 1050 Bruxelles, Belgium. (Canon Raymond Goor)

16. International Confederation of Free Trade Unions. Rue Montagne aux Herbes Potageres 37–41, 1000 Bruxelles, Belgium. (Mr. J. Vanderveken)

17. International Co-operative Alliance.** 11 Upper Grosvenor Street, London W1X 9PA, U.K. (Mr. Roger Kerinec)

18. International Fellowship of Reconciliation.** Hof van Sonoy 15–17, 1811 LD Alkmaar, The Netherlands. (Ms. Hildegard Goss-Mayr)

19. International Organization of Journalists. MON 1 St. Mesto, Parizska 9, Prague 1, Czechoslovakia. (Mr. Kaerle Nordenstreng)

20. International Peace Bureau.**# Rue de Zurich 41, Geneva, Switzerland. (Hon. Sean MacBride)

21. International Physicians for the Prevention of Nuclear War. 635 Huntington Avenue, Boston, MA 02115, U.S.A. (Dr. Herbert Abrams)

22. International Union of Students. 17th November Street, P.O. Box 58, 110 ol Praha ol, Czechoslovakia. (Rolandos Katsiaounis and Mr. Miroslav Stepan)

23. International Youth and Student Movement for the United Nations.** Pavillon du Petit-Saconnex, 16. ave. Jean Trembley, 1209 Geneva, Switzerland. (Mr. Jan Lonn)

24. National Nuclear Weapons Freeze Campaign. (U.S.A.) 4144 Lindell Blvd., St. Louis, MO 63108, U.S.A. (Ms. Randall Forsberg)

25. Pacific Concerns Resource Center, P.O. Box 27692, Honolulu, Hawaii 96827, U.S.A. (Mr. Roman Bedor)

26. Parliamentarians for World Order. Uganda House, 336 East 45th Street, New York, N.Y. 10017, U.S.A. (Hon. Douglas Roche)

27. Pax Christi International. Kerkstraat 150, 2000 Antwerp, Belgium. (Archbishop Dom Helder Camara)

28. Project Ploughshares. (Canada) 321 Chapel Street, Ottawa, Ontario K1N 7Z2, Canada. (Rev. Lois Wilson)

29. Pugwash Conference on Science and World Affairs.** 11A, avenue de la Paix, 1202 Geneva, Switzerland. (Prof. Bernard Feld)

30. Russian Orthodox Church. (U.S.S.R.) External Relations Dept., Russian Orthodox Church, Moscow Patriarchate, 18/2 Ryleev St., Moscow, U.S.S.R. (Patriarch Pimen)

31. SSD II National Liaison Committee for Nuclear and General Disarmament.** (Japan) Nihon Seinenkan 15, Kasumigaoka, Shinjuku-ku, Tokyo, Japan. (Mr. Senji Yamaguchi)

32. Soviet Peace Fund/Soviet Liaison Committee for Peace Forces. (U.S.S.R.) Kropotkin St. 10, Moscow, U.S.S.R./Soviet Liaison Committee for Peace Forces, Moscow, U.S.S.R. (Mr. Gregory Gretchko)

33. The Swedish People's Parliament for Disarmament. (Sweden). c/o The Swedish Association of the U.N., P.O. Box 15115, 104 65 Stockholm, Sweden. (Mr. Ulrich Herz)

34. Union of Arab Jurists. Damascus Street, P.O. Box 6026, Bagdad, Iraq. (Mr. Mansur Kikhia)

35. United Presbyterian Church in the U.S.A. 475 Riverside Drive, New York, N.Y. 10115, U.S.A. (Dr. William P. Thompson)

36. War Resisters' International. 55 Dawes Street, London SE17 1EL, United Kingdom. (Ms. Myrtle Solomon)

37. Women for Peace. c/o Romstad, Trudvangveien No. 12A, 1342 Jar, Norway. (Ms. Eva Nordland)

38. Women's International Democratic Federation.** Unter de Linden 13, 1080 Berlin, German Democratic Republic. (Mrs. Valentina Tereshkova)

39. Women's International League for Peace and Freedom.**# 1, rue de Varembe, C.P. 28, 1211 Geneva 20, Switzerland. (Ms. Katherine Camp)

40. World Association of World Federalists.** Leliegracht 21, 1016 GR Amsterdam, The Netherlands. (Rev. G. J. Grant)

41. World Confederation of Organizations of the Teaching Profession. 5, ave. du Moulin, 1110 Morges, Switzerland. (Mr. Willard McGuire)

42. World Conference on Religion and Peace.**# 777 U.N. Plaza, New York, N.Y. 10017, U.S.A. (Dr. Homer A. Jack)

43. World Federation of Democratic Youth.**# P.O. Box 147, 1389 Budapest, Hungary. (Mr. Miklos Barabas)

44. World Federation of Scientific Workers.** 40 Goodge Street, London W1P 1FH, England. (Mr. Jean-Marie Legay)

45. World Federation of Trade Unions. Secretariat, Nam, Curieovych 1, Prague 1, Czechoslovakia. (Mr. Ibrahim Abdallah)

46. World Federation of Teachers' Unions. Wilhaelm Wolss Str. 21, 111 Berlin, German Democratic Republic. (Mr. Daniel Retureau)

47. World Federation of United Nations Associations.** WFUNA/FMANU, Palais des Nations, 1211 Geneva 10, Switzerland. (Mr. Sidney Willner)

48. World Jewish Congress, 1, rue de Varembe, 1211 Geneva 20, Switzerland. (Mr. Edgar Bronfman)

49. World Muslim Congress. 224, Sharafabad, Karachi 0511, Pakistan. (Dr. Viqar A. Hamdani)

50. World Peace Council.**# Lonnrotink. 25 A.6. krs, 00180 Helsinki 18, Finland. (Mr. Romesh Chandra)

51. World Union of Catholic Women's Organizations.** 98 rue de l'Université, 75 Paris VII, France. (Mrs. Eleanor Aiken)

52. World Veterans Federation.** 16, rue Hamelin, 75116 Paris, France. (Mr. W. Ch. J. M. Lanschot)

53. Yugoslav League for Peace, Independence and Equality of Peoples.** Narodnog fronta 45, Beograd, Yugoslavia. (Mr. Aleksandar Bakocavic)

2. Research Institutions##

1. Centre for Conflict Studies. University of New Brunswick, P.O. Box 440, Fredericton, N.B. E3B 5A3, Canada. (Mr. Maurice Tugwell)

##One institution invited to give an oral presentation did not participate: Institute for Strategic Studies (Pakistan).

2. Center for Defense Information.**# 303 Capital Gallery West, 600 Maryland Avenue, S.W., Washington, D.C. 20024, U.S.A. (Rear-Admiral Gene La Rocque)

3. Council for Arms Control. 5 High Street, Windsor, United Kingdom. (Mr. Michael J. Davis)

4. Foundation for the Study of National Defense/French Institute for Polemology. Hotel National des Invalides, 75007 Paris, France. (Mr. Pierre Marais)

5. French Institute for International Relations. 6 rue Ferrus, 75014 Paris, France. (Mr. Dominique Moissy)

6. Gandhi Peace Foundation.** 221/23 Deen Dayal Upadhyaya Marg, New Delhi 110002, India. (Shri Radhakrishna)

7. Heritage Foundation. 513 C Street, N.E., Washington, D.C. 20002, U.S.A. (Mr. Burton Yale Pines)

8. Hungarian Institute of International Relations. Berc U. 23, 1017 Budapest, Hungary. (Mr. Gyula Gyovai)

9. Institute for Peace Research. Dr. Ignaz Seipel Platz 2, 1010 Wien, Austria. (Ms. Siegrid Poellinger)

10. Institute for Peace Science/Hiroshima University. 1-1-89, Higashi-Sendamachi, Naka-ku, Hiroshima 730, Japan. (Mr. Ohtori Kurino)

11. Institute for Defense Studies and Analyses. Sapru House, Sarahamba Road, New Delhi 110001, India. (Mr. P. K. S. Namboodiri)

12. Institute for World Economy and International Relations.** 2 Jaroslavskaya Ulitsa, d. 3 Korpus 8, Moscow 1-243, U.S.S.R. (Mr. Oleg Bykov)

13. International Institute for Peace.** Mollwaldplatz 5, 1040 Wien, Austria. (Mr. Gerhard Kade)

14. International Peace Academy. 777 U.N. Plaza, New York, N.Y. 10017, U.S.A. (Major-General Indar Jit Rikkhye)

15. International Peace Research Association.**# Faculty of Law, University of Tokyo, Bunkyoku, Tokyo 113, Japan. (Mr. Yoshikazu Sakamoto)

16. Israeli Institute for the Study of International Affairs. P.O. Box 17027, Tel Aviv 61170, Israel. (Mr. Mieczyslaw Maneli)

17. Nigerian Institute of International Affairs. Kofo Abayomi Road, Victoria Island, G.P.O. Box 1727, Lagos, Nigeria. (Mrs. Aderinsola Vogt)

18. Peace Research Institute-Dundas. 25 Dundana Avenue, Dundas, Ontario L9H 4E5, Canada. (Mrs. Ruth Klaassen)

19. Romanian National Committee of Scientists for Peace. Str. Roma 32, Bucharest, Romania. (Mr. Gheoghe Civcu)

20. Stanley Foundation.** 420 East Third Street, Muscatine, Iowa 52761, U.S.A. (Mr. C. Maxwell Stanley)

21. Stockholm International Peace Research Institute.** Bergshamra, 171 73 Solna, Sweden. (Mr. Frank Blackaby)

22. Tampere Peace Research Institute. P.O. Box 447, Hameenkatu 13 b A, 33100 Tampere 10, Finland. (Mr. Tapoi Varis)

Appendix F.
Enabling General
Assembly Resolutions

35/47

Preparations for the Second Special Session of the General Assembly Devoted to Disarmament.

The General Assembly,

Recalling section III of its resolution 33/71 H of 14 December 1978, in which it decided to convene a second special session devoted to disarmament in 1982 and to set up, at its thirty-fifth session, a preparatory committee for the second special session,

Reaffirming the validity of the Final Document of the Tenth Special Session of the General Assembly[1] and its conviction that disarmament remains one of the essential objectives of the United Nations,

Expressing its concern over the continuation of the arms race, which aggravates international peace and security and also diverts vast resources urgently needed for economic and social development,

Reiterating its conviction that peace can be secured through the implementation of disarmament measures, particularly of nuclear disarmament, conducive to the realization of the final objective, namely, general and complete disarmament under effective international control,

1. *Decides* to establish a Preparatory Committee for the Second Special Session of the General Assembly Devoted to Disarmament composed of seventy-eight Member States appointed by the President of the General Assembly on the basis of equitable geographic distribution;

2. *Requests* the Preparatory Committee to prepare a draft agenda

for the special session, to examine all relevant questions relating to that session and to submit to the General Assembly at its thirty-sixth session its recommendations thereon, including those in respect of the implementation of the decisions and recommendations adopted by the Assembly at its tenth special session;

3. *Invites* all Member States to communicate to the Secretary-General their views on the agenda and other relevant questions relating to the second special session of the General Assembly devoted to disarmament not later than 1 April 1981;

4. *Requests* the Secretary-General to transmit the replies of Member States relevant to paragraph 2 above to the Preparatory Committee and to render to it all necessary assistance, including the provision of essential background information, relevant documents and summary records;

5. *Requests* the Preparatory Committee to meet for a short organizational session of not longer than one week before the end of the thirty-fifth session of the General Assembly in order, *inter alia*, to set the dates for its substantive sessions;

6. *Further requests* the Preparatory Committee to submit its progress report to the General Assembly at its thirty-sixth session;

7. *Decides* to include in the provisional agenda of its thirty-sixth session an item entitled: "Second special session of the General Assembly devoted to disarmament: report of the Preparatory Committee for the Second Special Session of the General Assembly Devoted to Disarmament".

36/81A
Second Special Session of the General Assembly Devoted to Disarmament.

The General Assembly,

Recalling section III of its resolution 33/71 H of 14 December 1978, in which it decided to convene a second special session of the General Assembly devoted to disarmament in 1982 at United Nations Headquarters in New York,

Having considered the report of the Preparatory Committee for the Second Special Session of the General Assembly Devoted to Disarmament,[2]

1. *Endorses* the report of the Preparatory Committee for the Second Special Session of the General Assembly Devoted to Disarmament and the recommendations contained therein for the special session, to

be held between 7 June and 9 July 1982 at United Nations Headquarters in New York;

2. *Endorses also* the recommendation of the Preparatory Committee to meet in New York for the period from 26 April to 14 May 1982 in order to continue consideration of substantive issues related to the special session, including the implementation of the decisions and recommendations adopted by the General Assembly at its tenth special session, for incorporation in the document or documents to be adopted at the second special session on disarmament and any remaining organizational and procedural matters;

3. *Expresses its appreciation* to the members of the Preparatory Committee for their constructive contribution to its work;

4. *Invites* Member States to submit to the Secretary-General, not later than 31 March 1982, further views on the substantive issues related to the special session, including the implementation of the decisions and recommendations adopted by the General Assembly at its tenth special session;

5. *Requests* all Member States engaged in bilateral, regional or multilateral negotiations on disarmament issues outside the framework of the United Nations to submit appropriate information on such negotiations to the General Assembly, in accordance with paragraph 27 of the Final Document of the Tenth Special Session of the General Assembly,[3] the first special session on disarmament, before its second special session on disarmament;

6. *Further requests* the Secretary-General to render the Preparatory Committee all necessary assistance for the completion of its work.

REFERENCES

1. Resolution S-10/2.

2. *Official Records of the General Assembly, Thirty-sixth Session, Supplement* *No. 49* (A/36/49 and Corr. 1).

3. General Assembly resolution S-10/2.

Indexes*

BY INDIVIDUALS

*Appendix A containing the Final Document of SSD I is not indexed.

BY SUBJECT MATTER

27; civil disobedience, 176; communications, 24, 154, 157, 165, 166,
167, 170; consensus, 24; definition,
164, 180; demonstrations, 13, 27,
47, 168, 172, 181, 211–12; Final
Document, 164–65; future, 13, 216,
219, June events, 173–75; June 12th
demonstration, 175–76; NGO
Days, 183–202, 265–70; parallel activities, 172–77; petitions, 176–77,
182; preparations, 17, 172–73; Prep
Comm, 20, 22, 167, 168; rationalization of role, 179–81, 182, 218; religious activities, 177; role, 17, 20,
22, 35, 93, 165, 167–68, 201, 217;
SSD I, 164; Special NGO Committee on Disarmament, 166, 173, 182,
184; statements in Prep Comm, 22,
24; statements in SSD II, 25, 26, 40;
strategy, 13; WDC, 114–16, 118–
24, 171, 177–78, 199, 201, 218
NGO Committee on Disarmament,
126, 166, 170, 172, 173, 179, 181,
182; costs, 27; Disarmament Information Bureau, 174; *Disarmament
Times*, 171–72; NGO Days, 184;
NGO Media Center, 174–75
NGO Days, 183–202; Ad Hoc Committee, 50, 183–85; assessment of
SSD II, 217; common themes, 98,
200–01; Final Document, 183; list
of organizations, 28, 157, 265–70;
Prep Comm, 25, 28, 183–85; research institutions, 164, 185, 268–
70; SSD I, 183
Non-Proliferation Treaty, 47, 49, 62,
145; NGOs, 166
Non-use of nuclear weapons, 77; Indian initiative, 41, 76, 87, 88,
89; NGO recommendations, 178;
study, 152
North Atlantic Treaty Organization
(NATO); culpability, 205–06, 215,

218; nuclear freeze, 94, 103, 104,
105, 107–08, 109; Prep Comm, 19,
20, 23; preventing nuclear war, 88–
91; WDC, 114
Nuclear-free zones, 49, 63; NGO
Days, 201; studies, 152–53, 162
Nuclear power, 192
Nuclear weapons; study, 146

Officers of SSD II, 22, 23, 34, 36
Opening, 22, 33–48

Pacific Concerns Resource Center,
192, 267
Palestine Liberation Organization, 38
Parliamentarians for World Order,
100, 173, 174, 182, 192–93, 267
Pax Christi International, 161, 193,
267
Peace Research Institute, Dundas,
269
Pearl Harbor, 189
Plenary meetings; closing, 203–12;
general debate, 37–48; opening,
33–37; record, 157
Plowshare coffeehouse, 174, 177
Pomerance awards, 175
Preparatory Committee (Prep
Comm), 17–28; Ad Hoc Committee, 23–24, 25; agenda, provisional,
21, 22–23, 27; appointment, 17, 18,
271–72, 272–73; assessment, 22–23,
25, 52–53; bureau, 20–21, 22, 50;
chairmanship, 19–20; CPD, 23, 24,
25, 27, 28, 68–69; costs, 26–27;
dates for SSD II, 17, 18, 21–23, 272;
Declaration of the 1980s, 23; documentation, 21, 164; general debate,
22, 25; international atmosphere,
21, 22, 27; level of representation,
23, 25; machinery, 23; membership, 18, 19–20, 29–31; Non-
Aligned role, 17–18, 21, 27; NGO

BY COUNTRIES

Note on the Author

Dr. Homer A. Jack is Secretary-General of the World Conference on Religion and Peace (WCRP), an international non-governmental organization in consultative status with the U.N. Economic and Social Council (ECOSOC). He has been an observer at disarmament negotiations and deliberations for a quarter of a century and has been Chairman of the Non-Governmental Organization Committee on Disarmament (at U.N. Headquarters) since its establishment in 1973. He is author of *Disarmament Workbook: The U.N. Special Session and Beyond* (1978) and numerous articles on disarmament. A Unitarian Universalist Clergyman, he has also edited a series of volumes on religion and peace. The opinions expressed in this volume are those of the author and not necessarily those of WCRP or the NGO Committee.